Mini-budget, wage restraint, Razor Gang, ASIO, taxes, broken promises...

battler
PAPER OF THE INTERNATIONAL SOCIALISTS

No. 145 June 4, 1983 30 cents *(20 cents strikers, unemployed)*

AWWK !!
IT'S
MALCOLM
HAWKE

IS THE HAWKE Goverment trying to win a Malcolm Fraser look-alike contest?

Almost everything they've dished up to us has been in line with Fraser's policies ... or worse.

Bob Hawke is pursuing Fraser's holy grail of smaller deficit with a vengeance that must make even Malcolm shudder.

The mini-budget alone increased workers' cost of living by ten dollars a week, by cutting health and mortgage rebates.

Hawke has set up a Razor Gang just like Fraser's to chop back Government services. Except that Labor promises this Razor Gang will be effective.

The tax on superannuation lump sums upsets the retirement plans for thousands of workers. But the jobless aren't doing any better out of it. Under 18s still have to survive on the $40 a week Fraser gave them. Adults got a paltry $4 rise.

The sole "benefit" of Hawke's smaller Budget deficit will be to give business lower interest rates on their borrowings. Because Hawke is contracting the economy, we'll lose jobs despite the token "job creation" scheme.

The Summit was just a showy pretext for Hawke to extend Fraser's wage freeze. Later this year, he'll "restrain" us to a lousy 3 or 4% "catch-up".

It isn't just the economy where Hawke is outdoing Fraser at Fraserism. When the *National Times* ran secret documents exposing ASIO's dirty tricks, even Andrew Peacock applauded Hawke for his efforts to halt the articles in the Supreme Court.

Hawke subsequently sacrificed the career of one of his best mates, David Combe, to prove how ardently he supports the snoops.

On March 5th, millions of Australian workers and unemployed threw Malcolm Fraser out of office because we were sick of his discredited, right-wing policies.

Now we've got Malcolm Hawke instead.

If we want a better deal, we're going to have to fight this "Malcolm" just like the last one.

Registered by Australia Post — publication no. VBF 522

PAGE 4
MAY '68 revolt in France

PAGE 6

Reagan's America — living on billboards

First published 2020 by Interventions Inc.

Interventions is an independent, not-for-profit, radical book publisher.
For further information:
    www.interventions.org.au
    info@interventions.org.au
    Trades Hall Suite 68
    54 Victoria Street
    Carlton VIC 3053

Design and layout by Viktoria Ivanova.
Cover photo Maggie Diaz courtesy of Gwendolen De Lacy, Curator of the Diaz Collection.
Back cover cartoon Mark Matcott.
Frontispiece 'Awk it's Malcolm Hawke' The Battler 4 June 1983. Design Alec Kahn. With kind permission of Socialist Alternative.
Photo on dedication page courtesy David Main.
All front pages from The Battler and Socialist Action magazine used with kind permission of Socialist Alternative.

Title taken from informal badges produced by Victorian public service union activists in 1985.

Author: Liz Ross

Title: Stuff the Accord! Pay Up! Workers' resistance to the ALP-ACTU Accord
ISBN: 978-0-9945378-9-8: Paperback

© Liz Ross 2020

The moral rights of the author has been asserted.
All rights reserved. Except as permitted under the Australian Copyright Act 1968 (for example, a fair dealing for the purposes of study, research, criticism or review), no part of this book may be reproduced, stored in a retrieval system, communicated or transmitted in any form or by any means without prior written permission.

All inquiries should be made to the author.

A catalogue record for this book is available from the National Library of Australia

STUFF THE ACCORD!
PAY UP!

**WORKERS' RESISTANCE
TO THE ALP-ACTU ACCORD**

Liz Ross

INTERVENTIONS
MELBOURNE

Interventions is produced on the land of the Wurundjeri people of the Kulin Nation. We acknowledge the Traditional Owners of country throughout Australia and recognise their continuing connection to land, waters and culture. We pay our respects to their Elders past, present and emerging. Their land was stolen, never ceded. It always was and always will be Aboriginal land.

The title of this book is taken from badges produced by rank-and-file public service union activists during the 1985 pay dispute. They altered official union badges with the slogan 'The Accord says Pay Up!' to read, 'Stuff the Accord – Pay Up!'

To all those named and unnamed workers who stood up for their rights, who took a stand against the Accord against heavy odds, some losing their unions, their jobs and a decent future. This book is your story, your legacy of struggle for the future.

CONTENTS

	Acknowledgements	1
	Introduction	3
1	The Accord – 'A Transitional Program for Socialism'?	9
2	Unions and the New Right	33
3	Lights Out in Queensland	55
4	The Accord and Women – 'Sold a Lemon'	77
5	Robe River – New Right or Accord Neoliberalism?	99
6	The BLF – 'A Challenge they Must Crush'	123
7	The Public Sector – Strung up by the Accord	145
8	Pilot Unions – 'You go out and it's War'	165
9	Then There Were Three	183
10	Workers' Capital? Superannuation and the Accord	209
11	Enterprise bargaining – Accord Mark VII	229
12	'The Accord Gospel: Profits, more Profits'	247
	Acronyms	259
	Endnotes	265
	Bibliography	297

Author Liz Ross at BLF picket at Como building site, Melbourne, 1986.
Photo Janey Stone.

ACKNOWLEDGMENTS

Many thanks to all the people who made this book possible. Thanks in particular to people whose stories I have shared here who were part of the fight against the Accord – many builders' labourers, public service workers and nurses, Dean Mighell, Luke van der Meulen, Eris Harrison, Sue Jackson, Rob Cecala and Graeme Haynes. Also thanks to Tom O'Lincoln, Rick Kuhn and Tom Bramble for their important political and trade union analyses. Mark Matcott's brilliant cartoons add much to the text.

I also thank the Interventions team – Janey Stone, Graham Willett, Alex Ettling, Lisa Milner and Viktoria Ivanova – who put in so many hours of work and follow up into the editing and production process. A special thanks to Janey and Alex for photo selection and preparation. Thanks to Rick Kuhn for comments, Eris Harrison for meticulous copy editing and David Main for his photos.

Most importantly I want to acknowledge the political grounding I have had since the late 1970s, when I first joined the revolutionary left. This book is also an acknowledgement of the role of revolutionaries in the struggles under the Accord. Through my time in the Socialist Workers Party, the International Socialists, Socialist Action and now Socialist Alternative, I have learnt so much from the greats of Marxism – Marx, Engels, Lenin, Trotsky and Luxemburg, first among many. Strengthening this has been the inspiration, solidarity, highs and lows of the class struggle, the fight for a revolutionary socialist party, an unparalleled education that informs my unwavering belief in the power and potential of a revolutionary working class to overthrow capitalism and bring socialism to the world.

INTRODUCTION

Who was running the country? Early in the Accord years, one right wing politician claimed:

> We are now at the high point of trade union power in the history of Australia because of an agreement called the prices and incomes accord ... the trade union movement is running the country.[1]

If the unions were running the country during the 1983–1996 Accord years, it definitely was not in the interests of their members, the Australian working class. The Hawke–Keating social democratic government implemented the ruling class' policy for capitalist revival, neoliberalism, through the introduction of a prices and incomes policy, the Accord.[2] After the turbulent years of the Fraser government and the brutal neoliberalism of the UK's Margaret Thatcher and USA's Ronald Reagan, the 1983 Australian Council of Trade Unions (ACTU) and Australian Labor Party (ALP) Accord was seen by many in the labour movement as promising a better world of cooperation and consensus between labour and capital.

Economic failures and social upheavals around the globe during the late 1960s to mid-1970s left capitalism severely shaken. These mobilisations toppled dictators in Iran and Nicaragua and challenged for power in Portugal. They were met with brutal crackdowns, physical, economic or both, as the capitalist class fought to regain control and restore profits. Thatcher and Reagan led the pack in this neoliberal recovery.

In Australia, the economy moved sharply into recession from 1974. In 1975, conservative leader Malcolm Fraser usurped power through the dismissal of the Whitlam Labor government, amid scenes of political and industrial turmoil. He vowed that his government would break the power of the unions and restore business confidence. In that same year, ACTU president Bob Hawke envisioned a different world, saying to Storeman and Packers' Union (FSPU) research officer, Bill Kelty:

> What this country needs is a different way to go about change. I'm going to deliver to people a country that respects people, consults with people ... I'll be the Prime Minister Bill and that's what I want to achieve.[3]

High goals indeed; but Hawke's ACTU history of compromising, even selling out, at workers' expense proved a warning that workers would end up paying a high price, while the bosses benefited.

Key to Hawke's project was a social contract – an agreement between government and unions – to run capitalism in partnership through a prices and incomes policy.[4] This would be a caring, sharing and technologically innovative capitalism, where everyone stood to benefit. Because the nature of social contracts involves cooperation between employers and workers and their unions, most left wing commentators describe it as class collaboration; an irreconcilable difference between capital and labour is papered over, usually in the interests of capital. Nonetheless, social democratic Sweden and other countries with social contracts – except Britain, which was rarely mentioned in Australia – became the role models. In the UK, British Labour introduced two social contracts, the first in 1964 and the second in 1974, bringing record wage cuts, high unemployment and inflation, along with soaring profits. The 1978–79 workers' rebellion or 'winter of discontent' saw the end of this experiment and the dumping of the Callaghan Labour government.[5]

Then ACTU vice-president Simon Crean had a different analysis of the UK experience. Crean was convinced that social contracts needed to control wages, a critical feature of economic policy. With wages 'out of control' in both Australia and the UK from the end of the 1970s to the early 1980s, he was determined that Australia would, unlike Britain, control them.[6]

While 1983 marked a triumphant introduction of the Accord and Labor in government in Australia, both became so unpopular that Labor was turfed out of office in 1996, losing to a reactionary John Howard-led Coalition. Nonetheless, despite such an ignominious loss, both the Accord and the Hawke–Keating government have enjoyed decades of plaudits from all sides, left and right (though rarely from rank and file workers). At a thirtieth anniversary forum in 2013, attended by many in business, the labour movement and academia, Hawke reminisced about his time as Prime Minister:

> I felt a degree of pride – over recent times in reading the many independent analyses of the period of our government and the reforms that we were able to make – [we] made a permanent, constructive contribution to our nation.[7]

Although the Accord was part of the rightward trajectory of the ALP and ACTU after Labor's defeat in 1975, it was actually the Left unions and some on the Left of the ALP who drove the adoption of a social contract. Communist parties around the world, and the unions and intellectual milieu they influenced, gave up any pretence of a revolutionary program following the 1970s uprisings; they looked to reformism, even joining social democratic governments in some cases. Their programs, a left nationalist project of unions and the 'progressive' bourgeoisie combining to influence economic development, were tailor made for social contracts. The decline in class struggle saw the ALP looking less to the working class – and being less influenced by them – for its policies and membership. More and more, union bureaucrats, academics, lawyers and the middle class were writing the party's policies, joining up and becoming the face of Labor and some unions.

The Communist Party of Australia (CPA) travelled along that exact path. The CPA and Left Labor leaders of the unions were critical to the acceptance and implementation of the Accord. The Australian Manufacturing Workers' Union (AMWU), the Building Workers' Industrial Union (BWIU) and others laid the political basis for the class collaborationist politics of the Accord and were heavily involved in formulating it. In *Politics and the Accord*, the pro-Accord authors' preface noted that the viability of the Accord depended on the support from the Left: 'No other element in the Union movement had the power to break the Accord, since only the traditional militancy of the Left could disable an incomes policy.'[8]

It was the left wing leaders of the AMWU who surrendered the most during the Accord years. Left union leaders have never acknowledged how much damage the Accord's class collaborationist policies did to the working class, but employers were only too happy to gloat about the benefits to their class. At the thirtieth anniversary gathering – to the applause of Labor and union leaders present –Metal Trades Industry Association (MTIA) leader Bert Evans spelled out his side's gains:

> We opposed the first Accord, but then people said to us, 'what are you bloody doing? This is too good to be true. We have got industrial stability, we know what our costs are going to be, we have got the unions' cooperation, we were restructuring the award and we got rid of 380 classifications. It was restructured down to 14 so all the things enabled us to do all of that while the Accord was developed.'[9]

There was opposition to the Accord, both initially and throughout its term, within the ALP, unions and rank and file; however, Jenny Haines from the NSW Nurses' Association (NSWNA) cast the sole vote against acceptance of the Accord at the 1983 ACTU conference.[10] At each stage, there was workplace resistance, including on the wharves and in mining, transport, manufacturing and the public sector. A few Left unions and far left parties attempted to build a more political opposition through Fightback! conferences in 1987 and in their publications and members' workplaces, offering support for those unions and workers resisting the Accord. These oppositional forces didn't break the Accord, but they did teach us valuable lessons.

There are still many among Labor and in the union movement and academia who support, even praise and advocate, Accord-like programs, despite the massive contribution of the Accord and its associated political ideology to the current parlous state of the unions and the Left more generally. Most recently, superannuation has been touted as one stand-out gain of the Accord. In fact, the 2018 Banking Royal Commission thoroughly exposed the failures of this market-based retirement project; it has entrenched workforce

INTRODUCTION 7

inequality, leaving casualised and young workers, and women generally, with little prospect of a properly funded retirement.

This book is an argument against the neoliberal policies and reformist programs of the labour movement of the Accord years, which continue to this day. Unlike the plethora of pro-Accord histories and apologia, *Stuff the Accord! Pay up!* recovers the neglected history of working class resistance to the Accord – essential if we are to learn from history and rebuild a fighting union movement.

Chapter 1 introduces the Accord, and the following chapters detail key disputes of the Accord years. Chapter 2 describes two significant disputes: Dollar Sweets, in Melbourne, and an abattoir at Mudginberri in the Northern Territory (NT); both defeats were commonly attributed to 'New Right' forces among employers, but it was actually the restraints imposed on workers by the Accord and by the ACTU that were responsible.

Chapters 3 and 4 cover two major confrontations between the state, the state-based industrial relations systems and unions, nominally outside the Accord: firstly, the sacking of Queensland electricians at the South East Queensland Electricity Board (SEQEB) and the campaign run by the Electrical Trades Union (ETU), which had the potential to lead a breakout from the Accord but ended in disaster for the workers and for union strength; secondly, the inspirational 50-day strike of the Victorian nurses which comprehensively defeated the state Labor government's cost-cutting agenda but was quickly quarantined by the ACTU

Chapter 5 addresses the influential New Right agenda, specifically at the remote Robe River mine in Western Australia's (WA) Pilbara region. A dispute that could have been won was again undermined by the ACTU, continuing the Accord's record of union defeats.

Chapter 6 describes the destruction of one of the country's most militant unions, the Builders Labourers Federation (BLF), by governments, with the willing participation of the ACTU and other Left union leaderships.

Chapter 7 examines the fight within the federal government sphere, in the then Department of Social Security (DSS). The government's objective of cutting wages and conditions was resisted for some time by strong rank and file organisation but finally sold out by the union leadership for less than their claim.

Chapter 8 charts the brutal war against pilots in the Australian Federation of Airline Pilots (AFAP), a war directed by the federal government, ACTU and employers with the willing connivance of ground staff unions such as the Transport Workers Union (TWU).

Chapter 9 documents three key disputes from 1989 to 1992, showing how workers continued to fight back against the Accord, with varying degrees of success, right up to its last days.

Chapter 10 deals with one of the supposed gains of the Accord, superannuation, showing that it is essentially designed to benefit the financial system and prop up the economy at workers' expense.

Chapter 11 focuses on enterprise bargaining, supposedly the pinnacle of the Accord's neoliberal agenda. It divided industries and disempowered workers in both the public and private sectors.

Chapter 12 summarises the impact of the class collaboration of the Accord and returns to the main theme of the book, emphasising working class resistance and its continuing potential to change the world for the better.

CHAPTER 1

The Accord – 'A Transitional Program for Socialism'?

Described by the AMWU's Laurie Carmichael as a 'transitional program for socialism', the Accord emerged against a backdrop of workers' uprisings around the world.[11] The late 1960s and early 1970s saw a worldwide wave of uprisings: a surge in workers' struggles in France, Italy, Poland, Czechoslovakia and Britain; student uprisings; the massive anti-Vietnam war protests; and the explosive arrival of the black, women's and gay liberation movements – all culminating in the revolution in Portugal in 1974. The growth of the left included the revitalisation of a revolutionary left. Trotskyists who rejected the Stalinism of Russia and China wanted instead a new society won by workers themselves. Much smaller than the hegemonic communist parties, they were nonetheless able to play a role in some of the key struggles. Australia reflected all of this in local movements, left wing parties and protests, many involving workers. This peaked in 1974, with the highest strike figures since 1919, and it scared the ruling class. In 1976, the year before he became Governor-General, Zelman Cowen talked about the many challenges to authority:

> People mass, march, sit in defiance of government and law, there are clashes with police ... involving the mass resistance of people protesting about various political and social issues ... the use of industrial power for objectives which cannot be remotely described as industrial.

There was even 'a desperate concern with an increasing resort to violence' in Western society, where people must think they were 'in the middle of a civil war with those forces which wish to overturn it.'[12]

Cowan correctly pointed to the revolutionary nature of the struggle and the desire by many to overturn Western society. But it was not to last. The Portuguese revolution marked the highpoint; its defeat signalled the success of the ruling class counter-attack. Wanting to crush working class incursions on their power, bosses also noted that world capitalism was moving into economic crisis. The post-WWII boom had come to an end, and profit rates were falling. The rate of profit fell from around 17 percent at the end of the 1960s to around 9 percent by the mid-1970s and 6 percent in the early 1980s, rising to 9 percent again in 1986. In order to restore profit rates, employers had to cut into workers' share.

In Australia, the Whitlam Labor government came to power in 1972 on a reforming program but quickly implemented measures designed to punish the working class for capitalism's failures. By 1974, defying a massive strike wave, the Bob Hawke-led ACTU was quick to respond to the signs of a worsening economy with restraint, promising cooperation on all government measures. In particular, they signed on to the Autumn 1975 national wage case decision to implement quarterly indexation, which would gradually reduce real wages and bind unions not to pursue higher wages outside an individual enterprise or industry. Tom O'Lincoln points out:

> Once the unions had committed themselves to trading industrial peace for periodic pay increases, their officials were required to police the agreement and pressure increased on shop stewards to do the same.

The Hayden Budget of 1975 cut spending, public works and social welfare, while the government launched an ideological attack against workers, accusing unions of 'bloody-mindedness' in 'pricing thousands of Australia workers out of employment.'[13]

With Labor more on the nose with its supporters, the ruling class saw – and seized – its opportunity. Gough Whitlam's government was summarily dismissed by Governor-General John Kerr on 11 November 1975, a coup engineered by Opposition leader Malcolm Fraser, the Liberal and Country Parties' Coalition and their ruling class allies. The dismissal was met with an outpouring of anger on the streets. Millions of workers marched and struck around the country. Rather than turn this into a serious industrial campaign to unseat Fraser, the ALP and ACTU led workers into a purely electoral campaign, running the slogan 'maintain your rage.' Whitlam lost in a landslide to Fraser on 12 December.[14]

Class tensions simmered and often exploded during the Fraser years. The Coalition could not deliver on its promise of smashing the unions and significantly driving down wages and conditions to restore profits. When the resources boom of 1979 was met by a wages push from workers, the unpopular Fraser government was under threat; 1981 saw a breakout by Telstra workers, sparking a more generalised wages push and the formal end of wage indexation.

It seemed possible that the heady days of the early 1970s were returning. But it was not to be. Instead, by 1982, the world economy was again moving into recession. In Australia, the resources boom went into freefall: production dropped, unemployment and inflation rose, and profits fell. Fraser quickly imposed a wages freeze and rebuffed several ACTU offers for wage restraint deals to restore the economy. Workers initially responded with anger to the wage freeze and rising unemployment, and the momentum for action continued among unions and other social forces. For example, thousands marched in Melbourne in a militant 'Stop the City' protest over unemployment which ended with a stormy invasion of the ruling class Melbourne Club.[15] However, more unions were in retreat, choosing 'to forgo pay increases, to accept voluntary retrenchments, early retirements and Christmas shut-down in an effort to protect employment.'[16] Strikes and street marches were seen as disruptive barriers to boosting profits; buckling down to raise productivity became the union officials' mantra. When the union leadership backed the bosses' arguments that workers' wage rises were to blame for the crisis, and that increasing profitability and industry protection rather than shorter hours (on full pay) would help create more jobs, workers' confidence collapsed.[17]

Previously, the Left had opposed these right wing arguments and anti-worker solutions. But O'Lincoln explains that many on the left had long given up on revolution and were more intent on reforming capitalism.

Whitlam's defeat and the increasing employers' offensive, coupled with splits within the Communist Party and a shift to the right in the wake of an overall decline in workers' struggles after 1974, meant that most of the organised Left, including the Labor Party and its left wing, were shifting rightwards too.[18] These factors undermined the independent union committees of rank and file workers and shop stewards or shop committees in workplaces, ceding more control to union bureaucracies. Without this independent rank and file organisation, the impact of the economic crises left the militants ideologically disoriented, industrially weakened (even jobless) and effectively paralysed. They were no challenge to the officials' reformist and electoralist solutions. Many rank and file militants actually supported them.

Federal Labor continued its rightward direction after another electoral loss in 1977 and began entertaining ideas of a prices and incomes policy, or social contract between Labor and unions to regain workers' support. Labor MP Ralph Willis' senior economic adviser, John Langmore, presented a prices and incomes discussion paper to Labor's caucus, similar to one he'd drafted earlier for the Papua New Guinea government. Informal discussions began with caucus leaders, the ACTU and major unions before it was presented to the Labor Economists Conference in May 1979. In a paper on the 'Role of Incomes Policy', Willis emphasised that 'an essential aspect of a viable prices and incomes policy must be that it has a more equitable distribution of income, wealth and power.'

The social contract proposal was debated at the ALP's national conference in 1979. Some Left unions argued that it was just a disguise for wage restraint, but Left opposition was quickly neutralised; the conference voted unanimously in favour. A Labor government would, the policy outlined:

> With the understanding and cooperation of the trade union movement, develop and implement a policy which will encompass prices, wage incomes, non-waged incomes, the social wage, taxation reform and elimination of tax avoidance and which will achieve a more equitable distribution of our national wealth and income, with the commitment to supporting the maintenance of real wages by quarterly adjustments and the passing of the benefits of increases in productivity.[19]

The Accord in a nutshell!

Langmore described this social contract policy as: 'a realistic basis for consultation between the Labor Party and the trade unions about the moderation of wage claims' in return for various social wage, taxation and other policies. By the time of the 1980 elections, which Labor lost, this was the agreed position of both Labor and the union leaders. A working party of Labor MPs and ACTU officials met from 1981 to refine the paper. The resulting *Statement of Accord*, stronger on rhetoric than detail, was completed in June 1982, further revised and extended, then endorsed by caucus and a combined unions conference held during the election campaign in February 1983.[20]

Meanwhile, the Communist and Left Labor leadership of the AMWU had begun a process of re-educating members in the wake of the Whitlam government's defeat in 1975. Starting in 1976, the AMWU leadership brought out *The People's Budget* and went on to publish a series of pamphlets – *Australia Uprooted, Australia Ripped Off, Australia on the Rack* and *Australia on the Brink*.[21] These pamphlets, with their lurid 'pulp fiction' covers, forecast the death of the Australian economy – unless workers looked to the national interest rather than their own and collaborated with employers to modernise to lift production, productivity and profits. A key mechanism, introduced in *Australia on the Rack* in 1981, was a joint government–union prices and incomes or social contract policy, one that the unions argued could favour workers. The CPA explained in its paper, *Tribune*:

> There is always an incomes policy in existence ... There is one now [under Fraser] – a diabolical one that means workers get robbed ... The question arises whether the Labor Party formulates an incomes policy with consultation or regard for the trade union movement.[22]

But posing Fraser and Labor as the bad and the good misses the point of such incomes policies. British workers had discovered under their 1970s Labour government that signing onto such a policy would cause losses for workers if profits were the ultimate aim. Tom Bramble notes that these policies, with their nationalist proposals, struck at the heart of workers' strength and, in every case, 'eventually derailed the alternative – a class struggle response.'[23]

The 1981 ACTU Congress cemented the unions' acceptance of a social contract. Driven by the manufacturing and other Left unions to abandon their earlier unease about the British experience, they carried a resolution for wage restraint (although not in those exact words) in return for a social wage: tax cuts, superannuation for all and increased spending on welfare, education and health. The 1981 national metal (manufacturing) trades claim was the testing ground for the union movement's preparedness to implement such a social contract policy. The claim was for a $57 wage rise and a 35-hour week, but the AMWU leaders had agreed to half that: $27, a 38-hour week and a 12-month no-strike clause, with the promise of a social wage campaign to make up the difference.[24]

The bosses, naturally, wanted even more concessions – and they got them. The MTIA's Bert Evans told AMWU National Secretary Laurie Carmichael that he wanted a no-strike clause. Carmichael said that he couldn't deliver that, instead promising a no-extra-claims commitment. Carmichael explained that, if workers made no claims for extra improvements in wages or conditions after the deal was signed – as had been commonplace until then – there could be no industrial action. And Carmichael and the unions, not the bosses, would police the deal.[25]

Bert Evans got the MTIA mandate to sign the agreement with the AMWU, boasting to his club in the lead up to Christmas that he'd settled the strikes and helped set up a national disputes procedure. All through the Christmas break there were no strikes, but:

> when I got back to work after about 10 to 12 days, maybe 14 days and there were three claims or four claims. I rang Carmichael and I said, 'you had better convene this disputes panel because we have got three or four claims.' He said, 'no, I am not going to just do that, mate.' He said, 'you can forget it.' I never had a strike. He stuck to his word. He went out. He said [to his members], 'you bastards voted for this. You are going to do it. Drop it.' That then became the basis of the Accord. Hawke told me that he wouldn't have entertained the idea of the Accord if the metal unions hadn't proved they could be trusted.[26]

Evans commented recently, 'this was fantastic for us.'[27]

While the union leadership shut down any attempted extra claims, their social wage campaign was lacklustre, soon morphing into an electoral campaign supporting Labor and the new ALP–ACTU Accord.

A New Policy

With the election of the Hawke–Keating government in March 1983, the Accord experiment of class collaboration and neoliberalism began. This section will give an overview of key aspects of the Accord and briefly examine each stage. While union officialdom had been involved in the discussions and signed off on the deal, few workers had had any input to the Accord's content. Few had even seen the agreement before the election, and even fewer knew what it would mean for them. The messages they got from their union officials and the ACTU were promises of a better life, an end to capitalism's roller coaster ride of job losses, wage cuts and unaffordable services. One of the Accord's architects, then ACTU Secretary Bill Kelty, made typical comments:

> the philosophic framework [of the Hawke Keating government] ...... [was] Open up [the economy] to the rest of the world, increase productivity, promote competition – but part of the distribution would be powerful safety nets in national health care, superannuation and wages. In turn these super safety nets would promote adaption and change, thus increasing productivity.[28]

Such descriptions of the benefits of social contracts drew on the policies and experiences of some European and Scandinavian countries. The low rates of unemployment, equal education opportunities and social wage benefits of a thriving modern economy in countries such as Sweden were the role models for the Australian Accord. Austria's social contract, for example, was referred to by long-time CPA member Bernie Taft as the 'Austrian miracle.'[29]

Fairly soon, the positive Australian messages of social wage and workplace benefits turned into a focus on restraint, profits, productivity and competition:

For all the rhetoric of the 'social wage' in the 1980s, policy developments actually intensified the trend back to a selective welfare system, from which many workers obtain no benefit ... Secondly, the use of tax cuts as substitutes for wage increases benefited those in employment, but limited the available resources for social security initiatives.[30]

Eight Stages

The Accord went through eight stages, negotiated between the government and the ACTU. These stages more or less followed the national wage cases, each tailored to the needs of capital at the time – whether the economy was in recession or expanding, or how wage control was to be organised. Each stage left workers more impoverished, with lower wages, fewer conditions and rights, more anti-union sanctions and falling unionisation rates. At each stage, some workers did protest, strike and resist; because of worker opposition, not everything the employers or Accord partners wanted was achieved.

Each Accord agreement, the 'two-tier' system, award restructuring and enterprise bargaining, was part of a process of transforming the wages system. For the first two Accord stages, a centralised system, based on a national wage case before the Arbitration Commission, used the cost of living index and other economic factors to determine new wage rates for all. The Accord continued Fraser's wage discounting, resulting in an effective 18-month freeze, and invoked external factors, such as devaluation of the dollar and Medicare, to lower expected pay increases. It also dismantled the previous union practice of flow-on: the stronger unions winning wages and conditions in their sectors, usually by taking industrial action, which then spread to the weaker or less organised workers. By enforcing a no-extra-claims commitment from every union before the centralised increase could be granted, the Accord processes ensured that each rise was strictly quarantined and limited to a workplace or individual industries. The result was a growing wage disparity and a dramatic drop in industrial action, all of which weakened both strong and weak unions and the movement as a whole.

One of the most destructive aspects of the Accord was the undermining of the solidarity built up through such struggles. Workplace action was 'derided

THE ACCORD – 'A TRANSITIONAL PROGRAM FOR SOCIALISM'?

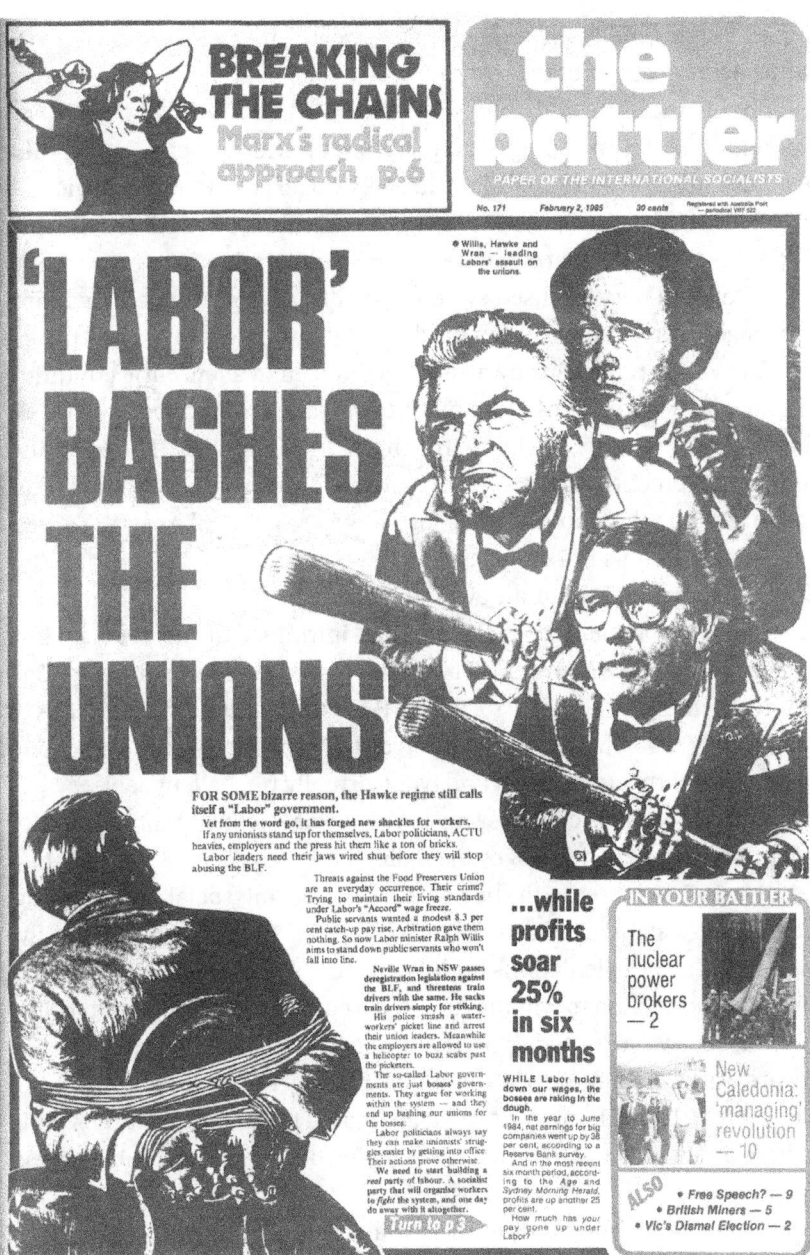

The Battler 2 February 1985

as defensive, sectional and counter-productive', often described as the selfishness of elite sections of the working class.[31] The liberal use of threats or actual enforcement of the anti-solidarity laws, – s.45D of the *Trade Practices Act* and other industrial and common law legislation which opened up unions to thousands and thousands of dollars in fines – backed up the ideological war against industrial action and solidarity with prohibitive sanctions

From a centralised arrangement, wage determinations were shifted step-by-step to a decentralised system – and finally enterprise bargaining – where wages were traded off for productivity improvements, enterprise by enterprise; where remaining awards were reduced to a few basic conditions, leaving workers the options of no pay rise or trading off even more. This led to the disastrous situation where, in enterprise bargaining: 'The inability of the union movement to exercise a collective approach to the labour market is demonstrated by the opportunities forgone during one of Australia's strongest economic booms in 1988–89.'[32]

Individual contracts put an even greater dent in workers' ability to win improvements or bargain collectively. First introduced from 1990 as Enterprise Flexibility Agreements (s.170NA), they were extended to include Certified Agreements (s.170MA) in 1992 and 1993 amendments to the *Industrial Relations Act (1988)*. Legally subject to certain safeguards, they nonetheless allowed non-union agreements and were virtually unchallengeable.[33]

The impact of these changes was to drive wages down. Using 1983–84 as a benchmark, by 1990 real wages had fallen by $1,032.21 on an annual basis, offset by a $57.07 increase in the social wage. Taking social and real wages together, living standards were lowered by $975.14, or 5.4 percent.[34] Even then, some of these calculations understated the value of the social wage: $17 million spent on trying to win the America's cup yacht race a second time, in the mid-1980s, was counted as part of the social wage.[35]

Award wages continued to fall in value, dropping by 5 percent between 1993 and 1996 and by a full 16 percent when compared to their value in 1983. Enterprise bargaining didn't deliver much, flattening out by 1996. Bramble notes:

> Even taking into account the social wage, only the top 20 percent of households saw any overall income lift in the decade to 1994 and income inequality registered a sharp increase under Labor.[36]

The Prices Surveillance Authority, introduced to keep a check on prices as wages were held back, was a toothless tiger, an advisory body with absolutely no power. Hard won workplace conditions, gained from decades of struggle, had to be traded off because wages became linked to productivity. These changes were part of a process of accommodating 'whatever industrial issue, economic challenge or social imperative that emerged which the Accord partners needed to address.' Exactly who was accommodated becomes clear; the Accord afforded employers:

> the 'courage' and the protection to raise some of the old 'sacred cows.' These long outdated practices, such as 'one in, all in' approach to the rostering of overtime had remained off limits ... until the Accord ... refused to justify 'such outrageous inefficiencies' that prevailed in the majority of workplaces.[37]

Like all neoliberal projects, the Accord aimed to weaken union power and undermine unionisation. Leadership-led compromises and collaboration resulted in defeat after defeat, until decline in membership was inevitable The decline 'occurred in almost every sector of the workforce, private and public sector, women and men, every age group, in every state and territory and in every industry except mining which employs relatively few people.'[38]

With falling union membership and a more complex industrial sphere, the unions' resources were strained. Amalgamation was just one of many plans dreamt up by union officials in trying to rebuild. *Future Strategies for the Trade Union Movement* (1987), *Unions 2001, a Blueprint for Union Activism* (1993) and other publications proposed a target of reducing the number of unions from around 300 to 20 large, industry-based organisations, offering new strategies, new services and more democratic union structures to revive union membership. Nothing was included about challenging the laws or taking industrial action – just more training, more meetings, more advice and something called 'social wage activism.' *Unions 2001* really just argued for the Accord, resolving that, if Labor lost the 1993 election, they would campaign for a new Accord in the lead up to the 1996 election.[39] There was to be no attempt to rebuild fighting unions from the workplace up, taking on employers, breaking the law and building solidarity. Backing the

The Battler 2 March 1985

government's attacks on unions produced impotence; time and again, the Australian Industrial Relations Commission (AIRC) ruled against them, and the employers went on the attack, even flouting the law.

Outlined in various phases of the Accord was a range of industry plans, promoted as providing a secure future for workers and the economy and a way for unions to intervene in the economy and have a role in determining policy. In reality, the focus was only on industries in sectors vital for Australia's export market or fundamental to restoring profitability to the Australian economy. Profitability returned in areas covered by the industry plans, but there was a massive loss of jobs, and lower wages and conditions, for workers in the waterfront, steel, textiles and meat industries and the federal public sector.

In the textiles, clothing and footwear sector, the tripartite plan was overtaken by the 1987 tariff cuts which crippled the industry. The steel industry plan saw the 'big Australian', BHP, paid $360 million in industry assistance between 1983 and 1987. Annual production rose from 175 to 260 tonnes per worker, while 21,000 workers lost their jobs. Millions of dollars from state and federal governments poured into the coal industry, but hundreds of workers were laid off and miners' conditions seriously downgraded. The 1989 Waterfront Industry Reform Authority (WIRA) pushed through 1,000 job losses and removed union control over hiring and allocation of labour. With the shift to company-based employment, workers' jobs were tied to the fortunes of individual stevedores, undercutting union solidarity and enhancing the ability of employers to hire and fire. Later, Labor MP Kim Beazley was to boast to parliament about these cuts. Union leaders not only backed the reforms, but were often part of the planning, implementation and enforcement against their own members' interests.[40]

The Accord revamped the industrial relations laws to accommodate the various changes to the wages system and union organisation. There were promises to revoke anti-union laws, but apart from abolishing Fraser's Industrial Relations Bureau (with the support of the Liberal Opposition!), the government made only a half-hearted attempt in 1984 to repeal these laws. Introduced just before the 1984 election, the legislation was quickly dropped when the Australian Democrats refused to support it. ALP Senator, Gareth Evans, told parliament that all the government was doing was 'paying lip service to a promise it made with the ACTU.'[41]

Overall, it was the economic benefits for capitalism through a neoliberal project that drove the Accord and its supporters. Elizabeth Humphrys convincingly argues that the Accord oversaw the introduction and implementation of neoliberalism. It contained several essential components central to neoliberalism, including 'wage suppression; suppression of industrial militancy; the implementation of capital-focused industry policy; and the introduction of deregulated industrial relations through enterprise bargaining.' In Australia, unlike countries such as the USA, UK and New Zealand (NZ) where incorporation was through coercive confrontation, 'the social democratic ALP and the union movement led by the ACTU, ensured that the Australian labour movement actively participated in and consented to its own disorganisation through a social contract.'

It was one of the most self-destructive steps the union movement in Australia has ever taken.

Accord Mark I

The first stage of the Accord was the first step in restraint, continuing Fraser's wage freeze, maintaining indexation (linking wages to cost of living increases) but delaying finalisation of the 1983 national wage case until the end of 1984. Bob Hawke also sent a warning to any workers aiming to restore the losses from the Fraser freeze. He told parliament:

> if a centralised system of wage fixing is to work, there must be an abstention from sectional claims except in special and extraordinary circumstances ... [leaving] no room for selfish claims from maverick sections of the trade union movement.'[42]

In reality, from 1983, 'the Accord years can be best viewed as being characterised as one in which the ALP employed a strategy of promise, promise, delay, delay.'[43] The Accord document had promised wage rises 'over time', and, from day one, delays were built into the processes.

Accord Mark II (September 1985)

By 1985, Australia was facing a falling dollar, a decline in the terms of trade, and inflation caused by higher priced imports. The ACTU therefore retreated from any commitment to full wage indexation, offering instead a wage–tax–superannuation deal. Wages would be discounted by 2 percent because of devaluation of the dollar, and this cut to workers' real purchasing power was followed a year later by a tax cut of around $5. Already there was talk of productivity-related pay rises, but this was converted into a 3 percent superannuation payment – in effect, a pay cut.

Even at this early stage, some unions had reservations about the superannuation trade-offs. The transport and coal unions started industrial bans campaigns for superannuation before the national wage case had agreed to the deal. They were pressured by the Commission, the government and the ACTU to back down, which they did. Hawke was adamant that wages had to keep falling. Delays in granting national wage rises had already benefited employers, saving them $250– 400 million; while the ACTU organised a day of protest, delays continued. The final decision was a 2.3 percent wage rise from 1 July 1986 and an unspecified amount from 1 January 1987, following a review in December 1986.[44] The Accord objective of maintenance of real wages over time clearly meant, possibly sometime in the future; definitely not in the here and now. According to Treasury, real earnings declined by 2.4 percent in 1985–6 following the negligible increases of the preceding two years.

Accord Mark III (March 1987) – two tiers

In November 1986, when the national wage case reopened, the ACTU presented its claim for a 6.7 percent increase in 1987, to be paid in two stages or tiers. The first tier would give two flat wage increases of $10 for all workers in 1987, and the second tier would be negotiated between unions and employers over the period, capped at 4 percent.

The wage indexation promise was ditched after just three years, and the debate on productivity trade-offs ramped up, laying the groundwork for enterprise bargaining. The government delayed promised tax cuts and pension rises, tightened welfare criteria, introduced student fees, increased taxes and sold off government-owned assets, aiming to achieve $4 billion in Budget savings.

For some Accord apologists, the two-tier system remained 'strategically the best course' for the ACTU in the longer term; in alliance with a future Labor government, under relatively favourable conditions, union organisation could be strengthened where historically it had been weakest – at the

enterprise level. And a more active presence in the workplace might stem or reverse the erosion of union membership.[45]

Nothing like this happened. Two years into Accord Mark III, only 20 percent of workplaces had won a second-tier rise. A 1989 review showed that all second-tier agreements involved trading away conditions such as penalty rates, a rise in casual and part-time staff, restrictions on the ability to strike and more managerial control.[46] Any work practices that were actually improved conditions were won by workers through their own struggles.

The second-tier deal was not popular, with rank and file opposition reaching government and private enterprises. Oppositional unions included the federal clerical unions, the Australian Public Sector Association (APSA) and the Administrative and Clerical Officers' Association (ACOA), the NSW Teachers Federation and the printers and manufacturing unions, PKIU and AMWU. At a Melbourne delegates' meeting, AMWU State Secretary John Halfpenny defended the decision and argued that more discussion was needed, adding: 'We have to start resuming some of our traditional activities so that we can get a proper deal.'[47]

A Government Ammunitions Factory (GAF) delegate told the meeting:

> We've been the bunnies. Profits have gone through the roof. They've cut our wages and the federal government has helped them. This time, we say no bloody deal! No deal until our members have a say! No deal until the government delivers.

This was only the beginning of the war on workers. Treasurer Paul Keating explained later that, while real wage cutting was exhausted by the late eighties, 'it served its purpose in restoring the factor shares, lifting profits and getting investment restarted.'

Accord Mk IV (1988) – Award Restructuring

Award Restructuring was the process that rewrote the awards (arbitration-approved agreements documenting job descriptions and wage rates) in every sector to suit the 'modern workplace.' In exchange, there was to be a pay rise. The Award Restructuring or Structural Efficiency Principle of the August 1988 national wage case decision explained how it would happen:

> Increases in wages and salaries or improvements in conditions allowable … shall be justified if the union … agrees to cooperate positively in a fundamental review of that award with a view to implementing measures to improve the efficiency of industry and provide workers with access to more varied, fulfilling and better paid jobs.

Trade-offs were required in career paths, multiskilling, hours and conditions, numbers of unions and the introduction of core and periphery employment (casualisation).

Union officials were quick to deny that this represented 'negative cost cutting'; rather, it would open up new opportunities for all. First to go would be the award clauses that stood in the way of multiskilling and flexibility. Training and retraining would open up a new career structure, with more choices and chances to advance. Workers would be paid extra for learned skills. Conditions

would be more flexible, giving workers greater access to part-time work and more control over their working hours and holidays. Federated Ironworkers Association (FIA) secretary Steve Harrison claimed that anyone could become whatever they liked. Tellingly, however, Industrial Relations (IR) Minister Peter Cook praised the restructuring for cutting the manufacturing trades skill levels from 300 to 14, describing how the 'task-based classification structure helped entrench a Taylorist system of production.'[48]

'Women only' jobs, those well-known ghettoes of low paid work, would disappear. In offices, for example, everyone would use keyboards, allowing keyboard workers to learn new tasks and 'aim for the top' like anyone else. Migrant workers would benefit from retraining. Sue McCreadie of the Textiles Union painted a glowing picture of award restructuring providing 'an opening for a significant shift in the balance of power in the workplace, from management to workers.'[49]

Others saw the benefit for the employers, because workers would be forced to rely on their individual abilities and ways to re-skill for any pay increase rather than a union-led general wage rise.

One unionist commented to me: 'things have got a lot worse since the job redesign, everybody's more competitive, it's not as cooperative as before.'

Multiskilling was another bosses' benefit, the paper wrote, because it 'alleviates short term labour shortages since individual workers will be more productive.' I explained at the time: 'In unstable industries – and even within the government sector – only a core of trained workers will be secure. For the rest we'll see a lot of less skilled casuals with no career paths, training or job security.'[50]

Many workers benefited little; some went downhill. In government-owned enterprises, employment fell 24 percent between 1987 and 1993, while labour productivity rose 100 percent. One manufacturing worker's experience of award restructuring was all too common. As a shop steward, he'd been really enthusiastic about restructuring, but he told me:

> Once they'd worked out how a certain number of workers could take on extra jobs and they picked the ones who weren't very union minded, they promptly told the ten of us we were redundant …So don't mention restructuring to me, it stinks to high heaven.

Australia Reconstructed, the 1987 report of a Department of Trade–ACTU junket to Western Europe, stated quite openly that the purpose of the Accord and award restructuring was to increase 'international competitiveness and productivity, rather than the maintenance of living standards.' The report also countenanced fines for, and limits on, strikes – a sentiment endorsed by IR Minister Peter Cook on the Accord's thirtieth anniversary.[51]

Accord Mark V (1989)

For this round, the government offered moderate wage increases, more tax cuts and social wage improvements. The importance of continuing award restructuring and, later, union amalgamations under the Accord was spelled out by Keating in an address to corporate Japan in November 1989:

> it is important to recognise that before we can develop greater flexibility in wages and working conditions across industries and enterprises, we have to rationalise the structure of unions and awards'.

The purpose of this exercise, he said, was to 'create a framework which can handle greater relative wage flexibility without generating destabilising flow-ons and wage break-outs'[52] (see figure 1).

Award restructuring continued, despite the loss by many of hard won conditions for little reward. For manufacturing workers, flexibility led to 12-hour shifts, no penalty rates, and annual leave only when it suited the employer. AMWU national industrial officer Chris Lloyd noted his members' unrest; they struggled 'to understand why, in a period of the eighties when there was substantial productivity and profit improvements in Australian manufacturing, they got such dismal results out of it.'[53]

UNION AMALGAMATIONS

In 1987, the proposal to rationalise the number of unions down from 326 to 20 through amalgamations came out of *Australia Reconstructed*.[54] The rationale was that having fewer, larger unions was critical for the future of unionism, ensuring better service, greater efficiencies and more effective recruitment campaigns. This so-called 'strategic unionism' would provide resources for unions to respond to a changing world, including taking greater responsibility for Australian economic conditions. In reality, amalgamations were a means of coping with declining membership (without recruiting members in the workplace, or fighting for workers on the job) and centralising more power in the hands of the top union bureaucrats and the ACTU.

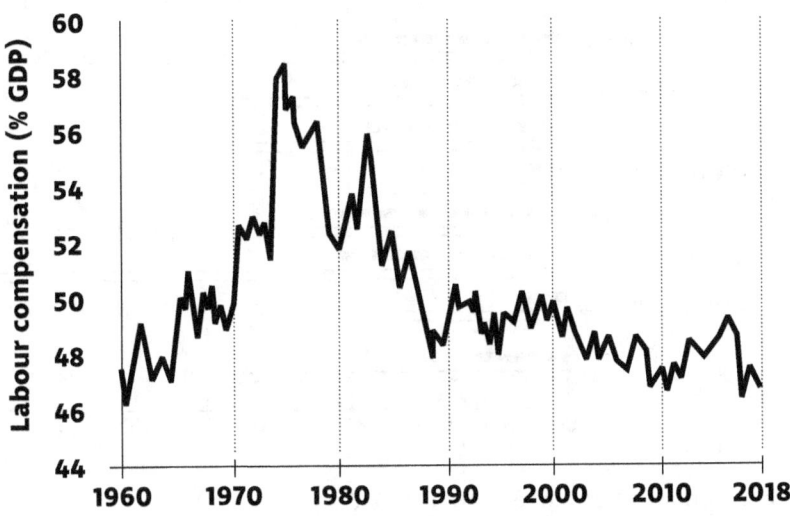

Figure 1. Wages as proportion of GDP. Source ABS

By mid-1996, 132 unions survived; 47 were federally registered and represented 86 percent of total union membership. While the majority of members did vote on the amalgamations, the ACTU decided which unions were to amalgamate and with whom. 'Principal unions' in each sector would remain, entrenching the biggest unions and forcing many into amalgamating with right wing unions. Those who did try to resist amalgamation or shift to more progressive unions were quickly rebuffed through *Industrial Relations Act* s.118 orders.

There is no evidence that the mergers contributed to greater union democracy, increased membership or better services. Ewer et al. argue that, faced with 'the concerted attempts to break unionism's role at the workplace through enterprise bargaining, it matters not one jot whether the program of union amalgamation succeeds.'[55]

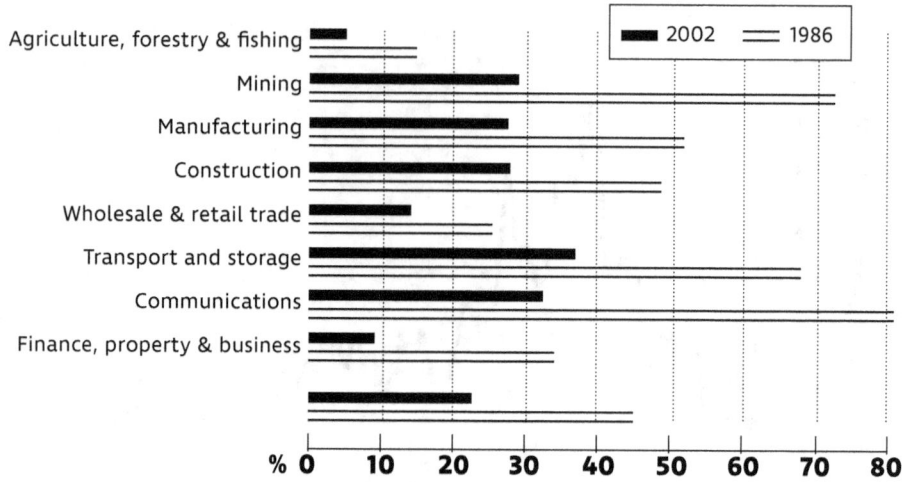

Figure 2. Union membership rate August 1986 and 2002 (%). Source ABS. After The Australian Financial Review 23 October 2003.

Accord Mark VI (Feb 1990, revised Nov 1990) – Flexibility

This was negotiated in the context of a forthcoming July election. It delivered a 2.5 percent wage rise, a continuation of award restructuring and a 'flexibility' clause. The deal promoted the future introduction of enterprise bargaining. For the rest of 1990, unions engaged in a mostly futile over-award campaign, which just delayed the 2.5 percent increase. The deal was really a safety valve for some in the workforce, but it backfired on those who did manage to win an extra rise – such as AMWU members, who subsequently saw their deals overturned, rewritten and reduced in the August 1991 national wage case.

Employment did grow, at an average rate of around 2 percent for full-time jobs and 6.3 percent for part-time jobs, with an increase in the female participation rate from 42.3 percent to 53 percent. However, the figures hid the decline in living standards and the loss of the purchasing power of a single income. Many of the jobs were low paid and lacking in career opportunities and access to skills training and affordable child care. The rapid rise in unemployment in 1990–91 demonstrated that the Accord's employment record was largely illusory.

Accord Mark VII (October 1991) – Enterprise Bargaining

In a damning assessment, the Australian union movement was described in 1991 as being 'associated with a program of privatisation, deregulation, real wage cuts and "reforms" to the welfare system which limit access to benefits.'[56] Next came an even greater transformation of the wages system.

The Accord itself was given an obituary by the *Australian Financial Review*. It had achieved 'an attitudinal shift among union officialdom and a moderation in aggregate wage outcomes through the 1980s.'[57] But the paper did not factor in the full impact of enterprise bargaining ushered in by Accord Mark VII, nor the shift by newly elected conservative state governments in Victoria and WA to scrap their state tribunals and introduce individual and non-union collective agreements, allowing only the barest of safety nets.

After rejecting the Accord partners' enterprise bargaining submission in April 1991, the Commission finally waved it through in October that year. To ensure that it would be an employers' picnic, the Commission pared down basic safety net conditions to four – annual leave, long service leave, standard hours of work and ordinary time earnings. Everything else was up for grabs when workers negotiated with employers, enterprise by enterprise.

The push for superannuation continued but met opposition from employers, with the Commission refusing to lift the levy from 3 percent to 6 percent. In response, the government legislated a Superannuation Guarantee Levy in 1992, but even this delayed the next increase; in 2020, it still lingers on 9 percent, with the promised rise to a 12 percent levy in limbo.[58]

This was another gift to employers. In 1983, the wages and conditions of around 85 percent of workers were set by federal and state awards. Two years after enterprise bargaining was introduced, fewer than one in eight workers were covered by enterprise agreements, the rest receiving only AIRC endorsed national rises. By 2012, only 16 percent were covered solely by awards, 42 percent had collective agreements, and 38 percent were on individual contracts. Almost 40 percent of enterprise agreements were made without unions. The role of unions on the job or in determining workers' wages and conditions continued to diminish[59] (see figure 2).

Accord Mark VIII (June 1995)

The final Accord agreement was reached on 21 June 1995, focusing on superannuation and national savings strategies. It was never implemented, because Labor lost decisively to John Howard's Liberal–National Party Coalition on 2 March 1996.

The Accord left a terrible legacy. By reducing power in the workplace, it laid workers open to more attacks by the Coalition and drove another catastrophic decline in unionisation. By 2019, experiencing stagnant wages and reduced conditions, in a low-growth economy buffeted by world instability and a continued anti-union onslaught, the ACTU and union bureaucracy have sunk to an all-time low of lobbying right wing senators, abandoning all pretence of a class-based struggle against the ruling class.

CHAPTER 2
Unions and the New Right

During the 1970s, predating the Accord, a loose coalition of groups and individuals founded explicitly political organisations such as the National Farmers Federation (NFF) in 1979 (which always denied any political role) and the HR Nicholls Society in 1986.[60] Dubbed the New Right during the 1980s, they were instrumental in pushing the boundaries.

The New Right played a significant role in various disputes, including Mudginberri, Dollar Sweets (Confectioners Union), SEQEB (ETU) and Robe River (AMWU, ETU, Australian Workers Union [AWU]). In 1987, the NFF backed employers taking on unions through the use of s.45D of the *Trade Practices Act*, especially in rural transport and grain handling. None of the unions was fined, but the threat of s.45D or common law torts ended industrial action. Union demands were defeated and employers victorious.[61]

John Howard, leader of the federal Liberal–National Party Opposition, praised the Mudginberri decision, declaring: 'let a thousand Mudginberris bloom.' Throughout 1985, Howard called for deregulation of the labour market, individual contracting and opting out of the award system, arguing: 'the right of individual Australians to make decisions in their own interests' as opposed to the influence of 'outside organisations' (unions) and the 'tyranny of collectivity ... [unions, who] believe they have an option to decide whether they will [obey the law] or not.' Mudginberri became a symbol for conservatives of 'individual freedom versus trade union power.'[62]

Dollar Sweets

Right wing journalist Janet Albrechtson relishes the history of the Dollar Sweets dispute, a reminder, she says, that unions had it too sweet for too long. 'A story worth telling? You bet. If only to provide an entertaining history lesson that rebuts the myth about the purity of collective action.' She describes Fred Stauder as 'one bloke just trying to run his small business in Victoria, making "hundreds and thousands", so kids could keep enjoying fairy bread at their parties.'[63]

This touching narrative is somewhat loose with the truth. Confectionery bosses, including Fred Stauder, were reaping big profits, and the union had won wage and conditions increases for its members across the industry. Stauder pulled ruling class forces together to fight the union at Dollar Sweets, and the union lost the confrontation. Fifteen workers lost their jobs, the union lost members and was fined, and the scab workforce continued to work for less money on longer hours than the rest of the industry. Stauder was the beneficiary, as was the company's lawyer, Peter Costello.

The dispute marked a significant breakthrough for employers against legitimate union actions like picketing. It exposed unions to common law claims and hefty damages claims.[64] Alongside the win at Mudginberri, it 'persuaded employers that a shift to enterprise bargaining was possible without exposing themselves to "union blackmail".' Aspects of the judgement were later incorporated into John Howard's WorkChoices legislation.[65]

Common law claims had been popular with employers much earlier in Australia's industrial history, but after the mass strikes – and defeats – of the 1890s, arbitration was introduced as an alternative to the civil courts. The option was still there, however; the laws were never changed, and it would take only a determined employer and legal team to test the system and take on unions. That employer was Fred Stauder, whose legal team included two new right wing lawyers, Michael Kroger and Peter Costello, backed by a number of high-profile heads of corporations, anti-union companies and organisations. Stauder was not exactly a lone crusader.

The story begins in September 1983, very early in the Accord years, when the Arbitration Commission began the first of many cutbacks of workers' wages. The Commission was prepared to grant a national Consumer Price Index

(CPI) linked wage increase, but only on the proviso that the unions make no extra claims on employers for better conditions, penalty rates or allowances before the next wage case. Each union had to provide this guarantee individually to the Commission before its members were granted the increase.

Frustration with the new Accord process grew during the first two years, as the Arbitration Commission used a variety of economic rationalisations to grant less than full CPI increases. It continued Fraser's wage freeze, delayed the rises by months and twice discounted the full amount. This round of wage cutting lasted through to March 1987, when Accord Mark III introduced another attack on workers, productivity-linked trade-offs of conditions for pay rises.

The Confectionery Workers Union (CWU), unlike most unions, had refused to make the no-extra-claims commitment for wage rises, so their members did not receive the September 1983 increase.[66] Instead, the union used strategic forms of industrial action to win better wages and conditions. Between 1983 and 1985, the CWU gained a 36-hour working week, four hours less than the award, with no cut in pay, for 90 percent of its 2,700 members.

At Dollar Sweets, Stauder offered workers the CPI wage increase in November 1983, on the proviso that they signed up individually to the Commission's no-extra-claims commitment. Without any union input, all 27 workers signed on the dotted line and were paid the wage rise. Since then, Stauder had not increased the workers' wages. Faced with the CWU demand for a 36-hour week in July1985, Stauder refused to lower the factory's 38-hour week, claiming that he could not afford it; he offered to show his accounts to the union but was rebuffed.

The CWU began an industrial campaign, calling its members out on strike. Stauder responded by demanding that workers add a no-strike clause to their current agreement or lose their jobs. Twelve of the 27 workers signed and returned to work. The 15 who refused were sacked on the spot. Stauder announced that they would never work at the factory again. He hired another 15 workers on the new agreement.

With no resolution, Stauder went to the AIRC. On 15 July, Commissioner Bain ruled that the industrial action must stop. The members refused and set up a picket outside the factory – an action that was to last 143 days. At this point, the CWU dropped the 36-hour claim in order to focus on reinstating the sacked workers.

The picket lines were solid, stopping most of the deliveries in and out of the factory. All major trucking companies refused to cross the line, and large suppliers would not sell to Dollar Sweets. It had a big impact on the company's bottom line; later figures demonstrated that a $10,000 profit for three months in the second half of 1984 turned into an $80,000 loss for the corresponding quarter in 1985.[67]

The striking workers and their union were subjected to a hostile media campaign, including allegations of damage to company premises and of violence against those attempting to break the picket line. Some of the strikers were charged and fined, including Carlo Frizziero, the CWU Victorian secretary, after confronting one of the truck drivers.[68] The dispute was the start of a concerted – and successful – attempt by the employers and Accord supporters to call for 'consultation' and 'compromise' instead of industrial action, in order to delegitimise effective picketing and prevent any wages break out.

The company demanded 24-hour police protection, which was refused. Dollar Sweets then employed armed guards.[69]

At the end of September, Dollar Sweets considered court action to sue the CWU for the costs of the dispute. ACTU Secretary Bill Kelty reiterated the union movement's (limited) support for the sacked workers, warning the company that taking this action would make the dispute harder to settle.

In October, Dollar Sweets, through the Arbitration Commission, offered the sacked workers assistance 'in finding alternative employment within the industry and also to supply references for these people.' Commissioner Bain recommended that 'those who have been picketing should accept the employer's offer and cease their picketing forthwith.' The sacked workers held firm and refused the offer, wanting their jobs back. Stauder then claimed to be seriously considering an invitation from the Queensland government to move his operations to that state.[70]

The union and the employer were in a stalemate. Support for the CWU was shamefully limited. Prime Minister (PM) Bob Hawke, as in other disputes, proved to be no friend of the sacked workers; he sent a message to Stauder encouraging him in his stand against the CWU. Despite the ACTU's expression of support, both Kelty and Simon Crean publicly condemned the union, saying that its claim was outside the Accord.

Against such an employer, real support from the ACTU could have helped to build a solid campaign for the Dollar Sweets workers. Solidarity action from other confectionery workers in the larger firms would have forced the manufacturers and their industry association to pressure Dollar Sweets management to make a deal. Instead, the ACTU ruled out solidarity actions, thereby signalling to courts and employers that they need not fear industrial retaliation.

Stauder, on the other hand, had the backing of the major employer organisations, including the Victorian Chamber of Commerce and the Confectionery Manufacturers Association, along with business leaders such as mining magnate Hugh Morgan. It was Morgan who directed Stauder to Peter Costello, a newly graduated lawyer with strong connections to anti-union businesses, company heads and Liberal Party members. Costello brought in Michael Kroger, a long-time friend and fellow right winger, and Alan Goldberg QC as lead lawyer.[71] This team recommended the somewhat risky common law option of suing the union through the Supreme Court of Victoria, an option Costello admitted he would not advise every company to follow because of the cost, time taken and the chance of losing.[72] The Victorian Chamber of Commerce, whose director, Andrew Hay, was a well-known anti-union business figure, financed the case.

In November 1985, the company began legal proceedings in the Supreme Court of Victoria. Stauder's team alleged 'torts of interference with contractual relations, torts of intimidation, torts of nuisance and conspiracy to injure the plaintiff' and sought injunctions and common law damages of more than $150,000. Stauder also sought an injunction to stop the union picketing.

On 12 December 1985, Victorian Supreme Court Justice Peter Murphy granted the injunction in a vicious ruling, calling the picket 'anarchy' and 'nihilistic', a 'nuisance involving obstruction, harassment and besetting.'

The charge of besetting, an 1875 law imported from England which criminalised effective pickets, was alarming. It had been threatened in the 1920s against the Timberworkers and was later used against the BLF in the 1980s, in the 1990s against union leaders in NSW and in the 2000s against anti-fracking protesters and Palestine solidarity activists.[73]

Justice Murphy described the union as trying to destroy the company.[74] He argued that the existence of specialist arbitral courts for industrial disputes was beside the point, claiming jurisdiction for the Supreme Court: 'This court is not without power ... and should intervene.' He issued an interlocutory injunction against the picket and ordered the union to pay damages. The picket was lifted on 13 December 1985. The damages case was finally settled in April 1988, with the union having to pay Dollar Sweets $175,000. It was the first time in Australia that a union paid common law damages to an employer for losses suffered through picketing, and its significance can't be underestimated. AMWU secretary Doug Cameron reflected, many years later:

> It was when the social contract between workers, business and government started to collapse. It became a cause célèbre for the big end of town and lawyers started to realise they could make money ripping off the pay and conditions of the workers.

When Cameron admitted this, in 2006, the dispute – and the Accord – were long gone.[75]

Costello revelled in the use of the law outside arbitration. He noted that arbitration was introduced with the express purpose of stopping the use of common law in industrial matters, with Henry Bourne Higgins calling it 'a new province for law and order.' For Costello, it was the reintroduction of common law through Dollar Sweets 'that ushered in, at long last, a truly new province for law and order.'[76]

Mudginberri Abattoir

The small Mudginberri export buffalo abattoir deep in the NT was not the obvious candidate for a pivotal role in the Accord years, but its name remains seared in Australia's industrial relations history.

CONTEXT

A number of factors combined to bring this case to the forefront: the Australasian Meat Industry Employees Union (AMIEU) campaign to win award conditions in the NT; the response of the Manager, John David (Jay) Pendarvis, a paid-up Country Liberal Party member; support for him from the NFF and from the NT and Queensland conservative governments; and the changed position of the industry employer group, the Meat and Allied Trades Federation of Australia (MATFA).[77] In the background were two key clashes which the unions had lost: the live sheep export dispute of 1978, involving the AMIEU, and the AWU shearers' strikes during 1982–83 over wide-comb shearing, which saw the intervention of the NFF for the first time.[78] David Trebick (writing for the HR Nicholls Society) argues that the live sheep conflict 'marked the turning-point in the handling of industrial matters in Australia after the decline which followed the O'Shea case in the late 1960s.'[79] For Ian McLachlan, NFF president from 1985, the message of the wide-comb dispute, 'which was a combination of workers and farmers shearing on in the face of a national strike, was that unionism – in the AWU of all unions! – became voluntary', delivering an 'absolutely vital national change.'[80]

The neoliberal political period was clearly a factor, encouraging the development of more politically and industrially active right wing forces.

There were also economic factors, of course, with the meat industry being important for export earnings. Rural industries in industrial capitalist societies go through cycles of prosperity and depression, generating not only hardship for agricultural workers and farmers but also bouts of rural political activism and protest.[81] One of the main forces playing a role in rural activism was the militant Meatworkers union, protecting its members with one of the highest levels of industrial action of any union.

LIVE SHEEP EXPORTS

During the 1970s, fluctuating wool prices led to peaks and troughs in the availability of sheep for slaughter. Coupled with a rise in live sheep exports, this cut a swathe through meatworkers' jobs. The meat industry became volatile in the 1970s and was the site of major clashes between the right (NFF) and left (AMIEU) from 1979.

The union took a stand against live sheep exports because of the impact on employment. The AMIEU banned it in 1973, leading to a federal government inquiry through the Industry Assistance Commission (IAC). The inquiry recommended weight restrictions and a ratio of live sheep to mutton carcases. For a short while, pickets were set up at ports, and industrial action targeted producers ignoring the ratios. The union also lobbied governments and employer groups. By 1977, when little progress had been made, the Meatworkers planned a national campaign, demanding implementation of the ratio system by March 1978 – or all livestock export would be banned.

That year, the Fraser government enacted amendments to the secondary boycott provisions of the *Trade Practices Act*, sections 45D and 45E, widening its scope to cover actions by unions, not just companies. The new sections effectively blocked union picketing whenever the workers' action would affect another or 'third' party (the shipping firms in this case); such a secondary boycott opened unions to hefty fines. According to some in the industry, the changes were designed specifically to deter industrial action on the ports over the livestock export trade by providing a lever to the employer side.[82] Unions could be quickly injuncted off the picket lines and then penalised for being in contempt. The s.45D action didn't proceed past the injunction stage in this dispute, but the employers had a new weapon which they would use at Mudginberri.[83]

With the employers' position hardening on support for the live export trade, pickets were set up in Adelaide and five ports in WA. Arrests on picket lines in WA led to a four-day national abattoir strike. But the AMIEU's actions were undermined, not so much by the employers' united opposition, but by fellow unionists. In some WA ports, Waterside Workers' Federation (WWF) members loaded the sheep in defiance of AMIEU pickets, seeing removal of the trade as a threat to their jobs on the wharves. In Adelaide, the AWU supported farmers in their rallies and public pronouncements against the blockade, fearing that a reduction in trade would affect the jobs of the shearers they covered.

There was no support from the South Australian ALP government, which favoured the live export trade. Federal Opposition Agriculture spokesperson, Senator Peter Walsh, openly criticised the AMIEU and backed the unrestricted export of live sheep. With no support from other unions or the public, facing a hostile press, the union suffered a bitter defeat.

Ian McLachlan, later to become a minister in John Howard's Coalition government, was exultant: 'The live sheep dispute showed that the union movement, even in the face of physical picketing and blockading, could be beaten.'[84]

The AMIEU's loss encouraged the more hardline players among the employers. In the meat processing industry, the NFF made its intentions clear as early as 1981. During an Industries Assistance Commission inquiry, Paul Houlihan explained that their submission's aim was to outline how to overcome what the NFF described as 'the extreme inefficiencies that exist ... due to the enormously powerful position ... [of] the AMIEU ... [and] the unit tally system.'[85] Mudginberri was to be the first step in a campaign to spread non-union contract employment throughout Australia. It later became clear that the NFF was preparing to take on unions in transport such as the FSPU, the WWF, rail unions and the TWU.

The NFF considered itself to be in a dispute for the long haul. The sheep shearing wide-comb dispute had illustrated their hardline stance.[86] Their strategic location, financial resources and strong ideological stance allowed that conflict to continue for as long as it did.[87] They had powerful allies, enabling them to intervene in the Mudginberri dispute politically and financially.

THE DISPUTE

By 1979, the beef industry was facing drought, infectious diseases outbreaks and a slump in demand and international commodity prices. All these factors and the live animal trade led to the loss of 35 abattoirs and 6,000 jobs between 1979 and 1982. By 1983, the federal IAC found that the industry was in serious decline. In Victoria, at least 4,000 AMIEU members were working fewer than five days a week, without any redundancy scheme or severance pay. In the NT, however, meat processing was doing well, employing nearly 1 percent of the workforce by the early 1980s.[88] Abattoirs were upgraded and new sites opened, although these were mostly non-union.

The AMIEU found itself struggling to save jobs in award strongholds, while scrambling to win conditions in a largely award-free growth industry in the NT. The union was determined to win a Territory-wide award. Union conditions were already under threat, with all but two abattoirs, Angliss in Darwin and Norwest Beef at Katherine, working on individual contracts. Failure to win an award would not only undermine the Darwin and Katherine plants, but could spread to other states. The union had sought to extend the Federal Meat Industry Award in 1981 to the Territory, but it was not pursued. The same year, Katherine abattoir management tried to bring in individual contracts. The workers struck, set up a picket line and held a

Mudginberri picket. Tribune July 1987. Photo Mitchell Library, State Library of New South Wales courtesy SEARCH Foundation.

500-strong march through the 4,000 resident town. The company backed down after 10 weeks.[89]

In 1982, AMIEU federal secretary Jack O'Toole toured the NT, arguing unsuccessfully to employers that they should adopt the award. In 1983, the union served a log of claims on around 10 abattoirs, based on the Katherine Meat Works Agreement or the Queensland Meat Industry Agreement Award, both unit tally systems.[90] As a counter claim, MATFA served its own log of claims, based on the Federal Meat Industry Award, but it was later dropped.[91]

In the abattoirs, work was organised along a chain system model based on Fordist production line principles, with payments by piece work – the tally system. First introduced into mutton processing in the 1930s and beef in the 1960s, the system was initially resisted by the union as a management tool to undermine militancy, but unionists soon realised that it could strengthen their power on the job by narrowing the pay gap and encouraging teamwork. By the early 1980s, through consistent industrial action, the union had won good wages and control over the pace of work and hiring and firing through industry awards; now, it was facing challenges from employers over new technology, individual contracting and opposition to the tally system.[92]

The stakes were high for workers. Meat processing was seasonal, only six months a year, so the money had to last, or the workers had to find other short-term jobs – a significant issue in small towns like Katherine. While a large proportion of meatworkers were union members, the seasonality encouraged itinerant workers more interested in the money, with little loyalty to the union, the town or the business. Contracting at higher pay often suited these workers, but it came without penalty rates, workers' compensation, holiday and sick pay, and there was no pay if the stock arrived late. Lower skill levels were a real disadvantage for a regular workforce.

For the employers, the benefits of contracting were obvious: few on-costs, such as tax collection or leave entitlements, and fewer skilled workers needed. At one abattoir, labourers earning $62.50 a day did slaughtering work which was normally paid at $350 a day. Point Stuart was one of the most extreme cases, with about eight skilled butchers instead of 23 and half the workforce of the Norwest Katherine abattoir, producing about the same output.[93]

At first, it was smooth sailing, although employer resistance was anticipated. During the April–July 1983 hearings in the Arbitration Commission under Commissioner Gough, the Meatworkers' O'Toole said that the union was prepared to negotiate on the tally levels, but not on individual contracts, because they allowed employers to have sole control of wages: 'it is a take it or leave it situation and our members frequently have two choices – to accept those terms or the dole.'[94]

MATFA agreed to use an interim award based on the Federal Meat Award Part III until the case was fully heard. The NFF, involved for the first time in a meatworkers' case, was silent. Then, in July, MATFA issued a statement calling for a non-tally award. At the same time, an employer-led push managed to install pro-business Commissioner Ian McKenzie into the hearings. The dynamic of the case changed dramatically, and the interim award offer was dropped.[95]

At the August 1985 Country Liberal Party Annual Conference in Katherine, the Jay Pendarvis Fighting Fund was launched. Pendarvis was later declared 'Australian of the Year' by the Murdoch Press' *Australian* newspaper. Afterwards, Pendarvis would try to distance himself from the anti-union push, claiming that the abattoir became 'a tool of the NFF', adding: 'It became a power thing [with the NFF] – we're going to destroy the unions.'[96]

More support was to come directly from the Territory government. On orders from the Minister for Primary Production, the NT Agricultural Development and Marketing Authority prepared to advance $992,000 – almost its entire budget – to Pendarvis and the abattoir. Fearing that the transaction would create political difficulties, the government arranged a $2 million loan from the Westpac Bank to Mudginberri; the government acted as guarantor.[97] In exchange, Pendarvis agreed to pursue the damages claim 'to its conclusion.'[98]

The Queensland National Party government, under the leadership of arch reactionary Joh Bjelke-Petersen, offered to arrange financial support for Pendarvis from non-government sources and finance for any Queensland abattoir affected by industrial action relating to Mudginberri.

For the rest of 1983, the AMIEU found that they were excluded from some meetings and generally sidelined, with the NT government invited to intervene for the employers. The AMIEU concluded that they were left with 'no choice but to look for industrial action.'[99]

The hearings ground to a halt in the first half of 1984, as the AMIEU unsuccessfully appealed to the High Court against the change of Commissioners.

In June 1984, at the beginning of the season, picket lines were set up at Mudginberri, Point Stuart and Alice Springs against the continued use of contracts.[100] There was a bitter fight at Point Stuart when the company tried to bring in strikebreakers, and armed security guards patrolled the site. Point Stuart and Mudginberri management applied for interim, and then permanent, injunctions under s.45D against the AMIEU. The pickets were injuncted off permanently on 12 July, although the union didn't lift them until 7 August, when the case went back to the Arbitration Commission.[101] The employers, as was common practice at the time, withdrew the threatened s.45D legal action to allow the case to be finalised in the Commission.

On 5 September, the Full Bench delivered its recommendation – contract workers should be covered by minimum award standards – but it was not enforced on unwilling employers. The tally system was ruled out.[102] Trevor Surplice, an AMIEU official, said that the ruling just confirmed what 'workers for years had always said, that the commission was the bosses' court.'[103] The NFF's Paul Houlihan boasted that it was his organisation's militancy that influenced the Commission in the employers' favour.[104]

But the case wasn't finished. The Full Bench recommendations were referred back to Commissioner McKenzie to prepare the new award for the Territory, which he handed down on 29 April 1985. Based on Part I of the Federal Meat Industry Award 1981, it was unexceptional except for additional clause 33, about payment by results. Again, it undermined the union, containing a clause allowing individual contracts without union input.[105] It was extraordinary for an award to allow wages to be determined without union participation, which the new clause 33(c) did.[106] A letter from Commissioner Sheather noted that the award 'cuts across the general pattern of awards in the industry' and is seen by some employers as 'a significant tactical breakthrough that will spread throughout the industry.'[107]

The union could not accept such a clause. The employers were determined to keep it in. The stage was set for the confrontation of 1985.

From 3 May 1985, new picket lines were set up at Victoria River, Mudginberri and Alice Springs, and AMIEU members were levied nationally. The action was endorsed by the ACTU on 17 May.[108] Although Victoria River workers were the worst off, getting only half the payments of Mudginberri workers, Mudginberri was the most difficult for the union and soon became the focus of the employers' push for individual contracts.

By all accounts, Mudginberri was a friendly place to work, with decent facilities, subsidised food and accommodation and a beautiful location inside Kakadu National Park. Most workers were union members and formed a 'close knit team.'[109] Manager Jay Pendarvis claimed that he was not anti-union, but insisted he couldn't run the place at a profit unless he paid contract wages and conditions. That raises the question of long-term viability. Indeed, despite the massive financial support it had from the NT government and the NFF, the meatworks collapsed within two years of the dispute's end.

At the Mudginberri union meeting after the new award was announced, the AMIEU's stance on the award was well received. The organisers argued that the award would deliver higher pay and better conditions and not the cuts in pay that Mudginberri workers had feared.[110] But after that first meeting, workers met with employer association representatives a week later and then the union again. This time, the workers were more hostile to the union case, in part influenced by the top three contractors who, it seemed, could lose from the new award.

Allan Anderson, then AMIEU Federal Research Officer, stressed the importance of convincing Mudginberri to join the action and see that 'what they were doing was in fact destroying the wages and conditions of meat workers throughout Australia – or at least the threat of destroying.' The AMIEU's Trevor Surplice believes that the union could have done more to convince the Mudginberri workers of the award's benefits, leading to a possible win as early as 1984.[111]

The Mudginberri workforce was not won over; the union lost the support of its members there. However, the union received strong support 'from other parts of the NT, especially from the Katherine meatworks, where the long history of fighting for good wages and conditions before their abattoir's shutdown drew them to the picket line at Mudginberri.[112]

The Mudginberri picket line did not include any of its workers, being made up of unionists from Katherine and other abattoirs.[113] It held because, on 10 May, the federal meat inspectors, necessary to certify the export licences, refused to cross the line. The inspectors were suspended without pay but maintained their stand for the whole dispute. The federal government did not direct them to cross the picket, nor did it bring in non-union inspectors, fearing a national strike of meat inspectors and a resultant economic blow to the meat export industry.[114] The union's Allan Anderson held at least 50 gatherings around the country, although he admitted that the high wages of abattoir workers were held against them by unionists not familiar with their conditions. Unionists who better understood the issues of isolation and the hazardous work were more supportive. Miners at Jabiru and TWU drivers backed the strike and picket lines, stopping some supplies. However, the Mudginberri workforce crossed the picket line and commenced production for domestic use on 24 June with the NT government sanctioned Territory meat inspectors.[115]

Compulsory conferences throughout May and June failed to resolve the dispute. Employers then commenced an 'avalanche' of legal proceedings.

The employer won a Federal Court interim order on 21 June, directing the AMIEU to lift its picket line. The union refused and was charged with contempt and subject to daily fines until 12 July, totalling $44,000. A writ was issued for sequestration of its assets. The Court instituted a permanent injunction against the AMIEU picket on 12 July, resulting in a further $100,000 fine, and imposed a sequestration order against the union's property and income.[116] In response, the AMIEU announced a campaign of strikes by its 20,000 strong national membership, meanwhile lodging unsuccessful appeals against the injunctions, the fines and the sequestration.

The legal onslaught rolled on through July. The employers began proceedings in the Federal Court under s.142A(2) of the *Conciliation and Arbitration Act*, attempting to exclude the AMIEU from representing all meatworkers in the NT. In August, the basis for the court action then switched to s.143, designed to deregister the union federally. These moves lapsed, but it was another cost, another issue for the union to deal with.

Faced with these threats, the union began its national campaign of industrial action, backed by the ACTU. The first national strike occurred on 25 July, followed by a second on 7 August with support from maritime and transport unions. While federal Labor did not condemn the AMIEU, it did argue that the union should not have taken industrial action against an Arbitration Commission decision. It did refuse to direct federal meat inspectors to cross the picket line, admittedly an important move, but offered no other support.

The ACTU's Simon Crean saw the clear attack on unions' right to organise, take industrial action and erode employment conditions, and the peak union body carried a motion of support at the September Congress. However, the industrial campaign and support from other unions and the ACTU was too little and too late to impact the legal juggernaut.

July also saw the Mudginberri Station itself target the federal government and the Department of Primary Industries, which had refused to force Commonwealth meat inspectors to cross the picket line.[117] On 19 December, in an unprecedented ruling, the Federal Court deemed that the department had no discretion in the matter; it had a duty (though not absolute) to provide services. While the court did not direct the government to force the inspectors back to work, it was a potentially dangerous ruling for the whole union movement, albeit not utilised since. In August, Mudginberri also began proceedings against the Meat Inspectors' Association (MIA) to force them across the line. That failed.

A major farmers' rally against federal Labor's economic policy on 15 July further politicised the situation; 45,000 farmers and supporters massed outside Parliament House in Canberra, coinciding with the government's Tax Summit. The NFF's Ian McLachlan used 'this highly visible and politicised occasion' to attack the AMIEU and accuse the Hawke government of backing the union against the farmers.[118]

At the same time, the NFF set up a fighting fund with a $5 million target for a range of causes, prioritising employer-initiated industrial campaigns such as Mudginberri. Within a year, it raised $10 million, much of it donated by non-rural business sources.[119]

The Hawke Labor government's main focus was to get the dispute into the Arbitration Commission. The government criticised both sides for not reaching agreement, but also slammed the NFF for pursuing s.45D prosecutions and inciting confrontation. Attempts by the government to broker a deal came to nothing. Employers refused to attend the 8 August meeting without the NFF. On the second attempt, 12 August 1985, employers claimed the matter was *sub judice*, making it impossible to meet, later boasting of their success in foiling the government. Instead, MATFA and other employer groups simply sent in their terms of settlement – removal of all picket lines, a two-year ban on strikes, legal costs and $2.5 million damages for Jay Pendarvis.

O'Toole commented: 'At that stage we knew we weren't dealing with people who were looking for a settlement so much as an overwhelming victory.'[120]

The union continued its national campaign, with a third national strike on 30 August. Throughout September, the dispute rolled on in the courts. The AMIEU refused to pay the fines and kept up the national strikes. However, the union campaign was then dealt a blow in Queensland. Under its controversial *Industrial (Commercial Practices) Act 1984*, the Bjelke-Petersen government obtained a Supreme Court injunction on 27 September 1985 prohibiting Queensland workers from joining the strike planned for 30 September. After a defiant stand, the AMIEU called off the action in Queensland following threats of a $250,000 fine and dismissals of employees in state abattoirs.[121]

Employers outside the industry stepped up their support for the Mudginberri and NFF stance, while 10 unions involved in transport, storage and the public sector met to discuss future tactics to support the Meatworkers. The TWU and airlines unions discussed meatworker bans on chilled meat transport. However, O'Toole admitted: 'whilst we put on a brave face ... we were looking for a way out.'[122]

On 27 August, the AMIEU applied to the Commission to vary the McKenzie award to allow union involvement in contract negotiations and strengthen union preference clauses. In particular, they wanted a change to the new s.33(c) which denied the AMIEU any role in wage negotiations. The change would enshrine the right of the AMIEU to negotiate with employers on behalf of workers. They did not intend to challenge the court's rejection of the tally system.

The pickets were lifted on 8 September to facilitate new Commission hearings, although it took a month before hearings actually started on 3 October. They were then adjourned to 17 October after a series of meatworker stoppages around the country, and continued through to December. The Commission's decision was handed down on 27 March 1986. It was another slap in the face for the union. Non-union individual contracts would still be allowed, but the union had to be notified and seven days given for the AMIEU to consult with members.

The Full Bench of the Commission dismissed the union's arguments against individual contracts, pointing to the fact that:

in the agreements negotiated to date, the AMIEU has only been excluded by the decision of the employees, including its own members. In the normal course of events, one would have expected the AMIEU to have been asked to act for the employees. The fact that it was not, speaks for itself.[123]

Further, the new award was not to be adopted outside the NT, which meant little in reality.[124]

It was a terrible defeat. The judges' comments about union members excluding the union and voting for contracts was a confronting issue for the AMIEU to deal with. Throughout the NT, all abattoirs, including previous union strongholds, adopted individual contracts. Management, having earlier supported the union award, hired only half the numbers, with few union members and all on individual contracts.[125] The strongest unionised abattoir in the NT had been broken.

One manager described contracts as a 'fresh new approach without the benefit of union involvement.'[126] But, despite employer claims that they needed individual contracts to survive, the new award did not always hold. Contract use dropped by 1990 in the face of skilled worker shortages. It also did not save the industry. Within two seasons, Mudginberri closed its doors. By 1998, there were no abattoirs left in the NT.

The union still had more pain to face with the secondary boycott damages bill.[127] Until Mudginberri, employers had used the threat of s.45D damages as a bargaining chip, with the threat alone curtailing union actions. The AMIEU hadn't held back, and it was about to pay the price. The union already had loads of writs under s.45D, dating back to the 1977 live sheep dispute:

> We could paper the walls of our offices with the paper from these writs, which were never gone on with. They were used, if you like, as a bargaining chip in the whole situation and withdrawn later. Now again, you can look back in hindsight and say, 'Well why couldn't we see that was going to happen?'[128]

The union leadership knew that the NFF was not bluffing, but they also recognised what was at stake: the tally system around Australia. This militant union had to draw a line in the sand to defend itself, its members and the wages and conditions of every abattoir worker. While MATFA told the ACTU that it would not seek damages after the pickets were lifted in September 1985, the NFF was on an ideological crusade to destroy, or at the very least weaken, unionism.[129] The NFF – or the employers it represented – were mostly out of reach of the AMIEU (having no abattoirs), leaving the union unable to retaliate directly against NFF actions without incurring even more s.45D penalties.

On 21 July 1986, Federal Court Judge Morling handed down the damages decision from the NFF claim. The union was to be fined $1,759,444 and costs under s.82 of the *Trade Practices Act* for contravention of s.45D. It could have been more; Morling limited the amount to the estimated losses from sales, not calculating the loss of goodwill and other business costs. The union's weak defence, that the loss was caused by the Department of Primary Industry's failure to 'ensure adequate inspectorial services' to license the meat for export, was dismissed out of hand.

It was a shocking result. For the first time since the 1969 Clarrie O'Shea case, a union had been penalised. 'There was to be no groundswell of protest to sweep aside the court decisions as there had been in 1969 during the Clarrie O'Shea case.'[130] The unions and ACTU were too wedded to the Accord processes. Rather, the ACTU oversaw the destruction of the union and the overall weakening of the union movement, both in numbers and industrially. The Hawke government, throughout the dispute, saw the Arbitration Commission as the only solution. Ralph Willis, IR Minister, told parliament on 20 August 1985: 'The fact is that this matter will be resolved only before the Conciliation and Arbitration Commission in an industrial sphere' – a sentiment echoed by PM Hawke.

The government and its Accord framework drove the union movement towards the legal processes of arbitration, resulting in a massive increase in penalties against industrial action. However, it is arguable that the AMIEU's action may have achieved a better result out of the new award and left them in a better position to fight on in the future.

The ACTU drew negative conclusions from this dispute. It sought to caution unions rather than build a fightback, claiming in the 1987 *Future Strategies for the Trade Union Movement*:

> It is important to appreciate that these cases [Mudginberri, SEQEB and the Plumbers and Gasfitters Employees' Union (PGEU) – see later chapters] constitute only the tip of the iceberg. Throughout industry, employers are exhibiting an increased willingness to seek legal redress (especially under s.45D and the common law) in dispute situations.

The ACTU then urged the movement to:

- carefully select targets for all forms of industrial action
- alert members and officials of the nature and extent of potential liabilities
- develop defensive (and offensive) tactics which can minimise the risk of legal intervention
- establish early warning systems to try to head off the possibility of legal action
- be prepared to beat a strategic retreat where that is the prudent course
- establish and maintain substantial fighting funds
- recognise that legal action can destroy a union.[131]

The AMIEU remained defiant. The union might have been bowed, its strongholds in the NT destroyed, but it was not broken. In a series of interviews with union officials and rank and file workers, Brian shows that a fighting spirit remained. One former Katherine meatworker still believes that 'it was worth it, because if we'd have all gone over and worked for contracts none of us would have been working in the industry the next year anyway.' Pat Roughan says of himself and Jack O'Toole: 'given the same set of circumstances ... we'd do the same exercise again ... it had to be done.'[132] The union lived to fight another day – as they did, several times in the early 1990s.

Mudginberri was an iconic struggle for two reasons. It was the first successful use of legal sanctions against a union since the jailing of the Tramway's Union leader Clarrie O'Shea in 1969, nearly two decades before, but it had a very different outcome. The union movement rallied around O'Shea to make the anti-union legislation a dead letter. In the 1980s, they retreated into caution and inaction, fearful of legal sanctions, weakening the movement.

Secondly, it became an important symbol for the right, 'a rallying cry for anti-union, anti-Labor and anti-arbitration forces', characterised by 'greater legal regulation, direct bargaining between employers and employees without the participation of trade unions or employer associations and reduced trade union power.' It was particularly marked by the notions of 'individual freedom' versus 'trade union power', where individual workers were seen as equal partners with employers in negotiating contracts of work.

O'Toole challenged this conception in the Arbitration Commission hearings on 14 November 1984, arguing that the union did not see any equality between workers and employers:

> the whole basis of the union's organisation and representation and provisions of the statute [the *Conciliation and Arbitration Act*] encouraging organisation is a recognition that a group of individual employees may not and certainly will not be in an equal bargaining position with the employer.[133]

The unions feared that the actions of activist, right wing employers and their industry organisations were the way of the future. Not everyone agreed; Mudginberri was 'in many respects unique', and 'it gave heart to anti-union forces in Australia but it did not become a "model".'[134]

The lack of serious union support for the Meatworkers and their members, along with the ALPs focus on arbitration, should cause alarm. Blaming the union movements' defeats on a New Right offensive misses the point; they pushed the boundaries, but the real danger to workers lay with the Accord.

CHAPTER 3

Lights Out in Queensland

On 7 February 1985, Queensland's ultra-conservative Premier, Joh Bjelke-Petersen, declared a State of Emergency over striking electricity linesmen at SEQEB sites. Backed by the government, SEQEB management sacked all 1,002 linesmen, withholding their superannuation and other entitlements. They would have to reapply for their jobs and be taken on as new employees, with no recognition of previous employment or entitlements, working on contract for longer hours and below award wages; they would sign a no-strike clause.

Outraged by the sackings, Queensland workers responded with strikes and other industrial action across the state, plunging Brisbane into darkness. Thousands of workers were stood down, costing business an estimated $1 billion.[135] After 14 days, with the power station operators still holding out alongside the linesmen, the government was on the ropes, ready to cave in.

It was the union movement's moment of truth. The dispute was theirs to win – or lose. On a verbal promise of reinstatement from Bjelke-Petersen, and reportedly with secret commitments given by the unions, the Queensland Trades and Labour Council (QTLC) capitulated and ended the power station operators' bans on 21 February. The next day, the government reneged. The linesmen were left with no jobs. Apart from outraged statements from the QTLC and ETU, it seemed to be over.

However, the anger was such that the dispute flared up again and again. Over the following months, workers had the advantage at key points and could have driven it home to defeat Bjelke-Petersen. Each time, the leaders of the ETU, QTLC and ACTU sabotaged, deflected and, ultimately, sold out SEQEB workers.

Although the dispute was state based, and consequently covered by Queensland's industrial laws, it had national repercussions. It was the first major test of the Accord, recognised as such not only by Labor and the unions but also by Bjelke-Petersen. The Queensland government was quick to blame the Accord for industrial disputes, while Bjelke-Petersen 'was happy to be seen by conservatives dissatisfied with the Accord as the one man who might break through it.'[136] For the trade unions, it was the first in a series of major defeats in the Accord years; for Queensland, it was the greatest blow to trade unionism in decades.

Business commentators also saw the SEQEB dispute as a pivotal moment for the Accord. The *Business Review Weekly* commented:

> The Australian labour market is at a crossroads. The trade union movement agreed to the prices and incomes accord which involves some restraint on wage demands. Yet what we are seeing now is a challenge to the very rights of unions to exist. The paradox of the situation is that if this challenge succeeds it will wreck the accord and hand union power to the people in the trade union movement who are already highly critical of it and are seeking to operate outside it.[137]

Context

Despite the social upheavals of the late 1960s and the presence of a strong, combative union movement, Queensland voted in the National Party, led by Joh Bjelke-Petersen, in 1968.[138] The party continued to hold power through to 1989, partly because of a gerrymander and a weak ALP Opposition, but primarily because the state's decentralised economy, driven by agriculture and, later, mineral exports, remained strong.[139]

The healthy state of the economy didn't stop the National Party from introducing harsh legislation targeting unions and civil liberties. In fact, the government was forced to respond to a combative workforce and a population with few electoral avenues for dissent. On 3 September 1977, the Premier announced that the days of political street marching were at an end, moving to amend the *Traffic Act* permit section on 14 September. Before he could act, a union rally of 6,000 took to the streets on another matter –successfully defending organiser Ted Zaphir, who was charged under the criminal code with 'threatening to cause detriment' for putting on a work ban. The union rally, including 400 students, was confronted by 10,000 police mobilised from around Queensland.[140]

On 22 September, 2,000 people demonstrated against the new ban. They were met by 800 police, who arrested 32 protesters. Thus began a two-year campaign that involved tens of thousands on the street – unionists, students and concerned citizens – and ended with hundreds of arrests. It was labelled 'the single most spectacular example of political resistance to the ruling class offensive.' As in many other civil liberties, anti-war and anti-uranium campaigns, Queensland unions were a prominent force.[141]

Bjelke-Petersen was forced to concede defeat. The marchers won the political battle, and victory gave them confidence that they could defy the law.

After a successful strike by Gladstone power workers in August 1978, the Premier began talking about outlawing strikes in essential industries. In October 1979, the National Party introduced the *Essential Services Act*, which gave the government wide powers to end a strike or prevent workers from withdrawing their labour. The Act's provisions included substantial fines, enforced by jail terms, and the right of people or companies impacted by industrial action to sue a union or individual workers.

In November, 200,000 stopped work, joining large rallies. In December, the power workers struck. In neither case did the government use its new powers. The provisions of section 22 of the *Transport Act* were invoked to declare a State of Emergency.

Despite the Act's reference to 'fire, flood, storm and tempest' as grounds for declaration, the State of Emergency section of the *Transport Act* was mainly used to crush civil and union dissent. Proclaimed by Labor in 1946, its usefulness to government was praised by Bjelke-Petersen:

> Declaring a state of emergency was often the key to it. The press would howl each time I did it and say, 'The Premier's gone mad – fancy declaring a state of emergency over a

thing like this', but the state of emergency gave me the power to deal with the problem quickly and effectively. It saved everyone a lot of trouble, including the unions themselves, because I would have beaten them in the long run anyway.[142]

The government also sought to disrupt union strength in the power industry by restructuring the electricity distribution network. In July 1977, the Brisbane Council (often a thorn in Bjelke-Petersen's side) was stripped of its control of electricity distribution (also an income source), which was then given to region-wide government controlled boards such as SEQEB. Since the redistribution, industrial conflict, often over the union campaign for shorter hours to counter rising unemployment levels, had increased.

In 1980, a 48-hour stoppage by the ETU won a decisive victory for a reduced working week. All sides considered this a humiliating defeat for the government. In 1981, there was another successful power dispute, followed by transport workers' action, where the government invoked the *Essential Services Act*. A near general strike over shorter hours followed in 1982, as workers across the board went on strike to support the railway workers' campaign. Again, the *Essential Services Act* was brought to bear against the railway workers, with 3,500 strikers suspended. The government applied to deregister 11 unions. Within two days, Bjelke-Petersen backed down, reinstating all workers and revoking the Essential Services provisions. Again, no one was fined, sued or jailed.

However, the collapse of a follow-up 48-hour strike called by the QTLC over the suspensions allowed the government to claim the successful use of the *Essential Services Act* and step up its anti-union rhetoric. Encouraged by the government stance, employers began a wave of sackings in the metal trades, with little opposition from the unions. Nevertheless, the union movement still had the upper hand. The *Essential Services Act* had not been as effective as the government had claimed or expected.

The tide began to turn in 1983. Industrial action dropped to its lowest level in many years. Economic decline from late 1982, with only a weak recovery in 1983–84, led to instability in the Queensland economy and consequent political insecurity. Queensland was the hardest hit of the states during this nationwide decline and did not recover as quickly. The government pushed an ambitious plan to revive the economy by attracting new industry investment, in part through the promise of lower energy prices. Lower power costs for industry and regional Queensland clearly spelled trouble for workers' wages and conditions in the mining and power industries.

Politically, it was risky; the government's policy of lower power prices shifted the cost of electricity from the countryside and regions to cities, where residents were already paying more than in any other state.

The economic decline made the government more aggressive and provocative in its approach to industrial relations. The Queensland National Party was also facing other pressures which drove its heavy-handed approach – the inescapable forces signalling its electoral decline. In fact, rather than indicating power and confidence, its actions reflected its weakness – something the union movement failed to capitalise on.[143] In 1983, the government attacked penalty rates and work practices in the railways and contracted out work in hospitals. It removed the requirement to be a union member for employment in the state public service, although the Queensland Industrial Commission (QIC) inserted a union preference clause into the award in August 1984, much to the government's fury. Encouraged by the Thatcher government's draconian laws, Cabinet approved the drafting of new anti-union legislation, and 1984 also saw the government initiate deregistration proceedings against the AWU and the PGEU. The unions backed down and abandoned their industrial action, and the government withdrew the deregistration threat.

Overall, though more on the defensive, unions were still a combative force. On the eve of the 1985 SEQEB strike, industrial action in the electricity industry had crippled the state 11 times. This time, however, the government was actively planning for a showdown that it intended to win.

The Dispute

A major source of conflict in the electricity sector was the attempt by management to introduce contract work to replace industry-wide permanent employment on award wages and conditions. Management argued that contract staffing would be more efficient, and no existing employees would lose their jobs; they threatened to pass the cost of not using contractors on to consumers.[144] Already, the union had seen a deliberate scaling down of full-time employment, with constant understaffing, fewer apprentices kept on at the end of training, and excessive use of overtime to fill gaps. The ETU rightly saw contracting as a major threat to the unionised workforce. Contractors on below award conditions would 'spread like a cancer through the whole electricity industry' once contracting got a foothold at SEQEB.[145]

In January 1984, SEQEB made its first move, announcing that its new Grantham depot would be completed under contract. ETU members at the nearby Gatton depot responded by banning all work associated with establishing Grantham. When the contractor continued working, the ETU threatened further industrial action, and SEQEB backed down.[146]

Throughout May, the ETU and SEQEB met and partially resolved the dispute, clearly in SEQEB's favour. The ETU agreed to lift bans, accepting contractors on Grantham as a one-off, but no overall agreement on contract labour was reached.

The government and SEQEB knew that their push for contracting was making unions more restive and creating the potential for a confrontation. As if to emphasise their determination to bring it on, the government appointed Wayne Gilbert, a hardline General Manager with a history of anti-union actions at the Carlton and United and Tooth's breweries, to head up SEQEB.[147]

Gilbert oversaw the development of a new workplace agreement which included contract labour, longer hours and a no-strike clause. SEQEB's overall aim was to cut the permanent workforce by 10 percent over two years. Gilbert made three attempts to win acceptance, in May, August and September 1984, but ETU members knocked it back every time. Following the May rejection, management announced in June that it was going to use contract electricians at five transmission lines. In October, after the third rejection of the agreement, SEQEB told the ETU that it would build a substation with contract labour. All its jobs were usually done by permanent SEQEB electricians on award wages and conditions.

The union put bans on all work involving contract labour and held stop-work meetings during November 1984. Negotiations failed, and the bans remained. In response, SEQEB sacked electricians who refused to work at the sites with the contractors; the ETU retaliated by calling out all SEQEB workers on indefinite strike.

Negotiations, cooling off periods, return to work, bans and stand-downs continued through December until 5 February. Throughout this time, the ETU returned to work when ordered by the QIC, but SEQEB continued working

ETU poster promoting strike fund for SEQEB strikers. Courtesy ETU.

with contractors on two of four sites, despite QIC orders to cease this work.

There was little faith on the union side in the ability of the QIC to resolve the dispute on anything but SEQEB's terms. Organiser Alan Doodney was blunt; the union only went to the Commission when ordered to: 'The history of tribunals like that aren't solving disputes … workers lose when disputes go there.'

Ken Vaughan, the local ALP member for Nudgee and a former electrician, spelled out employer tactics during such disputes. He told parliament at the end of February:

> What happens with monotonous regularity in the electricity industry … the electricity authority stonewalls, allows the dispute to roll on until it knows very well that people will be affected and then goes to the Industrial Commission, from which it knows very well it can obtain orders against the union. It then uses those orders like a club.

Countering this was what became a common argument from governments and employers alike during the Accord years: appeals to the rights of employers and employees to be free to choose to go to work unfettered by 'third parties', invariably unions. Deputy Premier Bill Gunn was typical:

> It is a measure of arrogance of the militant union bosses that they were prepared to deny the sacked SEQEB employees the right to regain their jobs … The union leaders, all in comfortable, paid positions, are OK. They received their wages … It was the poor little SEQEB workers who wanted to go back to work and who would do so tomorrow, who were denied their jobs and who had threats made against them.

On the same day, Russ Hinze, a notorious government minister, addressed parliament: 'I appeal to the rank and file of the workers to let their voices be heard above the threatening roar of mob rule.'

After the end of the final cooling off period, in the face of the failure of talks on manning levels and continuing provocation by SEQEB, a meeting of ETU shop stewards called an indefinite strike from 6 February. When workers defied an order to return to work on 7 February, the government threatened sackings, fines and deregistration. That night, a crisis session of Cabinet declared a State of Emergency. On 8 February, Cabinet sacked the linesmen for defying the return to work order and announced $1,000 fines and the loss of all their entitlements, including superannuation.

Bjelke-Petersen later wrote that he had deliberately closed down all the power stations in order to escalate the strike's effects, even at the expense of alienating powerful forces in the mining industry.[148] Behind that deliberate escalation was the government's resolution to 'use the settlement of the dispute as a lever to lift the electricity industry once and for all out of the industrial quagmire and place it in a strike-free situation.'[149]

The government authorised SEQEB to begin hiring, but only contract workers on lower pay and conditions. At this point, the QTLC stepped in to support the sacked SEQEB workers, issuing a leaflet 'Bjelke sacks SEQEB workers – You May be Next' and, along with the ACTU, calling workers around the country to take action supporting reinstatement and the right to take industrial action:

> The Trades and Labor Council of Queensland condemns the Premier's actions ... [and] Queensland now calls on affiliated unions to take action because of the Premier's provocation of the original dispute, his refusal to negotiate a compromise solution, his misrepresentation of the facts, his dismissal of ETU members for taking legitimate industrial action to defend their jobs and his advertising for employees to take the jobs of dismissed workers.
>
> The only way that this attack can be met is by a total unified approach by all unions in the Electricity Industry ... if we become complacent ... and forget about the sacked workers, then this Queensland Government will have successfully defeated the workers' industrial rights and set the precedent for other Employers to follow suit.[150]

Queensland workers did rally round the linesmen. ETU members at three coal mines and all power stations walked off the job. On 11 February, power station workers, coal miners in central and north Queensland and 200 power station staff at seven sites, including ETU members at other depots, joined the strike. Police were stationed at SEQEB depots.

ETU and QTLC officials still had hopes of a settlement, meeting with other unions, management and the government. Worryingly, the unions offered more compromise than challenge and rejected calls for a general strike. On 10 February, the ETU said that it would accept contracts on two lines, even placing five ETU members with the contractor on the substation. ETU Organiser Dinny Madden later explained: 'We compromised ... We'd given the whole lot away except for three blokes. We had already gone way past what the rank and file had decided.'[151]

The response from Gilbert and the Queensland Government was a contemptuous 'no deal.'

Day after day, the two sides slugged it out. The government remained publicly intransigent, raising the stakes with Supreme Court injunctions to force the power station operators to restore full power and beginning deregistration proceedings against the ETU. In the National Party, however, Bjelke-Petersen did not always enjoy unanimous support for his strategy. And the government was under enormous pressure from employers and the public, because the strike was bringing the electricity system to the verge of total physical breakdown.

Employers themselves were divided. Some were critical and occasionally openly hostile, wanting the government to abandon its strategy, reinstate the workers and return the dispute to the QIC. The Queensland Confederation of Industry had one of its spokespeople defending the government, while other member companies wanted nothing to do with the dispute. Mining companies were particularly critical, some arguing that the dispute threatened their entire operations.[152]

This pressure from business and unions, along with indications of waning public support for the government and increased support for the workers, saw the beginnings of revolt within the National Party. Metropolitan backbenchers warned the government that support was plummeting in Brisbane, the place hardest hit by the strike, and demanded that the Premier back down.

By 14 February, a crisis point was reached. Fuel and communications were cut off, and Mount Isa unions were on indefinite strike. Even Parliament House lift maintenance workers refused to work, forcing Bjelke-Petersen to walk up many flights of stairs. Coal supplies were short, and industries were shut down because power could no longer be guaranteed. The next day, the first of the $1,000 fines were sent out, and Cabinet suspended 400 railway workers for striking in support of the linesmen. At the height of the dispute, over one million workers were either on strike or stood down.

ETU Assistant Secretary Tom Barton told *The Australian* the next day:

> The best defence against the Premier's threats and actions are for the trade union movement to stand firm. There is no honourable solution in backing down. The survival of unionism is at stake.

His words ring particularly hollow in the light of the compromises which the union was already offering to Bjelke-Petersen.[153]

The crunch came on 21 February. Bjelke-Petersen announced a peace package, including re-employment of the linesmen with no loss of entitlements but with a no-strike clause. The *Daily Sun* reported: 'Ministers confirmed last night that Cabinet planned to reinstate the sacked SEQEB workers and restore their superannuation as the Government's fall-back position.'

However, transcripts of the Tribunal hearing on 21 February actually indicated that the QTLC accepted an offer to 're-employ', rather than 'reinstate', some, but not all, linesmen. The conditions of a return to work also included working at any depot in Queensland, up to 1,000 km from Brisbane, and being prepared to live away from home with no travel allowance. The sacked workers, if re-employed, would be treated as new employees with no experience allowances and no recognition of earlier sick leave, annual leave or superannuation.

That night on TV, Opposition leader Neville Warburton claimed that the dispute was over. The QTLC recommended a lifting of bans by power station operators on the basis of this verbal agreement from the Premier and as a show of good faith.

But next day, after five hours of negotiations, the government refused to reinstate the SEQEB linesmen. The ETU and QTLC were furious, claiming that they'd been sold out. Angry workers claimed that it was they who had been sold out – by the government and management as expected, but also by the ETU and QTLC. Reading through the new deal in the ETU office the next morning (22 February), workers demanded: 'Where is the deal? Where do we get what we want?' The realisation dawned that there was nothing there for them, that they'd been 'left like shags on a rock.'[154]

Union leadership had argued that falling support and morale justified lifting the action. In fact, Bjelke-Petersen's statements so angered Municipal Officers Association (MOA) members, the power station operators, that they were prepared to reduce power supply even more. The ETU and QTLC just played dead, refusing to call for further action.

Further betrayals came after more discussions between the unions and government on 24 and 25 February achieved nothing. The union told linesmen that their only option was to reapply for their jobs under the new contract conditions. No one would be reinstated, although the ETU held out the clearly false hope that taking the case to the QIC could result in a reinstatement order. A few days later, the government moved to shut off that option, introducing the *Electricity Authorities Industrial Causes Act 1985*, which placed SEQEB outside the industrial jurisdiction of the QIC.[155]

The fight against contract work was abandoned. Instead, the ETU sought to transfer power workers from state to federal award coverage – a shift supposed to protect their members from further National Party attacks. The ETU hoped that the Federal Arbitration Court, after granting federal coverage to the linesmen, would then order their reinstatement. It was the last gasp in their futile court-based strategy.

The resumption of full supply by power station operators, however, was by no means the end of the dispute. Neither workers nor the government were finished with the power industry.

With reinstatement not on offer, sacked workers attended mass meetings on 26 February and 8 March. They refused to accept the outcome and demanded that the QTLC call a 24-hour general strike. The day before the 8 March mass meeting, the strike committee burst into a QTLC press conference, accusing Secretary Ray Dempsey of betrayal.[156]

The Committee's *Strike Bulletin* wrote: 'It was at this stage that the sacked workers initiated pickets outside the SEQEB depots around Brisbane.' At least 100 workers and their supporters were arrested. One, Bob Carnegie, spent three weeks in jail for refusing to sign bail conditions to stay away from the pickets.[157] Queensland ETU officials refused to join the pickets until the WA and Victorian branches criticised them for failing to support their own members.

Workers were still outraged by the sackings, and many unions continued their industrial action in support of the SEQEB workers. The workers' mobilisation was among the largest in the post-WWII period and included three statewide strikes and an effective blockade of the state by transport unions. Seamen maintained their bans, railway electricians remained on strike, postal and telecom workers banned all government work, and coal miners were still out, remaining on strike for three weeks. Transport workers and MOA supervisors voted at mass meetings to refuse to work with the strikebreakers. MOA members agreed not to strike, but maintained bans and continued to raise money for the SEQEB linesmen. ETU maintenance crew at the power stations stayed out for another week and then imposed bans which lasted many months.

MOA rank and file members sent a message to the QTLC, criticising the union leadership for failing to consult with them and for making the decision to restore full power when the SEQEB workers remained sacked. They called the union leadership 'weak and unwilling to support us in the hour of our greatest need. Rest assured we will repay this let-down in kind.'[158]

The QTLC was not moved by workers' continued action, deliberately playing down the support the SEQEB workers had. The BWIU's Hugh Hamilton told a Broad Left seminar in 1986 that, throughout the strike, workers would not 'down tools, pen or pencil for someone else's fight', claiming that 'evidence of this lack of solidarity was as plain as day.' Others argued that the working class had lost its militant tradition, and the strikers and their families were 'demoralised, passive and doomed victims of forces greater than themselves.'[159] Untrue; but the QTLC strategy ignored truth in order to follow the ACTU's attempts to resolve the dispute through the court application for federal award coverage for power workers. They pursued this strategy to the bitter end, despite early legal advice to both the QTLC and the ETU that there was almost no hope of success in the courts.

STUFF THE ACCORD! PAY UP!

Leaflet from The Battler supporting SEQEB strikers.

The government was leaving no stone unturned in its process of transforming the industrial relations arena:

> Such powers have rarely, if ever, been used so ruthlessly and drastically as by the Queensland government in February and March 1985. The state government completely ignored parliamentary niceties and overrode awards and altered the entire basis of conducting industrial relations in the state. Through Executive Orders in Council and laws pushed through the unicameral parliament before the Opposition had read them, the government rapidly went far beyond the issues of the SEQEB dispute.[160]

The only solution was a concerted industrial campaign. And SEQEB workers were pushing for action, calling on all unionists to back them instead of wasting years waiting for the outcome of Commission and court cases. While the union bureaucracy stalled, the Queensland government stepped up its anti-union push, forcing the QTLC and the ACTU to call for another round of industrial action.

The government felt threatened by these protests, especially those involving the unions. MP Yvonne Chapman told parliament:

> The sooner we are made non-unionist, the better off we will be ... What right do these people have to tell us what we do? Have we ever voted for a union ... Why should they have a say in government?[161]

In early March, IR Minister Vince Lester forced through the first of six pieces of anti-union legislation. The *Electricity (Continuity of Supply) Act 1985* embedded in law the right of the Electricity Commission to take any steps considered necessary to ensure the restoration and maintenance of electricity supply. Alongside this draconian piece of legislation was the new *Industrial Conciliation and Arbitration Amendment Act 1985*. This included provisions to discourage union membership and involvement, broadened the definition of a strike and increased the provisions for union deregistration. Moreover, it applied to every union.

The *Industrial (Commercial Practices) Act 1984* mirrored the secondary boycott penalties of the federal *Trade Practices Act.* It made a variety of actions illegal across all unions, including industrial action over union membership.

Following pressure from the rank and file, the QTLC reconsidered its purely court-based strategy. The executive spent two days, 9–10 March, discussing tactics, once again rejecting a general strike. They apparently considered a guerrilla industrial campaign, but the ACTU convinced them to give the Queensland government one last chance to compromise.

On 13 March, Queensland linesmen and 300 Canberra ETU members demonstrated outside Parliament House in Canberra, demanding to see PM Hawke. IR Minister Ralph Willis fronted the workers, angering them by expressing the ALP's concern that an industrial campaign to support SEQEB workers might spread interstate!

Back in Brisbane, Ray Dempsey addressed a mass meeting of sacked workers who defiantly voted to continue their campaign. Two days later, despite attempts by Dempsey to head off a rally and illegal street march for 15 March, workers on building sites, metal shops and transport, as well as the sacked SEQEB workers, all joined in.

Unsurprisingly, Bjelke-Petersen rejected the union movement's last-ditch attempt to force a compromise. Instead, sensing weakness on the union side, the Premier ramped up his legislative war, introducing amendments to strengthen the *Electricity (Continuity of Supply) Amendment Act* on 19 March, followed by the *Electricity Authorities Industrial Causes Act* the following day.[162] When the *Continuity of Supply Act* became law on 28 March, it had added a prohibition on picketing outside SEQEB depots, police powers to arrest without a warrant and fines of up to $1,000. Police used these powers without hesitation, rapidly escalating the number of arrests, fingerprinting and photographing those apprehended.[163]

The scope of the new laws meant that every union was now threatened. The ACTU claimed that it had no option but to take 'the most serious industrial action'; as a 'last resort', it gave one week's notice of a 2 May national blockade of Queensland.

Bjelke-Petersen rejected an offer by the federal government for a meeting of all parties. Hawke and Willis wanted an end to the dispute; Willis told parliament: 'we are taking all the action which can be expected of a Federal Government to prevent this blockade and industrial action.'[164]

NSW transport unions jumped the gun, starting their own blockade on 16 April. Two days later, almost no freight entered Queensland. The state was cut off by air, sea and rail. Seamen, brewery and building workers struck, followed by the ETU, though not the power industry workers who'd been threatened with the sack by Bjelke-Petersen. Daily pickets at SEQEB continued. On 26 April, 1,000 rallied in Ipswich, marching single file to the courthouse to avoid the anti-street march laws. Tom Barton, ETU assistant secretary, later explained: 'We had to show that Bjelke-Petersen was the law breaker.'[165]

A second 48-hour transport blockade began on 2 May. On the same day, 26 members of the group Queensland Academics for Human Rights were arrested at a SEQEB depot picket.

A third blockade happened from midnight, 7 May. Southern transport unions refused to load cargo for Queensland, banning all forms of transport across Queensland borders for 48 hours. The freight blockade extended for another week, and a snap airline strike was called.

Meanwhile, on 10 May, the ACTU, QTLC, federal government and employers held secret meetings, without informing the ETU. The union was furious. Organiser Alan Doodney complained that the ACTU's role was:

> Piss poor! They came in as fix-it men but they never fixed it! ... Our members were absolutely outraged when they found out that Simon Crean [ACTU President] had actually been talking to the Confederation of Industry ... They weren't in a position to influence Mickey Mouse, let alone Petersen.

A mass strike began from midnight on 11 May. All shipping stopped for seven days. Australian Telecommunications Employee Association (ATEA) action led to a breakdown in telecommunication links. Only two days later, the ACTU called off the blockade, satisfied with a promise of federal government cooperation in securing the ETU federal award coverage. The ACTU knew that this would prove to be of no benefit for ETU members, but it served to satisfy the ACTU and QTLC's single-minded focus on a legislative solution and their determination to limit industrial action.

Once again, the union movement could have pushed its advantage against the Queensland government. The blockades had been very effective, and employers were becoming more wary of the government and particularly hostile to government attempts to abolish penalty rates – so hostile that Bjelke-Petersen was forced to back down.[166] But instead of pushing ahead, the ACTU did a deal with the Australian Democrats in the federal Senate. In exchange for reducing the waiting time before the Arbitration Commission could hear the ETU's federal award claim, the ACTU agreed to lift the blockades and force power industry unions to accept the no-strike clause in their awards. They also promised to retain a moratorium on industrial action for the duration of the Arbitration Commission process. The federal government reneged on a promise to get the SEQEB workers reinstated, declaring: 'there is absolutely nothing we can do ... The Arbitration Commission can't directly order reinstatement and will not give preference to sacked workers.'[167]

ACTU campaign coordinator Ian Court, who had promised that the unions would not desert the SEQEB workers, told an angry mass meeting that the ACTU would not be lured into the 'trap' of a general strike. Furious, the ETU's Alan Doodney hit back. The blockade, he argued, hadn't been allowed to have its full impact, was just used as a Mickey Mouse publicity stunt: 'Because they called it off! They managed to get it imposed and called it off!'[168]

Abandonment of the May blockade was a bitter blow. Still determined to fight on, workers travelled to Canberra on 1 July to meet with ACTU leader Cliff Dolan. Dolan had little but platitudes to offer:

> I have no suggestions except that ultimately we must get rid of Petersen ... the legislation must be defeated. This is the main concern of the ACTU, not getting the jobs back ... the only solution is a change of government and this is a political question.[169]

Even after this blow, Queensland workers did not give up. The federal award coverage process was dragging, so by 15 July, the QTLC Disputes Committee, under rank and file pressure, decided to restart the industrial campaign. The proposal for an August stopwork mass meeting met with overwhelming rank and file support.

Two days before the 20 August action, QTLC's Ray Dempsey told the *Sunday Mail:* 'Pressures are building again in the power industry as they were at the beginning of this dispute.' However, there wouldn't be fireworks from the union movement: 'It's a powder keg, but we aren't lighting any matches.' More accurately, they were tipping bucket loads of water on it.[170]

Despite Dempsey's attempts to downplay the action, 260,000 workers struck throughout Queensland on 20 August, coinciding with a new session of parliament. Statewide stopwork meetings were attended by 30,000 ETU members (although, again, the QTLC prevented power industry workers from joining in), and 13,000 unionists rallied at Lang Park in Brisbane, backing a campaign of industrial action. This was vetoed by the QTLC officials, but hundreds marched to parliament, where they joined the Coalition for Democratic Rights picket. National and ALP MPs looked on, some jeering the marchers from the balconies, as 102 protesters were arrested in violent clashes. QTLC executive member and former communist Hugh Hamilton condemned the protest, calling it a 'handful of misguided people who you wouldn't want to ask to shine your shoes.'[171]

The peak union leadership regarded the 20 August 1985 action as the last hurrah for the campaign, and the QTLC and ACTU called no more actions. There were some scattered protests by rank and file workers, such as one outside the ACTU Congress in Sydney on 11 September, and some bans remained after August; but, essentially, the campaign was left to die. The message now was: 'find another job.' Union after union raised the white flag, abandoning industrial action because, supposedly, everything had changed, and strikes no longer worked. Hamilton conceded defeat, offering empty rhetoric:

> We have to make a proper assessment of the situation and see that we need new methods of organisation and struggle. And these new methods should be spelled out through the collective wisdom of both the trade union movement and the community at large.[172]

Other union leaders insisted that it was impossible to defeat a government that introduced anti-union laws, arguing: 'You can't withstand what the state throws against you.'[173] The fact that the union movement had resisted the state many times and won, most spectacularly with Clarrie O'Shea in 1969, was ignored in this revisionist take on history.

Though the dispute was officially over, the bitterness and determination of the SEQEB workers and their supporters to fight on ensured that the issue did not leave the news. They recognised their dispute as part of a wholesale attack on unions around the country, from the Meatworkers at Mudginberri and the BLF through to local Queensland disputes such as the attempt to force contracts and no-strike clauses on Brisbane Council garbage workers:

> A defeat for any one of these struggles weakens the entire trade union movement. Our struggle is one struggle and the ETU Strike Committee pledges here and now that we will fight this through to victory.[174]

ETU official Bob Hendricks told the *Courier Mail* at the end of September that at least 300 sacked workers were coming to weekly strike meetings, and 600 were still seeking reinstatement.[175] As late as October, *The Australian* reported that ETU maintenance staff still had bans on some work at the power stations.[176] One year later, 200 sacked workers continued to meet in Perry Park, as they had done throughout 1985. SEQEB reported some picketing at depots until April of 1986.

Throughout the dispute, it was these rank and file workers from SEQEB and many other workplaces who had kept the pressure on the officials and on the government. An active ETU Strike Committee was run by rank and file SEQEB linesmen and produced its own *Strike Bulletin*. Other support groups, especially an independent Trade Union Support Group (TUSG) and a Women's Committee, played a crucial role in maintaining the momentum.

The TUSG, rank and file workers from other unions, helped SEQEB workers to travel round the country, addressing meetings of workers to raise funds and industrial support. In May, coinciding with the blockades and after a protest against Bjelke-Petersen' receipt of an honorary doctorate from the University of Queensland, the TUSG established the Queensland Coalition for Democratic Rights in an effort to broaden the campaign to many other causes, including Aboriginal and Torres Strait Islander rights and women's rights; SEQEB workers marched to support Greenslopes abortion clinic after it was raided by the police.

The SEQEB Women's Committee was indomitable – on the picket lines, raising money, having weekly meetings, marching on employer groups and National Party conferences, organising food supplies and speaking out at rallies. It had a radicalising impact on the women involved; one member, Robyn Burrow, said: 'It's changed my life, it's changed my outlook, it's changed everything.'[177]

At the 1985 International Women's Day rally, committee member Pat Spence told the crowd: 'I am proud that women are taking their rightful place in society and demand to be heard.' She saw clearly what needed to be done, telling Mark Sherry that business was getting organised, including individual capitalists such as Jay Pendarvis and Lang Hancock, and shaping up to destroy unions:

> These groups certainly recognise the power of unity and the force of might! The whole union movement is under attack, not merely the ETU in Queensland or the BLF … We are merely the most obvious examples of an insidious action against unions Australia wide, indeed world-wide!

This meant that workers had to organise too: 'It's time for the rank and file to take stock and analyse what we want in our work situation, job safety and conditions.'[178]

What of the much touted 'saviour' for ETU workers, the shift from state-based to federal awards? It was a dismal failure. Swift implementation was promised but blocked many times. There were adjournments because of industrial action; a Queensland Electricity Commission (QEC) appeal in April 1985 against the decision that an interstate dispute existed; the Queensland government's success in winning a stay of proceedings in the High Court against a compulsory conference to resolve the May blockade; a constitutional challenge in June in the High Court; and other government appeals. On 8 November 1985, the ETU was suspended for six months over some industrial action, further delaying the case. Finally, on 17 September 1986, 18 months after the sackings, the application for federal award coverage was rejected.

The impact on the remaining SEQEB workers was devastating. By 1987, there was a 30 percent cut in SEQEB's workforce, and 25 percent of workers were non-union. There had been no strikes in the industry since the end of the dispute in 1985. When one of the plants was shut down with a loss of 750 jobs, there was no response. In 1988, power station operators called for action over superannuation during the World Expo event. The government threatened sackings and loss of superannuation benefits, and the workers backed down.[179]

The lost SEQEB dispute helped foster the shift in union strategy that accompanied the Accord. In October 1985, a QTLC spokesperson said: 'The unions have not lost or gone weak in Queensland, but there is a new realism. We have recognised we have to radically re-think union strategy.'[180] This new realism meant moving away from industrial strategies to focus on the Commission and the courts – a strategy that had just proved disastrous.

CHAPTER 4

The Accord and Women – 'Sold a Lemon'

Unequal Pay

'We've been sold a lemon', was ACOA's Ann Sherry's blunt assessment of the Mark III stage of the Accord in 1987.[181] The two-tier wages system made it harder for women to get a wage rise. Closing the gap, when a 4 percent cap was set on increases, looked impossible. Brenda Forbath, Australian Teachers Federation (ATF) Organiser, commented: 'the decision simply entrenches historical differences in wage rates.'[182]

The Accord was supposed to bring real improvements for women. In *Freezing history: Women under the Accord*, Jo-anne Schofield showed that women barely made progress in wages, hours worked or employment during 1983–1988. The Accord years entrenched that position, still experienced by women to this day.[183] The Accord itself limits its mention of women to the section on education in relation to equal opportunity for women, rural and Aboriginal people. 'Issues such as childcare, equal pay for work of comparable worth, affirmative action and the high burden of unemployment borne by women are not mentioned.' Instead, everyone would benefit from the Accord's delivery of economic growth.

From 1983 to 1988, women's full time Average Weekly Ordinary Time Earnings (AWOTE) went from 80.1 percent to 82.8 percent of men's; women's full time Average Weekly Total Earnings (AWTE) went from 77.3 percent to 78.9 percent. When part-time workers were added, women's AWTE went from 66.0 percent to 66.4 percent of men's. One contributing factor to the continuing gap was the gender segregation of work in Australia, high on a world scale; work in these predominantly female sectors was low paid. Even where the same award applied, female classifications were paid at a lower rate than male. Schofield writes:

> In providing for CPI increases in wages, the Accord froze the differential between the wages of women and those of men. This meant that women were 'locked into' a wages system which had historically discriminated against them.

The two-tier system also punished women. In the August quarter during the 4 percent second tier industry-by-industry negotiations in the second half of 1987, men's wages rose by 1.9 percent, women's by 1.5 percent. In the November quarter, men's wages rose by 1.6 percent, women's by 0.8 percent.[184] Women also had fewer conditions to trade off for a wage rise.

Accompanying the hit on wages during this period were tax cuts. Higher paid workers received a bigger tax cut, which disproportionately impacted women workers. For weekly wages between $250 and $600, the cuts ranged from $5.80pw to $40.10pw; 91 percent of women earned below $600pw, and 21 percent earned below $240.

Similarly, women did not benefit from the 3 percent productivity-based superannuation payment in 1986 – a wages trade-off – because 75 percent of women were not covered by superannuation. There were significant delays in both awarding and spreading the coverage of superannuation, a problem that lasts to this day (see Chapter 9). Superannuation still penalises women workers more harshly: many part-time workers aren't covered; women often have 'time out' for children and lose continuity; and their superannuation pension often cannot keep retired women above the poverty line.

Employment of women as a proportion of all employed persons increased between March 1983 and March 1988 by only 3 percent (37.3 percent to 40.3 percent). Schofield argues that 'the employment policies of the Accord have had no significant impact on women's predominant status as part-time workers.' She points to the negative impact of the trend towards part-time employment, quoting one researcher:

despite the labour movement and Labor government's agreements through the Accord to maintain living standards, this rapid growth of part-time work is an unacknowledged reduction of work hours for many women and girls with an equivalent reduction in pay.[185]

The social wage – spending on education, welfare, child care and social benefits – was one of the major promises of the Accord, though not spelled out in the original document. Of particular relevance for women was affordable or free child care. During the Accord years, child care was privatised and funding cut in the name of economic efficiency. An initial promise of 20,000 new child care places in 1983 was undermined by a $10 million cut three years later. Had funding been maintained, it would only have increased the number of places available from 6 percent of all children to 10 percent. An analysis by Sue Jackson of the first three years of Labor in power examined one of the main promises of 'equitable and clearly discernible redistribution of income.'[186] The analysis showed a pattern that was to continue throughout the Accord years: a redistribution, but all directed from labour to capital. As profits soared, actual improvements in the social wage proved to be negligible. Australia's nett wealth increased by about 30 percent, but pensions and benefits remained below the poverty line, little was done to remove poverty traps in the welfare system, and the number of people living in poverty swelled to almost three million. Most damning of all, the social wage, because of cuts to public spending, was less in real terms than it was in 1975–76, with more cuts to come.[187] Major reforms, such as the introduction of Medicare, were more than paid for by workers, through wage freezes and delays in increases to social security payments in the mid-1980s.

> The social wage elements of the Accord at first appeared to represent an expansion of the trade union movement's interests and activities beyond the workplace. Many demands that community groups have been campaigning around were included. However, in practice these demands have been drawn into a process which makes any progress contingent upon 'economic growth'.[188]

The economic growth needed to fund the social wage always seemed elusive.[189]

The Accord also failed to improve women's situation in the fight for equal pay. After the 1972 Equal Pay decision, over 60 percent of employers reclassified women's jobs, so that they could still pay them at a lower rate. Many, in predominantly female occupations, weren't covered at all. A number of attempts to enforce equal pay were unsuccessful, so it is unsurprising that a 1983 government review concluded: 'The equal pay principle has had almost no impact on the gap between wages paid to men and women.'[190] The 1983 national wage case refused to grant increased rates for women to close the gap or to undertake a work value inquiry into women's work: in itself a tacit acknowledgement that women were being paid less than men.

At the beginning of 1985, the ACTU launched a new attempt, following pressure from groups such as the newly formed Council of Action for Equal Pay (CAEP), which had brought together a wide range of women. In November 1985, the application, with nurses as the test case, went before a full bench of the AIRC headed by Justice Barry Maddern. Jenny Acton, for the ACTU, asked the Commission to effectively reaffirm the 1972 principle of equal pay for equal worth, to enable it to grant the unions' case, while adopting the new concept of comparable worth as the equivalent of its equal pay principle. Rather than setting some arbitrary value, comparable worth entailed taking similar jobs with comparable skills and responsibilities that women and men do and equalising the pay rates.[191] The ACTU also asked the AIRC to rule that the claim was not bound by the current Accord guidelines of wage restraint. The CAEP provided significant research for the ACTU's case and backed up the claim with actions, like recreating Zelda D'Aprano's 1969 equal pay action of chaining herself to the Arbitration Commission building and later paying only 75 percent of the fare on trams. Their actions, including a 1985 Time's Up Conference, brought together women from unions, academics, labour lawyers and women's liberation activists.[192]

It was clear from the beginning that the claim breached the Accord guidelines. If granted, it would have a seismic impact on women's wages and the economy more generally. In the Accord years of restraint, it had no chance. In February 1986, Maddern rejected the comparable worth case and reaffirmed the Equal Pay decision, ruling that acceptance 'would strike at the heart of long accepted methods of wage fixation in this country' – precisely the point of trying to win an equal pay case! He said that the ACTU could pursue the case as an 'anomaly', as the Accord allowed. The ruling prompted the CAEP to remark that the decision had only confirmed that women's work was undervalued and would stay that way.[193]

The nurses' 'anomalies' case then went to the Victorian IRC, where the Royal Australian Nurses Federation (RANF) argued for a rise, winning a wages and new career structures deal in June 1986. The IRC gave its reasons as a shortage of nurses, changes in work value and the application of the equal pay decision – not comparable worth.

Effectively defying the Accord guidelines of quarantining the rise to Victoria, NSW nurses, with tacit ACTU support, used the June 1986 decision as the basis for their claim. After they won an increase, WA, Tasmanian and Queensland nurses also smashed through the Accord's restrictions on the spread of wage rises. Victorian nurses were now lagging behind and were actually in a worse situation, because the John Cain Labor government had reinterpreted the June decision from a win to cutting nurses' wages and conditions. Angered by Labor's move, Victorian nurses launched a new campaign – and won. Despite the state to state wins by nurses, the government and the ACTU never allowed this threat to the Accord's quarantining of wage and conditions increases to spread to other sectors.

Over the years, individual unions have won equal pay in their industries, culminating in the partly successful 2009–2012 Australian Services Union (ASU) equal pay claim, but figures show the wages gap remaining stubbornly high.[194]

Two legal gains for women – the *Sex Discrimination Act 1984* and the *Affirmative Action (Equal Employment Opportunity for Women) Act 1986* – have been updated over the years, but their impact has been limited because of inadequate funding and power to enforce the requirements.

At the end of November 1983, right wing politicians in the Senate went into meltdown at the prospect of legislation to prevent discrimination on the basis of sex or gender in Australia. Several states already had similar acts, but several senators nonetheless claimed that we were facing the end of the world as we knew it, because demands for equality had originated in Soviet Eastern bloc countries and were a communist plot smuggled into Australia.

Noted NSW bigots, Fred and Elaine Nile, took out full page advertisements, crying: 'Stop the Ryan Juggernaut' – a reference to Labor MP Susan Ryan, who was introducing the legislation.[195] The bill passed, despite the hysteria.

Affirmative Action legislation was passed in 1986, requiring 300 companies (Australian businesses employing more than 1,000 employees) to lodge annual reports on their progress as 'non-discriminatory employers.' The government claimed that the new Act aimed to remove barriers to equal opportunity; all it actually required was the appointment of equal employment opportunity officers and development of on-paper company policies. IR Minister Ralph Willis made it clear that 'the obligations are not intensive ... we would expect there to be a net economic benefit, because what we are about is trying to get the best use of employees.'[196] The only sanction was for employers to be named in a report to parliament. The real barriers to equal opportunity – lack of child care, education and equal pay – were not addressed by this Act, nor by any other actions of the Hawke government, despite minor social wage measures.[197]

By 1 February 1988, only one company, the Herald and Weekly Times, had complied with the Act, and its report was incomplete. Companies like BHP consistently fought all attempts by women to achieve equal opportunity in its steel mills, while publicly supporting the *Affirmative Action Act*. Only by taking on the company, and not relying on legislation, did women workers at BHP finally win.[198]

The Accord remained focused on income, and its other promise, price control, lapsed. Ann Sherry expressed the general frustration, felt especially by women on lower wages:

> it is absurd to talk about a wages strategy without talking about some sort of price control. We are constantly chasing our tails, despite having an alleged Prices and Incomes Accord in place for a number of years.[199]

Despite all the award restructuring, multiskilling, increase in proportion of women in the workforce, and anti-discrimination and affirmative action requirements becoming law, the Accord did almost nothing to improve women's situation: 'the position of women workers relative to their male counterparts deteriorated between 1984 and 1988.'[200] Both men and women suffered, because average weekly earnings declined overall by 8 percent under Hawke during this time, and the real value of the social wage dropped, but women were hit harder.

Women were getting angry. Joan Corbett, from the ATF, said: 'I get very pissed off with the argument that, to protect women workers, we have to wear whatever the ACTU determines.'[201]

Some women refused to wear what the ACTU determined. Among these were members of the Victorian Food Preservers' Union (FPU). At the Heinz, Plumrose and Rosella Lipton factories, the mostly female workforce imposed bans in their bid for a pay rise outside the Accord guidelines. At Heinz, the dispute lasted for 11 weeks. Workers were stood down, but they won. Workers at Rosella had the book thrown at them, including government support for employer attempts to cancel their award, but a number of unions in transport and construction backed their demands. They were forced to concede some demands, as were FPU members at Plumrose and later Nestlé, but the companies paid 'special allowances' soon afterwards.

In the federal public sector, women were in the forefront of the struggles in NSW.[202]

Victorian Nurses

'Florence Nightingale is dead – so how come we're still getting her wages?' It was a slogan that rang true during the Victorian nurses' strike of 1986, a year when working as a shop assistant in Myer paid more than a third-year nurse could earn in hospitals.[203] In Australian working class women's history, only the Tailoresses' strike in 1882–3 was longer.

The strike also broke through the stereotypical image of nurses, giving nurses the sense of their own industrial strength and bringing other workers out in solidarity. At the height of the dispute, *The Sun* newspaper reported:

> As if anyone needed further proof of the radicalisation of Florence Nightingale there it was at Olympic Park yesterday – a T-shirt pledging allegiance to 'Irene Bolger's Nurses' Liberation Front' … There was little doubt the striking nurses were going to hang tough. At times, between the laughter

and cheering, you could even hear talk of solidarity and the workers' struggle.

RANF state secretary Irene Bolger summed up members' determination. The ACTU, government and AIRC, she pointed out, accused the nurses of being naïve, of not knowing the system:

> Of course we knew the system, but we ignored it because it was their rules and their system – and we'd decided that it was time to chuck their rules out the door ... [our members] were fed up.[204]

The newly elected Victorian Labor government had begun a process of annual cuts to the health budget. Simultaneously, it encouraged the development of private health centres, shifting the cost for health care from the public purse onto individual workers, with profits going to the private health providers. Plans were in place for more cost cutting through reducing the numbers of higher paid trained nurses and replacing them with lower paid State Enrolled Nurses (SEN). It was never explicitly stated, but this restructuring of nursing was also aimed at breaking union organisation.

Government policy was already having a devastating impact on nurses. They topped the workers' compensation claims, 10,000 left nursing in the year to October 1985, and a further 8,000 did not renew their practising certificates. In 1986, the shortfall of nursing staff was 14,000 – the 10,000 who had left and half of those who had not renewed would be required to fill the gap.

So when the nurses took on their employers, the state government, they faced a determination they were forced to match. Match it they did, in one of the most rank and file controlled disputes the nurses had ever had; striking and holding the line to the end. One of the nurses at Peter McCallum Hospital said:

> The health system is one of the million things that are decaying at the moment. And Labor has got to a pitiful state. This is going to radicalise nurses across the country. There can't be an end until we get better conditions.

NURSES' HISTORY OF STRUGGLE

Australian nurses had taken strike action before. In 1946, in the middle of WWII, nurses at Kempsey Hospital in NSW struck over a sacking and won. Sporadic industrial action included some short strikes during the 1950s and 1960s. The Victorian RANF constitution explicitly ruled out strike action until 1984; in other states, particularly NSW and Queensland, nurses began taking more militant action from the early 1970s.

In 1970, Canberra nurses, then covered by the Hospital Employees' Federation (HEF), struck for six weeks over pay, understaffing and long hours of work. It was the first large-scale nurses' strike in Australia. Builders Labourers in Canberra supported it strongly, and delegations of nurses went to Melbourne, Sydney and Brisbane to speak at factories, building sites and the wharves. Workers at these meetings would then strike for the rest of the day. Overall, so much money was raised to support the nurses that their strike pay was as high as their wages!

Although the strike ended in only a partial victory on wages – nurses wore black arm bands as a sign of their disappointment – it was a major breakthrough and encouragement to nurses around the country.[205]

In April 1975, 4,000 angry Victorian nurses stormed parliament over pay and staffing. They marched along, singing 'We shall not be moved' and carrying placards saying 'Unite and Fight' and 'Dedication doesn't pay the rent.' They won a 12 percent increase and a further 9 percent, although their claim was for a (justified) 50 percent.

Next was NSW, where nurses rallied to Parliament House in 1976 in response to a pay claim of $9 per week; this had been granted in 1974 but was overturned in 1975 and 1976 following appeals from employers. Nurses burned their caps in protest and threatened to strike. They implemented bans rather than striking, but there were protest pickets which lasted for three days.[206]

Through 1977–79, nurses in NSW and Queensland marched, picketed and imposed bans over staffing and cuts to hospital bed numbers. Despite significant wage gains by the end of the 1970s, student nurses were still left in charge of entire hospital wards, experienced nurses got the same pay as cleaners, patient workloads were unsafe, and there were acute nursing shortages.

ACTIONS IN THE 1980S

As nurses became increasingly fed up with workloads and pay and more prepared to act, the new decade saw a marked increase in industrial action. NSW nurses began in 1980, with a 24-hour strike at three hospitals over the closure of the Eastern Suburbs Hospital – although it was not enough to save the hospital or its workers. After a short lull, industrial action around wages, conditions and staffing in NSW stepped up again from 1982, culminating in an all-out strike on 19 November 1983. One nurse commented:

> Sydney Hospital was ready to go out in April 1982. Since then there's been 18 months of discussion. The only way to prove anything to this geezer up in Parliament House is to withdraw our labour.

At the same time, the other major health workers' union, the HEF, had been industrially active in Victoria, winning wage rises for its nursing members, SENs. One placard at the time summed it up: 'RANF just play the game, while HEF strike and reap the gain.' Many nurses considered leaving the RANF and joining the HEF, but the RANF removed its no-strike clause from its constitution in 1983, putting it in a stronger position industrially.[207]

During the early Accord years of 1984 and 1985, nurses in NSW and Victoria again fought state government cutbacks. The Victorians won extra staffing by June 1985. It took NSW nurses until May 1986 to gain a 38-hour week, without wages and conditions trade-offs, from Labor Premier Neville Wran. At the beginning of 1985, the Australian Capital Territory (ACT) branch of the HEF, which also covered nurses, made a claim that was clearly outside the Accord guidelines. Their industrial campaign demanding a 30 percent pay rise and additional staff had a partial win. Underlying the preparedness of NSW and ACT nurses to fight industrially was the fact that union leaders Jennie Haines and Hedley Rowe were both publicly opposed to the Accord.

However, gaining 300 extra staff (mostly non-nursing, to take administrative tasks off ward nurses) in Victoria was only a first step; and there was a catch. The money to pay the wages of new staff was to come from nursing funds, so there would be an effective cut in nursing staff. Backed by the HEF,

THE ACCORD AND WOMEN – 'SOLD A LEMON'   87

Socialist Action November 1985.

the RANF kept the bans on. The government backed down, unconditionally offering 700 non-nursing staff.

With increasing workloads, changing work practices, new technology that increased the need for more specialised staff, and falling real wages, nurses launched a new campaign at a mass meeting in September 1985. To back up their demands, they imposed a series of bans and held further stopworks; a motion for immediate rolling strikes was only narrowly defeated. Health Minister David White came back with an offer – less pay than the nurses wanted, increased productivity and a three-year implementation process, including a no-strike clause. The Federation rejected the offer out of hand and kept up the pressure, working to the RANF staff–patient ratio from 7 October.

White retaliated by ordering Alfred Hospital management to scab – which they did. Nurses at the Alfred walked out immediately for 24 hours. Industrial Relations Minister Steve Crabb, who played a major role in smashing the BLF in 1986, fumed: 'It's outrageous! I've never had a strike pulled on me in the middle of negotiations.'

The nurses were even angrier. On 11 October, the mass meeting of nurses from every hospital slammed the government's 'offer' and voted for an indefinite strike from 17 October. Thousands took to the streets, marching to Crabb's office demanding 'Wage Justice Now.'

When the strike started, nurses all over Melbourne noisily picketed hospitals, handing out leaflets to passers-by and collecting money. One student nurse said:

> Nurses' conditions are so bad because people haven't fought to change them. But now nurses have changed. In the strike they're learning a lot about government tactics and union power.

They were determined to stay out until they won; but it was not to be. The strike ended after five days, with a token offer, really not much to show for their action. A significant minority opposed the return to work.

Escalation

From October 1985, there were skirmishes over the proposed recruitment of British and Irish nurses to solve the immediate staffing crisis and attempts to paper over the cracks in the system with 'enquiries' into the dire situation at both the Alfred and Royal Melbourne Hospitals. At the same time, the Victorian IRC opened hearings into how to implement the government's offer, as well as considering some of the nurses' claims.

In reality, this was a delaying tactic. The decision took eight months to deliver, being presented to the union in June 1986. It was a bombshell – a pay rise with a difference! Despite a brand new career structure with some pay rises, most nurses would get nothing. Many would be pushed down the career grades – losing money. Further hearings abolished qualification or certificate allowances, cutting wages even more.

The impact was devastating. Nurse after nurse faced massively downgraded pay and work levels. One of the picketers at Preston and Northcote Community Hospital (PANCH) had 16 years' experience, held three certificates and was in the process of finishing a university degree; she suddenly found herself classified at the lowest of the Grade One levels. At one hospital, management even backdated the cuts to January 1 and demanded repayments from nursing staff.

At mass meetings, nurses rejected strike motions, instead voting to impose bans again and to lodge a further list of claims. Management responded by standing down nurses, but this tactic was thwarted by some imaginative action by fellow nurses. After a union delegate was stood down, many called in sick at the Eye and Ear Hospital; at another hospital, work colleagues formed shields around targeted members until management left the ward; and in a country hospital, nurses took an immediate extended tea break, not coming back until management reinstated their stood-down colleague.

This stalemate continued for weeks: bans, stand-downs, mass meetings followed by reinstatements, bans lifted and continued negotiations with the government and hospital management.

Throughout the dispute, the state Labor government threw the book at the nurses, backed up by a strident press which compared nurses to 'terrorist groups' who 'played games with the fears of the sick.'[208] Days before the dispute was settled, the so-called respectable *Age* newspaper wrote:

> Militant nurses are no longer just exploiting the pain and suffering of the innocent in what has become an industrial war of extraordinary viciousness; they are now quite

> deliberately and callously playing with human lives as if they were pawns on a chess board.[209]

Earlier, Irene Bolger had hit back at some of this characterisation of nurses, telling the Melbourne *Herald* newspaper:

> There is an attitude in the community that nurses are going to be saintly and do not deserve the same conditions as other workers. They did not go into nursing to be nuns or priests. They went to do a job and if they are not rewarded they will leave.[210]

She also noted:

> We want to avoid a situation where nurses will be in charge and be paid at a higher rate, but their numbers will be halved and other workers will come in to do the bedside nursing and be paid lower wages.[211]

Government threats of dismissal, deregistration of the union, criminal and manslaughter charges, the use of the Essential Services Act, and even police action to disrupt picket lines, only strengthened the nurses' resolve. The government's promises to negotiate were a farce. They refused to budge on their 'generous' offer, and negotiations collapsed on 24 October – a year since the first strike in the nurses' campaign.

The time for working within the system was over. Nurses were now ready to go out. At the October 31 stopwork, 5,000 angry and militant nurses overwhelmingly endorsed a rank and file motion for an indefinite strike. Nurses reinforced their message with a noisy march through the city.[212]

On 1 November, the strike started in earnest. Nurses at Western General were the first to walk out. By the weekend, another 18 hospitals had voted to walk out. Nurses at the Alfred were the last, but they marched out on their way to the Health Department offices, singing 'Oh when the Alfred goes marching out.' Most metropolitan hospitals were picketed, although no goods were stopped for the first few days. During the dispute, public support was tremendous, with many visiting picket lines. Sue Jackson recalls that many in the women's movement supported the nurses, visiting picket lines, getting up motions in their unions, pressuring politicians and, through CAEP, supporting the comparable worth case.[213] Encouragement to 'toot in support' prompted almost continuous honking outside hospitals. Food, firewood and money poured in, and pro-RANF letters and telegrams (in the days before emails and texts) overloaded Australia Post's delivery service. At the government-run employment agency, the Commonwealth Employment Service (CES), workers refused to post nursing vacancies on their boards.

Early in the dispute, workers at several CBD sites marched off the job to join nurses' rallies; later, building unions held a one-day stoppage and marched through the city. Wharfies and construction workers levied themselves and held workplace meetings. Eight hundred public sector delegates unanimously backed a support motion, and over 1,000 unionists braved a downpour to attend a lunchtime solidarity rally. Unionists in the Latrobe Valley power stations twice offered support action and even proposed to shut down power supplies, but their union leadership headed that off.

The nurses' action broke through other myths and stereotypes. Arguments about 'losing public support' are often used to discourage public sector workers from striking, especially in female-dominated workplaces such as welfare and teaching. Support for nurses remained at 75–80 per cent throughout their 50-day strike.

'More could have been done to transform the largely spontaneous and fragmented sympathy into organised and directed support', wrote Janey Stone at the time. 'There was no official call from the RANF to other unions for support.'[214] Backing from rank and file workers of other unions for the nurses raised for their leadership the problem of their commitment to the Accord. Left wing newspaper *Direct Action* pointed out: 'Union officials who might have supported the nurses' struggle in principle were caught in a bind.' Having committed their unions to holding back on members' claims, 'The question "if it's good enough for us to strike for the nurses why can't we strike for a wage rise for ourselves?" would have to be answered.' Few unions were prepared to go out on a limb for themselves, let alone another union.

For the ultimate success of the strike, however, rank and file nurses' input was crucial. For the first time in the union, the militants effectively ran the dispute, both on the job and through a strike committee. The committee met

Nurses picket during 1986 strike. Photo Maggie Diaz courtesy Gwendoline De Lacey.

daily at the union offices to plan action and go over the previous day's events. Every day, the RANF ran a program on community radio 3CR and put out a strike bulletin. Morale and solidarity were maintained by regular picket line events and regular marches and rallies in the city. Groups of nurses toured the country regions daily, building support and keeping country members informed. One nurse said: 'I've never seen nurses so united and strong.'

Nurses were also confident that the RANF leadership would back them. In May 1986, a new secretary with a more radical, activist agenda, Irene Bolger, had been elected. But it was the rank and file who were calling the shots. The Epworth Hospital union delegate noted: 'Irene is our employee. We tell her what to do.' At the Wimmera Base Hospital, nurses resigned *en masse*, against Irene Bolger's advice; when they phoned to let her know that they'd resigned anyway, she told them that she'd back them 100 percent. This commitment to carrying out decisions of the rank and file won Irene Bolger standing ovations at most of the mass meetings. For her, it was the solidarity of the nurses, their support and unity, that kept her going.

Of course, the strike was not a bed of roses. Nurses faced many personal traumas. Many cried as they walked out and had nightmares afterwards. They would often slip away from the picket line and in the back door to visit patients they'd nursed. One charge sister commented: 'It's been horrible for the past twelve months, but I think unity has come out of it.'[215]

The government refused to negotiate, so the strike escalated. Picket lines began to stop non-essential items, and TWU drivers largely respected them. Premier Cain threatened to use police to break the pickets – and, on a couple of occasions, they did. At the Royal Melbourne Hospital, the picket turned violent when police forced the picketers back to let some aggressively driven laundry vans through.

Not all unions were supportive. Most problematic for the RANF was the hostile relationship between the Federation and the HEF, the result of a history of the RANF not backing HEF industrial action. Led by Les Butler, the Victorian HEF openly sided with the Labor government and instructed members to cross RANF picket lines. Some did, but at Prince Henry's, Queen Victoria and Western General Hospitals, among others, the HEF members backed the nurses. HEF meetings at Prince Henry's agreed not to touch any goods brought in by scabs and threatened a total walkout if police were used.

They carried motions supporting the nurses' strike 100 percent. According to Les Taylor, the HEF chief shop steward at Prince Henry's, the strike brought the two unions even closer at that hospital.

The Trades Hall Council leadership played as despicable a role as the HEF officials. Trades Hall secretary Peter Marsh claimed that he didn't want to take responsibility for assisting the strike because it affected the health industry. That didn't stop him from trying, the very next day, to force the RANF to hand over the dispute to Trades Hall. He patronisingly told the nurses that they needed help because they could no longer handle the dispute. Louise Ajani from Western General retorted: 'basically we don't think Trades Hall are acting in our interests.'[216] Fifteen hundred strikers personally delivered that message to Trades Hall after a rally on 7 November. Chanting 'No Trades Hall Interference', a contingent of several hundred nurses stormed a health unions' meeting and saw to it that delegates voted against Trades Hall intervention and supported the nurses' independence.

By 19 November, 40 hospitals were hit by the strike, and building unions were threatening to impose bans. The IRC finally backed down from its refusal to arbitrate while the nurses were still out, calling private talks with all parties on 21 November – to no avail. The government still believed that the nurses would go back. They were buoyed by the fact that, while some in the private sector did strike – and were viciously attacked by hospital management – most did not. White's ultimate offer demonstrated that the government's real concern was the political cost of any agreement, the potential for other workers to break through, rather than any financial cost.

The government remained intransigent, wanting the ACTU to control the nurses. The RANF Federal Council refused to agree to ACTU intervention, although talks continued between the two union organisations. The ACTU supported the nurses' claims 'in principle', but it wanted to divert their claim into a national claim for all nurses, masterminded by Bill Kelty. The nurses would be the key group in a general case for all female workers under the Comparable Worth provisions of the Accord. A Comparable Worth case would test a predominantly female occupation, for example, nurses, against a similar group of male workers, like firefighters. A case was ultimately tested and failed, as detailed earlier in this chapter; but the Victorian nurses refused to let their claims be overtaken during the 1986 dispute. The ACTU tried its best to undermine the nurses. ACTU President Simon Crean personally attacked the union on several occasions, accusing them of 'demanding more than was justified' and advising them to go back to work. Irene Bolger hit back bluntly: 'Simon Crean should keep his mouth shut. He doesn't know what is going on.'[217]

On 8 December, with no end in sight, the RANF again escalated the action. The union pulled its trump card: in a dramatic move, nurses walked out of critical care wards – wards they'd kept staffed throughout the dispute. Fresh from the daily picket line reps' meeting, one member at PANCH announced the walkout. Asked what nurses were going to do if the government didn't respond, she replied: 'Not work? It has to work.' Having pulled out their trump card, they had no strategy to continue building the strike if there was a setback.

Sadly, there was. Although a similar tactic had brought the Canadian government to the table in seven minutes, the Victorian government had much more room to manoeuvre, with 50 percent of hospital beds in the private hospital system. The government still refused to negotiate. In fact, three days later, White escalated the dispute on the government's behalf by announcing that one-year trained SENs would be instructed to do the nurses' work.[218] Necessary legislation to cover the SENs legally would be rushed through parliament.

He was assisted by the leadership of the Australian Medical Association (AMA – the doctors' union) and the HEF, with Les Butler saying that he had no objection to his members doing work usually carried out by RANF members. He topped this off by adding: 'As far as we are concerned it should have been done yesterday.'[219]

It was a step too far – effectively a full frontal attack on nurses' conditions around the country. It swung the dispute back in the nurses' favour, both in terms of public support and also within the RANF itself. It galvanised the rest of the ANF branches and the federal office to protest and threaten nationwide industrial action. It is likely that other HEF branches would have objected, and many rank and file SENs would have refused to take over RANF members' work – for which they were not trained.

The Cain ministry did not publicly back down on the SEN threat until 17 December. The government's only real weapon now was the ACTU. With the

IRC opening up a loophole for the ACTU intervention, the government was able to manoeuvre itself out of its dead-end position and leave it up to the ACTU to deliver the goods.

After lengthy discussions, the RANF and ACTU finally came to an agreement on a joint case to put to the Victorian IRC on 15 December. The RANF had made some concessions, but the ACTU agreed to all the RANF's major claims – so they told the union. But when presenting the case to the Commission, the ACTU's Jenny Acton started backtracking. When Irene Bolger tried to stop her, Acton accused her of being 'unable to understand the difference between substantial and total agreement.'

RANF members and their leadership understood the ACTU's treachery only too well. Irene Bolger reported to that afternoon's stopwork: 'There is nothing joint about the proposal – it is now just the ACTU proposal. I think we have been sold out.'[220] The nurses stayed out. The ACTU got the message and changed their position to one of total agreement with the RANF.

On 19 December, an agonising 11 days after the total walkout, the government comprehensively backed down and agreed to the nurses' demands, withdrawing the SEN legislation. The dispute was over. The nurses went back victorious, and the government and its economic rationalist policies suffered a decisive defeat.

The Australian concluded:

> Despite all the public posturing ... the nurses did prove themselves strong enough industrially to make significant wage gains. It took five weeks of strike action, but the government did finally agree

It was a sweet victory for the rank and file who'd thrown so much into winning the campaign. One nurse said it all: 'For the first time thousands of nurses here are finding that they do have power, that they can change their own lives.'[221]

Nurses won a victory in a time of working class retreat, during the 1980s, when the Accord was the framework for attacks on working class organisation, wages and conditions across the nation. And they won in the face of a relentless press campaign of vilification. Irene Bolger was chastised for 'changing a noble, caring profession into a hard-booted militant union.'[222] One *Age* editorial thundered: 'Nurses must not win', advising:

> They should direct their anger at their union for not telling them what happens if you go on strike over multi-million dollar pay claims outside the wage fixing guidelines when the economy is in recession. You lose.[223]

The government didn't hold back in its media campaign either, with advertising that Yvonne Barratt from the RANF described as 'patronising, chauvinistic and misleading.'[224] More seriously, Labor threatened to use the full force of the law against the nurses, including the options of dismissal, criminal charges including manslaughter, and the use of police against picket lines.

Although not covered federally, nurses were in the firing line of Accord-like policies as state Labor governments adopted the Accord's neoliberal agenda, cutting a swathe through the public sector. The implications of decisions about nurses' wages and conditions certainly had consequences for the Accord.

Ken Howard, then RANF's federal Industrial Officer, pointed to the potential from the nurses' win: 'A breakthrough for the nurses, or rather a breakout from the straitjacket of the arbitration system and the Accord would have had tremendous significance for all workers.'

The year 1986 started with the smashing defeat of the BLF and ended with a decisive victory for the nurses. The question then was, would the union movement realise the potential of the nurses' example, or would their fate be that of the BLF?

CHAPTER 5

Robe River – New Right or Accord Neoliberalism?

Robe River sent shock waves around the country.[225] Mining unionists had won good wages and conditions across the Pilbara in north-west WA. Now, they lost almost all of that in a union-busting onslaught at the Pannawonica mine and Cape Lambert port, owned by Robe River Associates. When Peko–Wallsend increased their shareholding to take over Robe in 1986, CEO Charles Copeman, a poster-boy for the New Right, launched a ruthless attack on workers, stripping them of conditions and, at one stage, their jobs. A long ruling class battle effectively deunionised the region – the country's largest export earner, with companies among the most profitable in Australia.[226] On its own, Peko–Wallsend, a minnow in the Pilbara, could not have won. Supported by many in the ruling class, the company used and ignored the industrial relations system at will. But what broke the fighting resistance of Robe River rank and file was the enforcement of the Accord processes by those who were meant to be on their side: the ACTU, their own union officials and Labor, both state and federal. After SEQEB, Mudginberri, Dollar Sweets and the BLF deregistration (see Chapter 6), unions should have met fire with fire to defeat such employer offensives. Instead, their own uncertainty and lack of solidarity drove a weak campaign. The Accord-locked ACTU enforced a crushing defeat. Graeme Haynes, an ETU shop steward at the Robe River mine from the mid-70s, pointed out: 'Robe River aren't the world-beaters they claim to be. It is only with the help of union leaders like Simon Crean that they and bosses like them retain their power.'[227]

Mining and Unionism in the Pilbara

Initially, the region was not predicted to provide its eventual massive resources and profits. Intermittent surveys over the decades had underestimated the extent of the region's iron ore deposits. From 1938 and over the war years, there were restrictions on mining and export from the region until pressure from overseas economies, such as Japan, and locally in Australia, encouraged further development. Mining and jobs expanded in the 1960s; profits rose, but workers did not share in the bounty: 'workers faced horrendous conditions, arbitrary abuse of power, low safety standards and wages … Trade union organisation was patchy.'[228]

Unionisation was not a given, even with the obvious hardships in such an unforgiving environment. Isolation, high labour turnover and attitudes of workers (from a 'take it or leave it' stance to 'only in it for the money') militate against unionism and can leave workers apathetic about, or opposed to, collective action in general. To break through these barriers and to unionise the workforce, a sense of injustice resulting from employer actions needs to develop.[229]

Graeme Haynes describes how the employers' actions encouraged unionism: 'Getting fellow workers to fight, in some ways it wasn't all that hard, the bosses were rubbing our noses in the class difference.' One example typifies this:

> We were doing all the shit work and dangerous work, facing the possibility of getting burnt, even electrocuted or minced up in the machinery and you'd come in hot, sweaty and dirty for smoko. We'd be lined up for a packet of two salt cracker biscuits and a styro cup of coffee. The boss, not a sweat mark on him, was having percolated coffee and tim-tams in an air-conditioned office, in full view. We were dressed in 'prison greens', he wore pressed khaki clothing. It's things like that that galvanise workers.

Partly because of the dreadful conditions workers experienced, but also because of a rising working class combativity, the unions made serious efforts to unionise the region during the late 1960s and early 1970s, sending up joint teams of organisers to get workers together, sign them up and establish shop stewards' committees.[230] The first Iron Ore Industry Award in 1967, under the WA industrial relations system, entrenched compulsory – or closed shop – unionism, including union preference in hiring, although union action was needed to enforce all aspects of the award.

Rising industrial action around the nation in 1969, including the national general strike over penal powers in May (Clarrie O'Shea), seemed to signal a turning point in the Pilbara too. A build-up of strikes in the region from 1965 led to significant levels of industrial action across all companies, by all unions. Workers increasingly won. A new award, handed down in 1969, was roundly rejected by all unions and resulted in a three-week strike across the Pilbara; they got a better deal. An outbreak of strikes in 1970, including wildcat strikes in direct defiance of the union officials, management and WA IRC (WAIRC) orders, won the workforce massive improvements in wages and conditions.[231]

Out of this emerged a rank and file leadership supported by workers willing to take militant action. By the mid-1960s, newly elected shop stewards and regular meetings of members built up over time to become shop committees, where all the stewards from each separate union would meet to discuss whole-of-site issues. By the late 1960s, each shop committee had elected a convenor, who worked full time onsite on union affairs at the companies' expense. Being closer to the members, these rank and file bodies understood the issues more readily and were more prepared to take action to fix up any problems, whereas Perth-based officials were likely to opt for hearings in the IRC to ratify deals with management and head off any disruption to production. One official commented that he spent all his time trouble-shooting – more on behalf of the companies than the workers. Another, AMWU leader Jack Marks, was known by workers wherever he'd worked as 'Back to Work Jack'![232]

In 1972, Robe River workers established the next level of union organisation, the Combined Union Committee (CUC), consisting of representatives of each union shop committee on site – usually the convenors and deputy convenors. The CUC also worked with the other CUCs across the Pilbara, coordinating action around common issues, including formulating logs of claims for new industrial agreements, housing, health and safety and the like.

These convenors became powerful worker advocates, dubbed Czars of the Pilbara by their enemies, and an alternative leadership to the Perth-based union officials. This democratic organisations of stewards and the union convenors, the Shop Committees and the CUCs, ensured solidarity between worksites, coordinated campaigns and became a byword for union militancy.

Haynes describes how effective the unions, in particular the CUCs, were – and not just on the job:

> We were getting tangible results. We got proper housing and set up a housing committee to stop queue jumping. We'd threaten a strike if they put a boss in ahead of the workers on the list. We got a child-care centre built, a workers' club and cyclone committees that could override a boss' decision.

Other gains included a level of control over work itself, where the miners elected their own leading hands and made decisions over which machinery was to be used and, consequently, which job and which workers were on site:

> We won all those things through the strength of our labour. If you didn't like how things were, you withdrew your labour and you got the things you wanted, the things you needed.

Almost all of this was to be lost at Robe River after the massive attack on unions in 1986–1987. Other employers in the Pilbara looked on and bided their time, later acting against the unions when it suited them, so that all mines were eventually deunionised and their wages and conditions slashed. Robe River would show the way.

Peko–Wallsend

Deunionisation began at Robe River because of Peko–Wallsend, the eventual owners of the mine and port. Of the four companies in the region, Cliffs Robe River in 1972 had been the last to begin production and was more vulnerable to market changes and industrial pressure because of its reduced ability to stockpile ore and its lower quality ore, largely sold at spot or short-term prices, rather than on the long-term contracts typical of other Pilbara firms. By 1986, the company was ready to engage in a major expansion, to cost millions of dollars. Despite having already notched up a record profit, management argued that this was no guarantee of future profitability under the current production processes, especially in the light of the mid-1986 slump in world market prices.

Headed by Charles Copeman, Robe River was now focused on cutting costs and increasing productivity to maintain and increase profits. And they were prepared for confrontation if necessary.

Copeman's own ideological leanings were a factor in management's attitude. He won considerable, though not always overt, support among businesses for his actions. He was no lone agent or maverick, as many claim; he had aligned himself with that section of business which did not support the Accord and what they saw as its entrenchment of union power. He was a founding and vocal member of the New Right HR Nicholls Society, believing that so-called 'restrictive work practices' – union-won conditions – were holding back profits. A year after Robe River, in an address to the Society, Copeman thanked his co-thinkers: 'You all played a vital part in giving me the encouragement to initiate what we did at Robe River.'[233]

This is somewhat disingenuous of Copeman; under his leadership, Peko–Wallsend had already chalked up a number of confrontations with unions around the country. Earlier in the 1980s, Peko had taken on unions at Ranger, Tennant Creek gold and copper deposits, at Ellalong and Pelton mines and on King Island, and won on every site. While Peko was still battling the unions at Robe, the company summarily closed down its 500-strong Besco Batteries plant in NSW in October 1986, giving workers just 30 minutes' notice. This was no novice at union-busting.

When Peko–Wallsend initially acquired a 35 percent interest in Robe River in 1983, they reviewed employment levels at the mine and port and judged that there was significant overstaffing. Robe River management rejected the report. After gaining majority shareholding in early 1986, Peko directors again reviewed operations, this time in the middle of negotiations for a new, region-wide industrial agreement in the Pilbara. Copeman claims that they found 'an appalling state of affairs, including the list of 284 restrictive work practices ... and the outrageous food concessions which later attracted such public attention.'[234] He argued:

> By June [1986] the project was making a loss, major maintenance had been seriously disrupted and union bans that ensured low levels of stockpiles at the port were the cause of long delays to shipping, with costly demurrage charges.

Robe River acquired additional ore reserves in 1985, adding to its costs. In 1986, the company claimed to need 'the freedom of management to introduce new and more competitive working methods', to offset the cost of development of the additional ore body and return a profit.[235] Some caution is needed here in assessing Peko–Wallsend's claims of low profitability and high costs. Peko had borrowed heavily at high interest rates to buy Robe River and to fund the subsequent expansion. Consequently, it was able to offset its borrowings to push down its recorded profits in its accounts statements. It was all strictly legal accounting and showed the company's proposed cost cutting to have an impressive impact on the bottom line. The *Financial Review* reported that Peko–Wallsend tabled a healthy $50.22 million consolidated operating profit for 1985–86, an 84.3 percent improvement on the previous year's result. The newspaper noted that the 'creditable' 10.7 percent return on shareholder funds was high for an Australian mining company and was Peko's best result for many years.[236]

The dispute that led deunionisation in the Pilbara began on 31 July 1986 with mass sackings, although the conflict had actually been brewing for some time. Workers were defiant, one claiming: 'If they drive us out, they'll never mine another ton of ore at Pannawonica.'[237]

According to Peko management, an incident on 28 May sparked their 31 July anti-union onslaught. The incident was the resetting of a power switch by powerhouse superintendent Ray Knapp during a 24-hour national wages strike. ETU members at Robe demanded that Knapp be suspended for five days for failing to call an ETU tradesperson, a requirement earlier agreed upon by unions and management. When a two-day suspension was ordered, ETU members went out for six days in protest. Earlier, there had been another strike over a similar incident of staff doing a unionised worker's task. Robe workers' actions coincided with strikes at BHP's and Rio Tinto's Mount Newman and Hamersley, all of which threw the region into turmoil and caused days of delays in ore export from the ports.

While management of the other companies were cautious in their response to strikes at their mines, they were carefully watching Peko's actions, setting up their own management reviews. There was support, if sometimes muted, outside the Pilbara too; employer groups such as the Business Council of Australia (BCA) expressed support for Copeman's demand for 'management's right to manage', adding that the arguments of the New Right were persuasive. Director Geoff Allen told the *Financial Review*:

> There may be some differences within the business community about the precise tactics of Peko–Wallsend, but many businessmen in the mainstream of business life share Charles Copeman's frustration about restrictive work practices, operational absurdities and excesses of union power.[238]

After the 31 May action by ETU members, Peko issued a 48-hour notification of stand-downs to the CUC at Cape Lambert and Pannawonica, warning that unless industrial action was lifted by 19 June, with a guarantee of no further action, the whole operation would be progressively stood down. Workers reacted angrily to management's move, but, through a mixture of threat and appeal, union officials forced a return to work.

Peko–Wallsend management under Copeman had never hidden their aim of running an award-free operation, excluding both the IRC and unions. It was striking, however, that they used the WAIRC and any other legal institution at will during the 1986 dispute, implementing decisions when they suited, ignoring those that did not. Now, after the June warnings, they felt ready to act. On 31 July 1986, they made the move that quickly earned Copeman the label 'Rambo of the Pilbara.' Led personally by Copeman, the new management swept through the Perth office, sacking or demoting all six managers and installing their own team. Under the new General Manager Operations, long-time Peko staffer Ian McCrae, they issued a flurry of memos and letters, including to union state secretaries, announcing that they wished to withdraw from award negotiations and from all local agreements in favour of 'procedures ... solely determined by the Company in accordance with sound management practices.'[239]

All workers were to work strictly as directed within the registered awards and agreements only, or they would be sacked. None of the roughly 200 site agreements, established over the years through practice rather than registration, would be honoured. Under the new regime, workers could be transferred by managers to different jobs, classifications (often downgraded), sections or shifts, or put on a 38-hour week; contract and piece work were introduced. Furthermore, union convenors were told that they could no longer be full-time workers with union facilities; they had to return to their regular jobs, with supervisors only granting strictly limited time for union business. A year later, Peko applied, unsuccessfully, to transfer all awards from the state to the federal sphere, a move that was designed to further cut wages and conditions.

Workers' immediate response to the 31 July 1986 ultimatum was to refuse to work as directed. Sixty were sacked on the spot, and others refused duties over the next few days, precipitating further sackings. The mining unions did not accept the company's decision to renege on all current, legally binding agreements. But, instead of striking and calling in industrial support from the rest of the Pilbara, union officials decided to go down the more cautious legal path to the Commission. On 5 August, the WAIRC, under Commissioner Coleman, ordered the parties to restore the status quo existing before 31 July 1986 for a period of 30 days. The company appealed the next day, at the same time ignoring the WAIRC order, continuing to sack any worker who would not work under the new conditions.

Meetings of management, union officials and the Commissioner continued. On 11 August, Coleman issued a further order directing the company to reinstate the sacked workers, without loss of entitlements, and restore the status quo for the whole site.

Starting from night shift on 10 August, workers attempted to work to their original conditions, leading to a somewhat chaotic day. Management responded by claiming that the site had become dangerous. They closed down the whole operation, then sacked the entire workforce. Copeman later insisted that, for the company:

> the only course of action left was to dismiss promptly the entire award workforce of 1,180 people that evening, lodge

an appeal against the Order the next day, and then start to get people back to work again on the terms set by management on and since 31 July. To have acceded to the Commission's Order would have lost all the initiative which had been achieved on 31 July.[240]

Unions submitted to the WAIRC that the changes introduced on 31 July should not be made and that all workers should be reinstated with compensation. But the union leadership did little else to fight back. Union officials 'decided on a strategy of passive resistance based on the premise that the dispute could not be won' by the workers. For the first time in Pilbara industrial history, a mass meeting accepted the official recommendation to allow Japanese ships waiting at Robe's Cape Lambert to be diverted to Port Hedland and loaded with Mt Newman ore. The meeting asked the federal government to use export licensing and legislation to force Robe back into compliance with the WAIRC, but Hawke refused to act.[241]

Haynes argues that this was a key backward step in the strike. Jack Marks and an entourage of ministers flew in, appealing to rank nationalism against rival international ore firms:

> Marks gave a terrific spiel about how we should let the ship go with good Australian ore, or it'd get filled with nasty fascist South African ore. Think about the terrific PR if we let the ship go, he said.
>
> About 11 of us delegates let fly then, but we were denounced as company plants and saboteurs and because the members still had faith in the officials, they let the ship go.[242]

Thompson and Smith argue that it was at this meeting that 'unionists gave away any thought of immediate confrontation or widespread Pilbara action.' Instead of fighting management, the officials, with workers' agreement, seemed more concerned to save the industry and 'placate demands for the abolition of restrictive work practices and help the Japanese receive a stable, secure supply of iron ore.'[243]

The lockout continued. Robe offered, on 17 August, re-employment with no continuity of service on the basis of the 1979 registered Agreements and awards, but on nothing signed since – provided workers signed an acceptance form the next day. The offer, along with the continued examination of work practices and a safety audit, was the basis of an agreement between the state Minister for Minerals and Energy, David Parker, and Robe. The workforce rejected it out of hand.

On 21 August, the Commission again ordered Robe to re-employ the workforce. Robe appealed, meaning that the only offer on the table was the one already rejected by the unions. The next day, 22 August, a hearing of the Industrial Appeals Court quashed the return to work under the status quo order of 5 August, making it clear that the 11 August order would also be quashed.

The company had won the first round.

Throughout the dispute, unionists were hectored constantly by hostile newspaper reports and opinion pieces from the whole range of players – Labor, the Coalition, union leaderships, employers and the press – criticising the dispute and undermining morale and solidarity. The *Financial Review*, for example, wrote:

> The unionists in the Pilbara know they cannot win the fight with Peko–Wallsend. What they don't know is how much they will lose ... The reality is that the unions want the mine to reopen, even if it means there will be fewer jobs and far fewer of what the company describes as 'wroughts' [rorts].[244]

The ruling class sensed the weakness of the union bureaucrat-led response too; the article continued:

> The mildness of the response demonstrates the difficulty for the unions in trying to compete with Peko's tough tactics. The dilemma is that attempts to punish Peko also punish them. In that sense Peko's action succeeded as soon as it began.

The *AFR* quoted an anonymous official: 'It's like playing a board game with all the blocks except one. And that one says – you lose.'

The paper claimed:

> A general strike in the Pilbara would not only unite the companies, it would ensure that when the people eventually did return to work, it would be to a much smaller industry, with fewer jobs and even more difficulties selling to Japan ... 'We'd just be cutting our own throats,' said one union official.

Haynes argues that the workers were prepared to fight, and the dispute could have been won. He recalls a meeting of the CUCs at Karratha, where the WATLC secretary Rob Meecham, dressed in suit and tie and carrying his briefcase, argued for the unions to allow the ore to be loaded and shipped from the ports in spite of bans. Meecham was told in no uncertain terms that there'd be no ore leaving the ports; AMWU convenor, Bob Dalrymple, told him that barnacles 'as big as his fucking boofhead' could grow before the ships would be let go. Dalrymple got a huge roar of approval, and Meecham left with his tail between his legs. Robe River unionists held the line that time, but it was not to last. Instead, a process of wearing down the workforce and refusing to broaden the dispute to stop all iron ore leaving the Pilbara made defeat inevitable. For Robe River, the union leaders isolated the dispute to Wickham (the township at Cape Lambert) and Pannawonica, preventing other sites' industrial action in solidarity and merely seeking financial support from the rest of the region – a very unpopular move, says Haynes.

Formation of a workers' dispute committee at the beginning was crucial to the longevity of the dispute:

> We set up finance, food and welfare and PR committees and organised radio contact throughout the region ... This committee, which had women and men working together, was the hardest working of the lot and had a terrific effect on morale. In fact, women played a key role all the way through the dispute, from shop stewards to the food and welfare committee.

The committee decided to hold a tour of the Pilbara calling for industrial action.

> The union leaders had to stop this and they did by cancelling the tour and making it impossible for us to get on the sites. They told us we were living in cloud cuckoo land for thinking we could organise a walkout of the Pilbara.

In the end, Graeme concludes, 'Despite all our efforts, we lost. We lost because we couldn't win on our own. We needed the support of the rest of the union movement.'

After the 22 August decision, management still weren't prepared to take back any of the workforce, except on their own terms. The lockout continued, while the case for reinstatement was still before the Commission. Finally, on 3 September, the WAIRC under Chief Commissioner Bruce Collier ordered reinstatement on the company's terms and prohibited industrial action until the end of the year.

Even then, Peko took the dispute another step further. On 3 September, the first working day at the end of the company lockout, it directed staff to do the work of blue-collar workers and start operations up again before the first shift of workers returned to work. Staff walked through picket lines to begin the start-up, with the blue-collar workforce finally lifting the pickets and returning to work later that day. Though critical of the company's provocation, the AMWU's Jack Marks announced the union leaderships' capitulation, saying they would not play into Peko's hands by striking. At every opportunity, remembers Graeme Haynes, Marks would tell workers they wouldn't have to worry about the company sacking them: 'If you idiots go on strike, you'll be sacking yourselves!'

At the same time, the ACTU met with the BCA and Confederation of Australian Industry (CAI) in a work practices summit, where all parties agreed on the need to remove restrictive work and management practices to enhance productivity, best achievable at the plant or enterprise level.[245] No chance, then, of the ACTU taking it up to Peko–Wallsend on behalf of rank and file unionists.

Graeme Haynes, activist in 1986 Robe River dispute, outside Melbourne BLF office, with supporter Janey Stone. Photo Janey Stone.

Workers, however, did have something of a victory, winning non-taxable compensation for the three weeks they were sacked in August. Haynes explains:

> The only success from the dispute was that we won *some* money back for the time of the lockout. But we were re-employed, not reinstated after the lockout. So many people were reclassified into lower paying jobs and we lost a lot of accrued rights, including seniority and payments.

In their fight to retain conditions, the unions put up 32 matters common to all workplaces for the Commission to investigate and ratify, rather than the contested 284 claimed by Copeman. On 6 December, the WAIRC ruled that only six were allowable, and two were let through because of no opposition from Robe. The unions had lost, and the officials made no further attempts in the WAIRC to regain the rest of the work practices cancelled by the company.

Peko endured some criticism from the WA Labor government – mostly rhetorical, and more concerned about markets than workers. Premier Brian Burke threatened various legal moves to make the company recognise the threat to business with Japan. Halfway through the dispute, federal IR Minister Ralph Willis praised the 75 percent reduction in disputation in the Pilbara over the previous two years, complaining: 'The actions by the company threaten this industrial stability and also pose major threats to the continuity of Australia's iron ore exports.'[246]

Others, including union officials, talked about the danger of the loss of markets to Brazil if there wasn't an early end to the dispute. For Graeme Haynes, the Burke Labor government 'paved the way for Peko with a heavy campaign to reduce strikes in the Pilbara, tying unions up in bodies like the Iron Ore Consultative Council with company and government reps.' Haynes told a left wing union *FightBack* Conference in Melbourne in 1987: 'There was also what I call industrial conditioning. Unionists were sent off on government sponsored tours to Brazil to see the competition.' Robe workers had refused to buy into this Council, refused to go to Brazil, and had taken industrial action when Robe management sent workers' reps to a Council report-back.

Prime Minister Bob Hawke threw around some colourful language in his attack on the company and the HR Nicholls Society, accusing Copeman of inviting a return to chaos in Australian industrial relations and painting the Society as 'political troglodytes and economic lunatics ... whose confrontationist style will lead to industrial relations chaos.'[247]

However, the workers were pawns in the ideological warfare between the government and its Accord supporters and oppositional sections of the ruling class. The workers were of little concern to Hawke, as he focused on an orderly shifting within the industrial relations framework from a centralised system to one based on enterprise agreements, while controlling wages in the interest of profit making. Industrial action was 'a fly in the ointment' for Labor and the ACTU; during the Accord years, they did their best to crush any attempt by workers and unions taking action to protect or extend wages and conditions.

After the lockout ended, there was an uneasy truce in the townships of

Pannawonica and Wickham. Sackings continued, while the militants and unions were isolated. Two new crews were appointed by the company to employ workers who continued to refuse to work as directed. First was the Special Project Group, who cut up old steel from the breakup of the pellet plant, outside in the sun; and then the infamous Clean Up Group or 'grot squad', which worked around the mine site and townships and was designed to shame and break workers who dared to challenge management control. In other cases, workers were ordered to do work totally outside their previous job descriptions, like some older canteen workers who were directed to do heavy outdoor yard duties or clean cars.[248]

By October, 400–500 workers had quit the mine and the towns. They were not replaced. The townships shrank in size and became company, rather than union, towns. It became impossible to hold meetings, because Robe owned all the meeting halls. New workers were screened and hired on contracts; the union could not be sure that they were getting award conditions. It marked the beginning of the 'fly-in, fly-out' or FIFO workforce, living outside the region and flying in for fortnight-long working stints, further dividing the towns and workforce. Union membership dropped as low as 60 percent (still high by today's standards).[249] Meanwhile, the company, with 500 fewer staff, forced up production from 100 tonnes per worker, per shift, before July 1986 to 200 tonnes by November – a massive increase in such a short time.

From the beginning, the new management at Robe appealed decision after decision of the WAIRC, up to the Industrial Appeals Court, until they got the decision they wanted. One of the last fights was at Pannawonica over the number of power shovel drivers per shift. The practice was two per shift across the Pilbara, with regular breaks, but Peko wanted a single-driver operation. The first action was a stopwork by Federated Engine Drivers and Firemen's Union (FEDFU) members, followed by a walkout when Peko moved in scab staff drivers. The train drivers struck in sympathy, and Peko moved in more staff to scab on them too. After a week, the whole of the Robe River workforce went out on indefinite strike, although the vote was close – 160 to 110 at Cape Lambert. Other workers in the Pilbara levied themselves for the strike fund. In a vital move, the Seamen's Union banned Robe River iron ore.

Robe River workers locked out at the gate 19 August 1986.
Photo courtesy Graeme Haynes.

However, this was not the unified dispute of earlier days. Peko's divisive tactics had fractured the workforce and deepened some rifts between union reps, the Perth officials, the ACTU and Labor.

Bradon Ellem describes what happened on the ground during the strike:

> A group called 'concerned workers' set up a network and newssheet attacking the strikers; the unions struck back with the *Pekobusters* and their *Resist to Exist* sheets and the occasional (and very funny) *Scabline*, a response to the company's *Jobline* sheet.

Reality was more grim than funny. When Robe brought in staff to do the work, some members of the AWU and FEDFU continued working alongside them; however, when this ore was then loaded and transported to the port by staff, maritime workers walked out.[250]

Robe upped the ante in early 1987 by issuing writs for damages against 10 unions under the *Trade Practices Act* and 18 individuals for breach of contract, including union officials and convenors at both the mine and port. This put the maritime workers and their unions in grave danger of being hit with s.45D writs, the ones that had brought down the Mudginberri meat workers and threatened SEQEB electricians. Because port workers weren't directly employed by Robe, their strike could be deemed to be a secondary boycott and illegal under the Trade Practices legislation. The union lawyer also warned against solidarity action from other Pilbara workers – or indeed any other worker around the state – who would fall under the same ruling. The company would not hesitate to use this weapon.

The battle continued on the ground. While the ACTU negotiated with Copeman, the company advertised 32 workers' jobs and then broke a 100-strong picket line, with police, at Cape Lambert. On 5 January 1987, a delegation of Perth union officials went to Melbourne to seek support from the ACTU, which agreed to establish a million-dollar fighting fund to pay for legal expenses and an extensive publicity campaign. ACTU President Simon Crean arranged a meeting with Charles Copeman. The two agreed to a set of proposals to present to the striking workers, while the company would withdraw all writs. Included in the deal, which was approved by state union officials in Perth on 14 January, were the following:

- Work would be resumed and all writs withdrawn.
- The company would have regular briefings with the workforce.
- All those returning to work would have their jobs and classifications as at 16 December 1986, with no loss of rights.
- Staff labour and contractors would only be used for essential services and specialist skilled jobs.

On 16 January, Crean and state union officials presented the proposals to meetings of striking workers at Cape Lambert and Pannawonica. The reception given to Crean is captured by *AFR* journalist Jenni Hewitt:

> When he landed there at 8.30am … the industrial relations climate was baked as hard and as hot as the red earth and the straggling spinifex …. The deal was overwhelmingly rejected.[251]

Further negotiations produced some minor changes.

The threat of s.45D damages finally drove a return to work after mass meetings on 24 January. Mining workers were guilt-tripped into feeling responsible for the fate of maritime workers and the punishing s.45D fines they would get if Pannawonica refused the deal. They returned on 25 January, after five weeks and five days on strike, with little to show for their action. Quite a few workers were disgruntled; Kim Metcalfe, an AMWU shop steward, expressed the anger: 'How much more are we supposed to take? It's about time we started doing it our way.'[252]

Both sides claimed victory for their brand of industrial relations. The New Right celebrated its confrontationist approach, while the Accord partners claimed victory for regulated, AIRC-controlled decision making. While overtly critical of Copeman and his crash-through tactics, the Accord partners were more concerned about having his revamping of workforce practices implemented in an 'orderly' fashion through the industrial relations institutions than about workers' rights or maintaining their wages and conditions.

For Simon Crean, Robe River proved that there was a right way and a wrong way to go about change; Jenni Hewitt explained:

> Despite being cheered on by the hardline element of the New Right, the action taken by Robe River did not succeed. They had to get a resolution with the help of the trade union movement and through the State tribunals … Robe translated the New Right's agenda into practice. No dignity for the workforce, no say for organised labour, conditions imposed by management and no room for negotiation.

Reflecting the pro-Accord take on the dispute, Hewitt was also somewhat critical of Copeman's crash-through approach, noting that no other major company has adopted it:

> Companies that went about achieving change sensibly through cooperation and consensus have achieved it without the social cost and the damage to relations. Even if that cost isn't apparent immediately, it will become so over time. A happier, more participative workforce has to be an asset to the company.[253]

Hewitt's suggestion that it is fine to smash workers' wages and conditions and deunionise a workplace, if you do it through cooperation and consensus and through the proper IRC process, reflected in a nutshell the Accord partners' position.

This was not the end of disputes in the Pilbara, but it was the defining loss that set the scene for the effective de-unionising of the region.

During the rest of Accord years, workers' rights, unionisation and wages and conditions were eroded throughout the Pilbara, despite some spirited resistance, including at Robe River.[254] After the disruption of Robe River, Rio Tinto's Hamersley Iron CEO, Gordon Freeman, exclaimed: 'Gentlemen, there has to be a better way.' He told Hamersley Iron workers that their counterparts at Robe were miserable, fearful and intimidated, 'leaving a legacy of mistrust that is not conducive to quality of life and reasonable working conditions.' His concern was not maintaining workers' rights, but maintaining the company's share of the Japanese market through reliability of supply against Brazilian and Indian competitors. Within four years, as Chinese demand expanded, Rio Tinto at Hamersley Iron went down the deunionisation path, enforcing individual workplace agreements (WPA) after threatening strikers with fines under tort law, using exactly the same tactics as Robe River.'[255]

Jeff Kennett's anti-union Coalition government won in Victoria in 1992, and Richard Court's Coalition gained power in WA in February 1993. Both immediately introduced new labour laws which restricted arbitration and union rights and promoted individual contracts.[256] The war continued against the Robe workforce too; on 23 August 1993, Robe secured cancellation of the award and set up their own WPAs. Almost all Robe River employees signed the agreements, with 97 percent of the workforce still on these agreements in December 1996, when Robe was again before the Commission resisting the continuation of an award payment for sickness and accident insurance for just five members of the AWU. Every attack on workers at Robe since 1988 happened under BHP management, who enthusiastically continued Peko–Wallsend's approach.[257]

From 1999, BHP offered individual contracts to workers at Mt Newman. This was the last unionised site in the Pilbara, and unions and the ACTU ran a campaign over the next five years to hold onto it. The company took the unions to the Federal Court and defeated them. The court ruled that, while workers were free to join unions, companies were free to ignore them. 'In other words, freedom of association, unionism itself, was robbed of its effects.'[258] In fact, if not in law, union recognition was removed.

Several attempts to reunionise, even a proposal for a single Pilbara Mineworkers Union, have come close to winning, but a combination of intransigent employers, state and federal labour laws and one union's moves of sabotage have enabled the companies to hold the line. Today, with FIFO, automation and the use of visa workers in the construction phase of new projects, workers are more isolated and fewer in number. Unions are yet to develop strategies to combat management's control.[259]

The disputes and outcomes at Robe River and its predecessors (Dollar Sweets, Mudginberri and SEQEB), represented a push by New Right forces within the ruling class to reshape industrial relations in Australia in the interests of profit and their own class. However, had the Robe River dispute not fallen under the framework of the ALP–ACTU Accord, results might have been different. WATLC Assistant Secretary Rob Meecham publicly repudiated the workers' case, agreeing with all the company's arguments – that change was inevitable, that productivity had to be driven up, that the company would otherwise become unviable. His only concern was that their confrontational approach was unnecessary: 'They [productivity gains] are achieved elsewhere without it.'[260] Indeed, they were.

Labor brandished the threat of the New Right to workers and employers. Hawke warned companies against risking the achievements of the Accord by accepting the rhetoric of the New Right, highlighting similar gains that had been made under his government – a reduced level of industrial disputation and increasing productivity.

Days after workers returned to Robe in September 1986, the *Financial Review* argued:

> The government has turned the New Right challenge into a catalyst for a campaign of sustainable change in the labour market, which gives it the opportunity to work out the pros and cons of deregulation on equal ground … After the New Right intervention the ACTU can more readily hold up to its constituency the dangers of leaving the Accord and jeopardising the government.

The paper explained that the ACTU could offer the government greater productivity, through improved work practices as a potential trade-off for continued discounting.[261]

Like old generals reliving an old battle, the millionaire press keeps on going back to Robe River to gloat; *The Bulletin* announced that 'Robe River has been made to work.'[262] The report reads like a press release from Charles Copeman's office. It rehashes all the 'rort' stories, with rapacious unions and money-hungry workers who lived a 'year round frolic' of 'swimming, snorkelling and sail-boarding.' The six flavours of ice cream myth was revived.[263] According to *The Bulletin*, following Peko's union-busting exercise, morale was:

extremely high, say middle management people, who plainly relish being in control once more ... The real lesson of Robe River is that sufficiently tough-minded management can bludgeon the system to produce a tolerably fair and reasonable efficient result.

Robe River workers tell a very different story. 'Fair for who?' retorts Robe River militant Graeme Haynes, who looks at the human cost:

> Four hundred people have left, with no redundancy payments. Many others would leave if they could afford it. I don't know any unionist who wants to stay. For morale they have dislocated communities, suicide and miscarriages, heartbreak and disenchantment. And conditions are going backwards faster than it took to establish them.

He points out that the famous 284 'restrictive work practices and conditions' were merely ways of making the harsh Pilbara environment tolerable for daily living, which Peko had been happy to allow. The reports of 'rorts' were invariably distortions:

> What actually happened is that the price of iron ore fell ... Even with the widely publicised 'restrictive work practices', they made vast profits ... If the price falls again, they'll have to find some more restrictive practices. Perhaps they'll think eight hours' sleep is too much.

Socialist Action May 1986.

CHAPTER 6

The BLF – 'A Challenge they Must Crush'

There are pivotal moments in history when the class war surges to the forefront, demanding that all participants take sides and openly engage in battle. The year 1986 was such a defining moment, when one of the country's most militant unions – the BLF – was deregistered.

The BLF had experienced attacks, but it faced the fight of its life in 1986. The state, aided and abetted by the ACTU and many other trade union leaders, including those on the left, turned on the BLF. The federal Labor government and its counterparts in NSW and Victoria legislated to deregister its strongest and biggest branches, allocating its members to other building unions. No one outside the union expected it to survive this onslaught. However, even as its enemies claimed that it was 'dead and buried', and the BWIU and the Federated Engine Drivers and Firemen's Association (FEDFA) took its members, the Federation continued to fight on the job and in the streets.

Because the union stayed true to its famous slogans – 'Dare to Struggle, Dare to Win' and 'If You Don't Fight, You Lose' – it survived. Even after its organisers had been arrested hundreds of times, officials jailed, many of its activists blacklisted, the Victorian office raided and its assets seized; even after its deregistration was extended in 1991 for another five years; the BLF kept its doors open. It ceased to operate as a separate union only when the Victorian branch followed its interstate branches in amalgamating with the Construction, Forestry, Mining and Energy Union (CFMEU) in March 1994.

As the militancy of the 1960s and 1970s ebbed, and capital went on the offensive, the crucial question was: which way would the workers' movement go? Would workers take the lead from unions like the BLF, prepared to fight whatever the boss threw at them? Or would they collaborate with employers and the state to restore capitalist profitability and supposedly benefit workers longer term? That vision of class harmony scathingly described by BLF member Bob Mancor as a place where capital and labour walked together 'arm in arm into some lovely world' had taken the form of the ALP–ACTU Accord, the 'transitional program for socialism.'

The smashing of the BLF fitted more into a vision created by Canadian poet Thomas McGrath about the ruthlessness of capitalism:

> *In the chill streets,*
> *I hear the hunting and the long thunder of money.*[264]

Attempts to deregister the BLF began in 1981. Malcolm Fraser set up the Winneke Royal Commission into allegations of corruption against the union's national leader Norm Gallagher, and the NSW and Victorian Liberal–National Party governments lodged a joint application to the Federal Court to deregister the Federation.[265] The move on the BLF was part of Fraser's open anti-union agenda, like the Royal Commission into the equally militant Painters and Dockers union and attacks on the closed shop in the Victorian Tramways or factory jobs covered by the militant AMWU.[266] Unions united against Fraser and his agenda, but then united around the Labor Party as it entered the 1980s and adopted a neoliberal economic agenda. The call for workers' restraint came from Fraser; from the new federal ALP leader, Bob Hawke; from the employers; from Bill Kelty and Simon Crean of the ACTU; and from Communist Party leaders of the AMWU and the other building unions. Unions were told to stay within the system or face severe penalties.

Labor, with its Accord and its union connections, had the credibility to sell this 'pain for gain' plan to workers. Journalist Michelle Grattan explained: 'Mr Hawke is also talking about the need for people to make sacrifices; he is not leaving all the hard ground to Mr Fraser', but Hawke dressed up the call for restraint in 'the guise of sharing, equality and consensus.' The question then was, would hard times seem more bearable under Hawke?[267]

Like all unions except the NSW Nurses' Association, the BLF signed the Accord. In practice, they opposed it and continued to take industrial action in defiance of the Accord's strictures. So BLF members stopped work nationally on 7 March, before the new Hawke Ministry was formally sworn in, demanding shorter hours and an end to Fraser's wage freeze. Immediately after the 24-hour strike, bans went on around the country. Victorian members took an extra day off a month, continuing their pre-election campaign. With their leader still in jail after a provocative move by the Fraser government in the pre-election period, BLF officials told a 'Free Norm' rally: 'Now the election is over, all bets are off.'

On the day of Hawke's April National Summit in Canberra, all building unions nationwide were striking for the shorter week. Two days later, delegates from seven NSW unions endorsed a national campaign of strikes and bans for a pay rise and a 36-hour week. The new Prime Minister was furious: the wage demands threatened the Summit's 'spirit of consensus', and these unions could find themselves expelled from the ACTU. Then journalist Bob Carr wrote that the action presented the ALP and ACTU 'with a challenge they must crush';[268] if building workers won, the ACTU could find it impossible to stop demands spreading, first to oil workers, then manufacturing workers. Wage rises would spread around the country. Labor, he predicted, would then lose office, stripping the ACTU of any role with government on future wages and incomes strategies. Carr also bemoaned the prospect of the ACTU's ability to police the union movement being undermined.[269]

The building unions, Carr insisted, had misunderstood the Accord. The deal had been settled 'in the white heat of the election campaign', but 'it was not clear then what the deal was, apart from the commitment to maintaining real wages "over time" through an indexation system ... Only [later] did the building union leaders realise it meant living with the loss of real wages.' Like everyone else, they should wait until the next national wage case in August, where they might get 3 to 4 percent; all they could expect the following year was a rise limited to indexation.[270]

There were other significant national economic reasons for both the Fraser and Hawke governments to rein in the BLF. The industry still accounts for almost one in 10 jobs and roughly 5 percent of the economy and has a disproportionate influence on employment rates, manufacturing and other economic indicators. Consequently, it has a major political impact. Strategic pump priming of building and construction has helped to deliver political power to Coalition and Labor governments alike, underpinning Howard and Costello's 'gangbusters' economy in the 1990s and Labor's boom times during the 1980s. IR Minister Ralph Willis told parliament in 1985, when moving to deregister the BLF: 'the government has deliberately encouraged the industry as a major force in renewed economic growth since 1983 and activity is expected to continue to grow strongly in 1985–86.'[271] A vibrant industry would encourage employers' attempts to increase productivity – and consequently profits – by restructuring the entire work process, even doing away with labourers altogether. SA state secretary Ron Owens had no doubt that the BLF, by this time the largest and most militant union in the industry, was an obstacle to their plans.

After the ALP won government in March 1983, the Federation still faced the Federal Court deregistration case and corruption charges. The Royal Commission's findings had landed Norm Gallagher and organiser Bob Dalton in court in September 1982 on 43 counts of corruption, with 10 other charges listed against other union officials. The union was forced to scale back industrial action during this period; the ACTU warned: 'back down or we'll support deregistration.' Hawke dangled the prospect of pulling out from Federal Court case if the BLF stopped their campaigns. The government's establishment of a regulatory National Building and Construction Industry Committee kept up the pressure on all building unions, and the Coalition later followed this example by creating the Australian Building and Construction Commission (ABCC).[272]

In these first months of the Hawke government, building unions were learning about the meaning of wage restraint. The result was a sporadic campaign for a Building Industry Agreement (BIA). Lengthy AIRC hearings during 1983 dragged the building unions' wages case on for months. The claim was rejected, then finally granted on 14 November, but with only two increases, both discounted. The remaining $9 component, the Building Industry Recovery Procedures Allowance (BIRP), was refused. The AIRC ruled that the employers didn't have the money. Even if they did, there was the danger of the rise spreading to other sectors, which was not allowed under the Accord. The unions were furious, with Pat Clancy from the BWIU threatening 'anarchy in the industry.' However, the BWIU soon joined forces with the ACTU to put up an amended claim. The rejected BIRP claim would become the basis for a superannuation scheme, to be lodged in 1984. The amended agreement was rushed through the AIRC and approved on 6 December 1983.

When the new BIA was signed, it appeared that the government and employers had forced the BLF into line – without having to deregister the union. So, at the 12 December Federal Court hearings, while employers stayed put, the federal Labor government finally pulled out.[273] Some in the Federation believed that the union was safe, but others understood that the BWIU and Labor were still planning the BLF's demise. Norm Gallagher claimed victory: all the government's attempts at crushing the union – Fraser, jailing Gallagher, spending millions on the Royal Commission and threats of deregistration – had got their opponents nowhere. But Gallagher was too optimistic.

The ALP, the employers and the unions were laying out their plans. Canberra BLF secretary Peter O'Dea was cautious; the ALP had 'pulled out of the court case because it was a flawed process ... They had to re-group.' According to NSW Master Builders Association (MBA) chief Ray Rocher, the employers only withdrew from the Federal Court case in 1984 because the government offered to pay all the legal costs.[274] The BLF's main rival, the BWIU, had already signalled what they were prepared to do. BWIU federal secretary Pat Clancy is quoted by Norm Wallace, BLF Treasurer, as saying during a dispute in the 1970s: 'If we can't get you this way – through agreement, we'll get you the other way – through force.' Wallace says: 'So all along we knew we had no ally in the BWIU.'[275]

In August 1983, leading British magazine *The Economist* spelled out what could – and did – happen: not every union would abide by the Accord, so there would be clashes with the government; mostly, these would be worked out 'behind closed doors', with the ACTU 'leaning on those unwilling to cooperate'; with some, there would have to be a public showdown. Deregistering such unions wasn't enough, because the BWIU and BLF had survived an earlier attempt. *The Economist* noted that other unions would have to be ready to 'cannibalise the deregistered one's members ... They have to be eaten up before they are dead... If Mr Hawke is serious about saving the economy, he had better have his cannibalisation plans ready.'[276] He did.

The attacks on the BLF escalated during 1984. Employers, Labor and Liberal politicians and other unions demonised the Federation, calling it 'the enemy', 'a cancer', prone to 'unacceptable behaviour' and 'not fit and proper' to be in the union movement. The union faced dangerous enemies in the NSW and Victorian state governments. In NSW, Neville Wran's Labor government deregistered the union in October 1984 over a major dispute on the Sydney Police Centre site. With the full support of the Trades and Labour Council – one parliamentarian claimed that it was 'at the request' of the Council – Wran framed his deregistration legislation in February 1984 and brought it on just eight months later, when the BLF was in dispute at the Sydney Police Centre site. *The Industrial Relations (Special Provisions) Act* was passed by Christmas 1984, proclaimed on 2 January and gazetted on 11 January 1985. Although Wran told parliament that the bill singled out the BLF, the government soon threatened unions such as the train drivers' Australian Federated Union of Locomotive Employees with the same legislation.[277]

In Victoria, the union's opponents used a similar dispute around the Melbourne Cricket Ground to target it. At the end of 1984, Victoria's John Cain said that his 'loaded gun' was pointed at the Federation; his legislation to 'wipe out the BLF' was drafted and ready to go through parliament at a moment's notice. 'If Gallagher comes up again, we will whack him again.' Norm retorted: 'Let them just try it. We have seen governments come and go and we are still here. This will be no different.'[278]

With Hawke still in power nationally, and the Cain team re-elected in early March 1985, the next legislative steps could be taken; both announced deregistration bills in July. The timing was crucial: throughout 1985, the BLF – and their industrial power – was essential to the ACTU's superannuation strategy. Victorian official John Cummins said: 'Gallagher was able to deliver to Kelty troops out of the trenches on ACTU campaigns. I don't really know of too many occasions where Gallagher knocked Kelty back.' Once superannuation was won, adds BL Don Rust, 'then they burned him' and the union he led. ABC commentator Max Walsh agreed; for the future 'preservation of the Hawke government [Labor] decided the BLF has to go.'

As the legislation was being drafted, Housing Minister Stewart West recalls the Cabinet meeting on 16 July that decided the union's fate. 'Hawke came in and he sat down abruptly and looked around the room … he said, "We're gonna smash those bastards. We're going to deregister the BLF!" Just like that.' Willis announced that the federal government would have its legislation ready by 20 August, the first day of the Spring parliamentary session.[279]

The new Act would give the government sweeping powers against the union. The minister could cancel the BLF's registration, denying members award rights such as pay or hours of work. The Federation could not negotiate any new awards nor cover new areas of work. The BLF could also be banned from coverage wherever it remained registered; all its state organisations were vulnerable. The government could shift members from deregistered branches into another union of the government's choosing! Willis threatened remaining states with the axe, if they took any action to support the three targeted branches. *Tribune* labelled the bill almost a carbon copy of the MBA's 'preferred industry view' of what should be done with the BLF and its members.

Also on 16 July, Victoria's Labor Caucus voted 51:17 for the state's *BLF (De-Recognition) Act 1985*. The bill passed the Lower House and was timed to act simultaneously with federal legislation.

The state deregistration and derecognition legislation was as harsh as the federal bill. Many in the BLF regarded it as the real 'dagger in the heart.' It gave government the power to destroy any union where BLF members had a majority and prohibited any organisation made up of ex-BLF members. Federation members would be forced to sign statutory declarations declaring that they weren't in the union, before they could step onto any building site. The bill gave police extra powers to enforce these provisions on the job, while employers got immunity from legal action. There would be no rights of appeal for the BLF.

Corruption at the top of the union, violence, and intimidation by BLF heavies were the banner headlines, editorials and articles, justifying why the BLF had to go. The major players knew that this was window dressing. At stake was the profitability of Australian business, especially in construction – several governments' lifeline to a buoyant economy. The BLF's determination to 'brazenly challenge the restrictions', as 'the most effective industrial fighting machine in Australia', threatened profits the ALP–ACTU Accord was designed to safeguard, as Treasurer Paul Keating told an overseas conference:

> Do you think that facing an economy this strong ... with non-farm growth of the order of 5% and a 20% depreciation, that the Liberals could secure a 6% award wages outcome? Not a chance. And that's why the markets will vote through their pocket and support this government.[280]

Union militant Dave Kerin says: 'this was very much the state intervening to reshape the market, freeing up the processes by which capital could invest and extract money.' The Labor Party was in advance of capital, 'very, very cleverly sniffing the wind as to what lay ahead ... laying the basis for globalisation.' They understood that 'the state has the capacity of disciplining, in military style, the population to the extent that the market doesn't have.' The *Financial Review* noted, early in Labor's term of government: 'The Hawke government has become a jailer for unions which dared to buck the Accord's consensus and the ACTU has become an industrial police force.' Such behaviour came as no surprise to BLs like Don Ward: 'they'll always use what's necessary ... They'd planned it for a while, they set it up, unlimited amounts of money.'[281]

Deregistration

With all the legislation in place, it was no surprise that an AIRC hearing into the BLF, set up in September 1985, produced a damning assessment of the Federation. On 4 April 1986, Judge Terence Ludeke reported that the BLF had engaged in 'serious industrial misconduct' in seven listed cases, acting first and negotiating later. The union had breached the Act by failing to 'promote goodwill in the industry' and failing 'to encourage and provide means for conciliation with a view to amicable agreement, thereby preventing the settling of industrial disputes.' The judge launched into the BLF, saying that it:

> has no standards as that word is commonly understood ...
> Instead of a rational policy designed to advance the interests of the members, the Federal Management Committee is addicted to slogans, such as, 'Dare to Struggle, Dare to Win', 'Most Harm to the Boss, Least Harm to the Members' and 'An injury to one is an injury to all.' It is under such archaic banners that the Federal Management Committee has waged campaigns leading the rank and file from one disaster to the next.

'The case against the Builders Labourers Federation is overwhelming', the report concluded.[282] A triumphant Steve Crabb, dubbed 'Minister of War' by *The Sun*, got front page coverage the next day wearing a boss's white hard hat and 'beating into submission' a staff member dressed as a gorilla wearing BLF paraphernalia.[283]

Within minutes of the Commission's declaration, Willis announced that he was bypassing the earlier 1985 legislation because it gave the BLF too many rights. Instead, the government would bring in a new law that would deregister the union immediately, handing over its members to other unions to stymie any possibility of union pressure on builders or appeal to the courts.

The BLF was shocked. Addressing a protest rally outside BLF headquarters, Gallagher angrily accused the government and Arbitration Commission of 'fascism', adding: 'It's no longer "Hi Aussie, it's Hi Hitler".' But Simon Crean claimed: 'The BLF has now isolated itself ... They are on the nose with other unions.' Far from being an overall attack on unions, it was a 'necessary response' to the Federation's 'constant breaches of agreement.' Questioned on the denial of appeal rights, Crean laughed, saying that the union was 'getting a taste of its own medicine.'[284]

On 14 April 1986, the Federal and Victorian bills were proclaimed simultaneously. The BLF was to be shut out of building sites from 16 April, 1986 – Deregistration Day.

'They have got us by the neck and by the balls,' protested one angry BLF member on Deregistration Day, as Federation members, determined to stay on their BLF union tickets, went to work. Johnny O'Connor remembers turning up to work, to be greeted by very upset shop steward Gerry O'Shea, saying: 'we've been deregistered ... that's it, John.' Johnny asked what he meant. O'Shea replied: 'look at the coppers.' Press reports painted a grim picture:

> BLs arriving at work yesterday were faced with a combination of government officials armed with 'union transfer' documents, organisers from other unions, police on a number of sites and employers who had themselves been threatened.

Members were told that the BLF had no legal status and no industrial rights, and so could no longer protect their wages and conditions. Rank and filer Andy half joked: 'For a person to go to work and the coppers or security guards tell you, you gotta join another union, that's when you've got a problem!' But he added, 'That's where I met the best blokes I ever met in my whole

life. They just turned around and said, "Don't tell me to sign a paper I don't need to sign".'

When BLs turned up to work on Ivor Lawrence's job, they were told to quit the union and join one the government picked for them, if they wanted to work. Instead, they stuck with the Federation's tactic – refuse to quit, refuse to sign over. Ivor began organising: 'I called a meeting of the members on the Chia's job and we walked off for the day … [some of us went] to the office and there were already meetings and demos starting to form.'

Battles flared around town:

> They had a garrison of police at Cranbourne shopping centre. There would have been 25 to 30 coppers on one side, 25 to 30 on the other and people had to walk through that line of coppers to get into the front gate. So we said, 'No-one's going in there. No-one's going to 'run the gauntlet.' And we all stayed out in the carpark. This was going on all over the place. It was ugly, it was terrible.

BLF members and supporters at picket at Como building site Melbourne. Photos Janey Stone.

It was weeks before workers on this job finally returned to work.[285]

BLF militant Bob Wilson said: 'A lot of sign over forms had false names and under "Name of Union" to join said things like dingo's union.'

The union in Victoria began to haemorrhage, and the tactic of staying on the job on a BLF ticket was in tatters. In Canberra and NSW, the story was more devastating. Union and local support enabled BLF members to hold out for some months in Canberra on some jobs. The branch continued to operate for some years, with only a few active members, and had little impact on the sites after 1986. In NSW, a Gallagher-led federal intervention in 1974 and the crushing of the Mundey-led branch had left a bitter legacy of division. A big showdown towards the end of April at the Grosvenor Place site, with thousands of scaffolders refusing to sign over, could not stave off huge losses. There were enough members for the branch to survive until at least 1987. Organisers visited sites and were arrested and jailed, and a Defend the Unions committee built some solidarity actions. However, NSW was a pale shadow of Victoria, and the branch's weakness seriously compromised the BLF in its fight against deregistration. It left the Federation defeated in the country's biggest state and relying on one branch, albeit its most militant, to fight for everyone.

After several days of heavy losses, the Victorian branch had to make some hard decisions. 'The original strategy was "We don't sign the thing. Bugger them. They need Builders Labourers to work it",' explains Don Ward. 'Then we worked out that they were going to get Builders Labourers in there.' So, from 21 April, starting with Jack Chia's South Yarra Como workers, the union directed members to begin signing the other unions' membership forms. John Cummins reasoned:

> We decided that we'd have to try and retain a footing in the job. Because if you're outside while people are inside doing your job, you're about as effective as throwing snowballs at Ayer's Rock.[286]

The decision was hotly debated at the May general meeting, along with proposals for an industry-wide strike with mass pickets and a strategy to spread the dispute nationally. Former official Marco Masterson, among others, called for a stopwork. But Gallagher opposed it, arguing that it would 'finger' the members and get them the sack: 'National strikes have never achieved anything. The lesson of the coal strike in Britain [of 1984] should teach us this ... General strikes don't lend themselves to our industry.' Mick Lewis was convinced: 'we will win on the job, not off it.' The union feared the fate of SEQEB workers, abandoned by the ACTU, with all their jobs handed over to scabs. When George Despard quipped: 'Pitched battles went out in 1066. It is hit and run guerilla warfare', John Cummins agreed. 'We want to win the war', he told members. 'At this time we are not able to rely on the other unions. We would like it to be different, but we must win it ourselves.'

Joining the other unions had its upside too, argues Bob Wilson: 'If anything the government enforced 100 percent unionism.' And BLs were used to being union activists. They were getting along to branch meetings, challenging the BWIU. 'We were asking all the hard questions ... "How come the rank and file members of the BWIU haven't got any say in the way the union's run?"' And many were still in the BLF. 'You go and tell them that the BLF is still alive and kicking', claimed a defiant Norm Gallagher from jail. 'Survival is the name of the game and we are surviving.' One month after deregistration, 4,000 Victorian members, according to the union, had signed a Federation 'duress' form declaring themselves still BLF, despite being forced into the other unions.[287]

There were enough members to keep the branch going – with a rank and file committee, monthly meetings, rallies and poster runs. One BL said:

> It was incredible ... Every day you'd go to work and there'd be another poster or leaflet. I don't know how or when they got on the job, but we always knew what was going on.

The BLF was just as active externally, with involvement in the closely aligned Defend the Unions and Women's Committees, strike support for the 1986 Victorian Nurses dispute and the Carlton Brewery drivers, and regular visits to workplaces, ALP branches and community actions.

In the lead up to May Day 1986 – the 100th anniversary of this international day of workers' solidarity – the BLF organised a national public statement called 'It's Time to Draw the Line.' Signed by rank and file unionists, officials and a range of supporters, it appeared in *The Australian* at the beginning of May. The BLF was also out in force on the May Day marches around the country. In Melbourne, the march was the biggest in years. The lead banner read: 'Workers of the World Unite.' The Federation's contingent, including several members chained inside a prison cage, was cheered by other marchers, many of whom carried solidarity placards. Pro-BLF speakers drew the crowds at the end of the march, while BLs handed out thousands of leaflets.

In Sydney, a large, noisy pro-BLF contingent made up well over half of the 2,000 attending. Unionists handed out leaflets – a 'May Day Manifesto: Defend the BLF.' The official platform, loaded with anti-BLF speakers like ALP MP Bruce Childs, was booed into silence. But when pro-BLF speakers – Steve Black, state Labor MP George Petersen and Victorian Bill Hartley – got up to speak, the truck which held the stage started driving off. Two of the speakers were arrested defending their right to be heard. Predictably, the papers reported 'BLF violence.'

Keeping up the fight was essential, argued Bob Wilson. The organisers visited as many sites as they could. 'You just kept going back ... and it works.'

> If you get pinched you keep going back – wear them bastards down before they wear you down ... Management would say 'you have no rights'. You'd say 'I'm here. Your job's a pigsty. When are you going to get it fixed?' Mostly you'd ignore management and go straight to the sheds, the shop steward. You'd be saying 'I'm your organiser. And it's BLF.' And that's it.

Referring to his own record, Bob grinned, '111 charges of trespass – not a bad score.'

The union fought deregistration in the courts, but to little effect. Outside the courts, the BLF was getting support from some other unions, at least in Victoria. In July, the MBA in Victoria (MBAV) told members: 'The ETU is currently supporting the BLF in various ways ... Until recently several officials of the Plumbers Union were pushing a similar demand.' Some organisers and officials of the Amalgamated Carpenters and Joiners of Australia (ASC&J) and Bricklayers were also supporting the BLF, the employers noted. In Canberra and NSW, there were some signs of a resurgence. 'The rank and file support us – even the tradesmen are starting to support us', said BLF organiser Nick Harris after meetings at Parliament House and White Industries sites in Canberra, where workers voted no confidence in BWIU secretary Rod Driver. In Sydney's CBD, Federation organisers visited six different jobs around the end of August; when the police were called, everyone walked off.

Before the end of April 1986, 'Defend the Unions, Defend the BLF Committees' (DTU) initiated by the Federation were operating in the three deregistered states. Straight after the May Day march, Sydney DTU held its first public meeting, 'BLF Deregistration: A threat to the working class.' Over 400 people heard NSW BLF secretary Steve Black, Victorian Plumbers' secretary George Crawford and other prominent labour movement figures. The crucial thing was building 'unity around the basic principles', Steve Black told the crowd, 'it's a matter of class struggle, not class collaboration.' By the end of the year, the Committee had 700 members in Victoria, with groups in Melbourne, in regional centres in the west and south east and the Latrobe Valley. The Melbourne DTU, the most successful of the groups, formed subcommittees and held weekly meetings of up to 40, discussing everything from the role of the state and police to the nitty-gritty of the next action.

DTU members around the state went on BLF marches, protest actions and pickets, with occupations at developer Jack Chia's and Crabb's offices keeping the resistance in the news. Members leafleted mass meetings of other unions and intervened in major disputes such as the nurses' strike, brewery drivers, Channel 7 and Nestlé, joining picket lines. Melbourne DTU organised solidarity tours by striking workers from Robe River, FEDFA members from the Bjelke-Petersen Dam and SEQEB electricians. Members spoke at workplaces and trade union meetings, with TAFE[288] and secondary school teachers delegating several teachers to the DTU. ALP branches, campuses, community groups and ethnic groups were addressed. The union was heavily involved in a series of Fightback! conferences over 1986–87, designed to cohere the anti-Accord left into a more political response to the Accord.

The BLF Women's Committee was a major support. Canberra women set up the first group well before deregistration hit, inspired by similar groups organised for the SEQEB workers and the British Miners. After the BLF was outlawed, meetings were thrown open to any woman prepared to back the union. An early move of the Canberra committee was to publish a declaration of support. Robyn Hohl, who was part of the Sydney Committee, asserted:

> I'd rather have a husband alive on the picket line fighting for his life and our future, than one who's forced to work in unsafe conditions, for reduced wages and is continually in fear of the bosses.

Victorian committee members spoke to the media, joined rallies and initiated their own direct action – 'taking a leaf out of the BLs' book!' They sat in at the ACTU, the MBA and at Jack Chia's offices in town, marched into Lewis Construction headquarters over one of John Cummins' many jailings, and once followed IR Minister Steve Crabb around Parliament House, calling out 'What about the BLF? What about the BLF?' Margaret Kane remembers husband Jim's role in a crane occupation at the end of April 1986: 'I was so proud of him, he took a stand.' After the men came down from the cranes, the May Day march was on. The women and kids 'hightailed it into town and we marched proudly … We wanted to be seen supporting the solidarity of the men.'

BLF women support committee, probably Mayday 1986. Photographer unknown.

This support and its own organising strengthened the BLF in its industrial heartland. In 1987, said *The Australian*, the BWIU now had 'within its ranks a hard core of unionists who were and still are, believers in the BLF – and more importantly, believers in the tactics employed by Gallagher.' The next national wages round was due, along with the unions' log of claims for the 1987 BIA covering superannuation, severance pay and shorter hours. The BLF pushed employers on a number of sites, but the BWIU let the campaign drop. The BIA finally included the 3 percent superannuation deal and kept most of the conditions. However, the agreement came in seven months late, and the BLF, although still legal in four states, was excluded by the ACTU from negotiations.

The defeat of the PGEU claim for an extra $70, shorter hours, a 2.3 percent national wage rise and 3 percent superannuation, without a restrictive no-extra-claims commitment, saw them forced back into the Accord straitjacket on a three-month good behaviour bond. They faced a fine of over $400,000. The union was defiant, claiming that it had won the $70 on many sites. Secretary George Crawford had no regrets about the campaign, although the union paid a heavy price. No other construction union followed the Plumbers, and the union itself stayed within the system for the remaining Accord years.

The BLF Melbourne office was raided on 13 October 1987 by 150 Special Operations police in full attack gear. 'It's World War Three! They've smashed the office like you wouldn't believe, had a go at the staff, the women, cut the phones, tried to seize all the assets!' yelled one of Andy's mates over the phone. Raiders seized what they could, bashed some of the organisers and left a trail of mindless destruction behind. The government immediately appointed a custodian to oversee the union's operations until 2002, when the Bracks Labor government finally agreed to hand back all remaining funds and property of the union.

Word spread. A crowd built up outside the union office, and senior cops started to worry. At 12.40 pm, just as suddenly as it had begun, the raid stopped. As the police left, the crowd set off around the city calling out members at various building sites, before marching on Parliament House. Terry Egan, Victorian secretary of APSA, was arrested by police as he attempted to go into parliament to talk to his local MP. Waterside workers went out for three hours, holding up 13 ships. On 15 October, Trades Hall delegates condemned the raid. Former Tramways union leader Clarrie O'Shea, jailed in the 1969 struggle against anti-union laws, declared to a demonstration in the Bourke Street mall that the ACTU and Trades Hall weren't 'worth a crumpet ... Kelty and Crean – who have grubbed on the workers and pretend to represent us. They are bosses' men and ... all bosses are bastards!'

The Accord process continued to weaken union organisation. By August 1988, coverage in the building industry fell to 47 percent, strike days fell by 18 percent, and workers' compensation claims increased. Because militancy had fallen off so dramatically, the 1986–1988 boom years had not benefited workers. 'I've been in the game since '49', said Kyran Nicholls:

> I can't remember any boom, at any time that we didn't get something out of it. This was the biggest boom of all and we went backwards, thanks to the BWIU, the FEDFA, ACTU and mainly the Labor Party.

In March 1988, Kelty admitted that Australian workers were 'right in the trough of the decline in living standards.' From 1988–89, all signs pointed to the bust of the building boom.

The government continued to pursue Gallagher and Cummins in the courts, charging Gallagher with contempt for saying that industrial action had forced court decisions, and dredging up old charges. Both were in and out of jail for months during the whole deregistration process. Gallagher was convicted on corruption and given an 18 months' sentence and a $66,747 fine. The bosses, who'd offered Gallagher the 'corrupting goods', got a slap on the wrists, ordered to pay an unspecified amount into the court poor box.

Union amalgamation was on the agenda for 1989, along with redoubled efforts to exclude the BLF from the union movement and weaken its influence in the BWIU. Within the Federation, coming up to the end of deregistration in April 1991, the consensus was that they were in good shape. They were still the second biggest building union in Australia, with about 3,000 active members in Victoria, and growing interstate.

In early 1990, the federal government extended the deregistration of the BLF for another five years and barred any post-1986 BLF member or branch from acting on the union's behalf in the AIRC. The BWIU could go for coverage of labourers' work in the registered states – as they were in fact doing – and neither the BLF nor its members could oppose it. The WA branch's attempt to gain federal registration, one of the BLF's plans to re-establish a national federally-based union from April 1991, was thwarted by this bill.[289]

The BLF was hit hard. Victorian membership plummeted to about 400–500, while the building slump meant that many of the union's militants were unemployed. The union was losing influence on the sites. In May 1990 came a further blow: the Victorian branch, desperate to pick up new members, signed a deal with the notorious labour hire firm, Troubleshooters Available, to cover their workforce. This disastrous tactic cost the Federation much support. This was a union that had done a lot to keep labour hire out of the industry. Other attempts by the Federation to develop new strategies were immediately undercut when the federal government delivered an ultimatum to the registered branches: stop trying to delay the merger with the newly amalgamated CMEU or face an AIRC hearing over industry coverage. To agree meant an end to independence, but knocking it back meant being stripped of the right to cover labourers' jobs. IR Minister Cook gave them till 18 January 1991, just nine days, to agree.[290]

In October 1991, long-time leader Norm Gallagher fought against

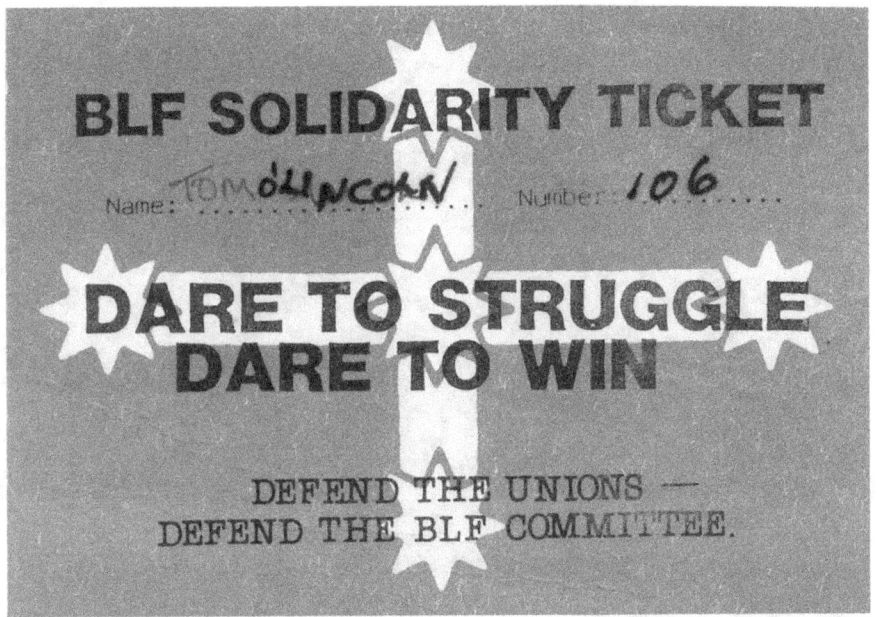

BLF supporter solidarity ticket. Photo Janey Stone.

amalgamation. While many shared his misgivings, most understood that the union had no other options, and Norm provided no new strategy. The situation in the branch deteriorated, amid accusations by Gallagher of financial mismanagement. The branch executive was forced to act against him, voting in John Cummins as secretary. Gallagher fought, but he was removed from the General Secretary position on 5 May 1992. In November 1992, he lost BLF membership. Norm Gallagher was out of the union he had given his life to.

On 30 March 1994, the BLF itself was no more. Amalgamation with the CFMEU was signed off. The BLF did not give up its commitment to members or its support of militancy. John Cummins told the last Victorian branch executive meeting on 6 April 1994: 'Now the work starts. We have to improve the situation for building workers and get as many of our blokes back on the job as we can.'[291]

There's no doubt that the state was prepared to use whatever it took to smash the Federation. It's also clear that the BLF itself made some costly mistakes in the initial stages of the fight. Underestimating the opposition left the membership underprepared for deregistration and floundering about

Socialist Action October 1986.

the issue of signing over. Despite the union's often political approach to the system, there was no strategy to fight the Accord. Accord promoters, like the AMWU, had already spent several years educating their members.

For all its faults and political weaknesses, the BLF's strengths are the lasting legacy of the struggle against deregistration. John Cummins summed it up:

> Builders Labourers lost their jobs, they lost their families, they lost houses, they gave it their all ... they were the source of inspiration, not only to their own workmates, but to those of us who were officials. And it's had a great impact in terms of still being around, still being in the game ... If we hadn't fought, hadn't run the distance, it would all have been lost.

Ever since the origins of capitalism, when the working class and capitalists faced off against each other, workers have had to determine for themselves the best way to wage that struggle. While the workers' own organisations, the trade unions, can ultimately only win reforms within the system, the way they win can either open up the basis for the possibility of revolutionary change or leave unchallenged a society of exploitation. In the 1970s, like militant unions around the world, the BLF took the fight to bosses and opened up possibilities for challenging the capitalist system itself. This militant resurgence by workers was feeding into the political organisations that carried the banner of revolution. The Federation taught members to stand up for their own class interests. The union's journal contained outspoken political commentary, such as this in December 1982:

> Those capitalists who control a country seek one of two ways out of their crisis of overproduction. They either make a war to use up the excess goods, or they make the workers take wage cuts ... Either way, it is the workers who suffer, not the few with the riches.

The back cover broadcast a rallying call to: 'Oppose the wage freeze cut! Make the Rich Pay.'

The BLF's class consciousness set it apart but also made it easier to isolate. Journalist Michael Gawenda, touring building sites a few months after deregistration, noted:

> The quintessential union leader is Simon Crean...
> [Somebody] who has no difficulty fitting into a smartly tailored pin striped suit, a man who can tell at a glance the difference between a good and bad chardonnay [whereas] the men on the building sites ... are so aggressively working men! They are so conscious of the gulf which separates them from the bosses, so aware that their interests and the interests of employers are in fundamental conflict.[292]

'There's still a sense that you were a member of something really important in Australian history,' Ivor Lawrence says. 'The influence of the BLF – at its peak having a national membership of around 55,000 – its influence on the trade union movement and through that, Australian society, was absolutely enormous.'

CHAPTER 7

The Public Sector – Strung up by the Accord

Suddenly, there we were – just one year into the Accord – public sector workers on the front pages of the papers, along with the BLF and the doctors, crippling the economy and threatening the Accord! That was exactly the impact of the three federal public sector unions' 1984–85 action over pay. Unionist Paul White wrote:

> By this time about $589 million worth of revenue had been blocked, according to the government. A week later Ralph Willis was complaining that about $41 million was held up in Telecom, $4 million in Australia Post and over $1 billion in the Tax Office.[293]

How did it reach this point?

The changing nature of the public sector

A post-WWII economic boom saw greatly expanded federal government control over functions such as tax, education, social welfare, communication, immigration and Indigenous affairs. By 1970, the Australian Public Service (APS) workforce had grown from 2.4 to 6.4 percent of the civilian workforce, with total government employment rising from 13.7 percent to 19.6 percent.[294] As the sector became increasingly important to the general economy, it also became a significant battleground between public sector workers and their employers – the government and departmental administrators. Fuelled by increased numbers and automation-led routinisation of work, white-collar workers in the public sector had become proletarianised by the 1970s. Contributing to that was the radicalisation of youth by the Vietnam war and, later, the Whitlam coup, with many of these students newly employed in the public sector.

The unions threw off their inactive stance. Reform groups, such as the ACOA Reform Group, replaced more right wing leaderships.[295] In 1979, the ACOA Reform Group won control of the Victorian branch after three years of campaigning over industrial and social issues. The new leadership drove a more militant stance under the Fraser government, imposing bans and, in 1979, holding the union's first ever national 24-hour stoppage.

Once in office, the reform groups, usually a mixture of left and right forces, turned their sights to staying in power – winning elections, rather than building rank and file militancy. More militant workers formed small rank and file groups, such as Public Servants Action Group (PSAG) in 1978 in NSW, appealing to an activist minority of public sector workers. They began a four-page national newspaper, *Grey Collar*, and held a national conference which attracted 60 activists. In the mood of rising struggle, PSAG formed in Canberra and Brisbane, but not Victoria.[296]

In NSW, the group included clerical workers in ACOA and APSA, with occasional members of the Federated Clerks Union (Tax Office Branch; FCU[TOB]), and met weekly to discuss disputes in their workplaces. They also met as a caucus before delegates' and mass meetings during the 1981 sector-wide staffing dispute, leading a walkout by 150 Tax Office workers after stand-downs for refusing to lift bans in that dispute.[297]

The high point for PSAG/*Grey Collar* style groups was 1981. This more radical type of rank and file organisation was disbanded soon afterwards, although other groups of activists followed and attempted reform.

Some of these new groups were responding to a rightward shift of the new reform-minded union leadership, who grew more reluctant to respond to government attacks. 'Rank and File Action' (RFA) in NSW focused on branch elections and stayed to the left of the leadership, but mostly shied away from more controversial policies. That group won two positions in the 1985 Branch elections, that of state secretary, filled by Trevor Deeming, and deputy president, filled by Alison Adler. Defying the old Reform Group leadership in the union office, who often resisted membership calls for action, Deeming and Adler backed members' calls for industrial action and stayed with them – up to a point. They had some power to call strikes and book venues for mass meetings. It remained to be seen what they could achieve, and how far they were prepared to go

The Fraser Years

The Fraser government armed itself with legislation specifically targeting government workers taking industrial action, introducing the *No Work as Directed-No Pay Act* (NWAD-NP) and the *Commonwealth Employees Employment Provisions Act 1977* (CEEP). If bans were imposed, workers could be stood down under the No Work Act. If the bans were lifted, nothing else would happen, but you could eventually be sacked if you didn't comply. It was the soft option. CEEP was much harsher. It gave the government complete power to suspend and then sack workers taking any sort of industrial action. Reinstatement was entirely at the government's whim and on whatever terms they chose. CEEP was not enacted until two years later, when it was used against Commonwealth employees engaging in 'go-slow' action.

DSS ON STRIKE

One of the centres of rank and file activism was the Department of Social Security (DSS), now Centrelink part of the federal department, Services Australia.[298] Because the department dealt directly with welfare recipients, decisions made by government for new programs and less staffing had an immediate, often political, impact on both staff and clients.

The Fraser government was infamous for its crackdown on welfare. As unemployment rose towards the end of its term, pressures on workers from increased workloads and staff cuts became intolerable. The Hawke government expanded welfare but made access to it more restrictive and its administration more punitive. Under the Accord, the government through department heads never increased wages, staffing or other conditions without a fight. And Social Security workers did fight.

One of the most significant pre-Accord industrial actions was the fight for jobs in 1981. It became the iconic staffing dispute in DSS, whose memory – and political lessons – were frequently invoked in later struggles. It started

THE PUBLIC SECTOR – STRUNG UP BY THE ACCORD

1988 DSS dispute. Clockwise from top left: strikers seeking support from other workers; strikers picketing a workplace in Chatswood, Sydney; strikers voting at a mass meeting; strikers marching along George St to the Sydney HQ. Photos courtesy David Main.

as an APS-wide campaign defying Fraser's anti-union agenda and a cut of 17,000 jobs. Fraser used NWAD-NP and CEEP to stand down DSS workers the year it was introduced.

NSW rank and file activists in PSAG argued for a sector-wide industrial campaign for more jobs. With no rank and file groups interstate to support the PSAG position, the national union officials pushed a policy of fighting the cuts with work bans, department by department and state by state.

Management smashed through this tactic in mid-1981, standing down unionists in Tax and Immigration under NWAD-NP. Workers walked out wherever the stand-downs occurred, complying with union policy. It was essential for the walkouts to spread quickly through each department and to other departments, to prevent isolation of those in the firing line; this had misfired in DSS in 1979, where restricting action took the strongest activists out of the campaign. The focus inevitably shifted to lifting stand-downs instead of building the campaign.[299] In 1981, 150 members in Tax walked out after being stood down. Their mass meeting voted for a public sector-wide meeting and further action. The officials refused to mobilise more support. Rightly feeling abandoned, first Tax and then Immigration workers lifted their bans.

DSS' lengthy bans action had been ignored by government to this point; now it was their turn to get the full government treatment. On 9 November 1981, Minister Fred Chaney began stand-downs in DSS, with 180 stood down that week in NSW and Victoria. The union refused to call out the entire department or extend action to other states. In NSW, the strategy was for rolling strikes, but the officials refused to call any after the first one. In Victoria, the only action taken was walking out to avoid stand-downs, returning when management left. Both strategies weakened the struggle. In Victoria, some offices attempted to escalate the action by staying out instead of returning to work; the union officials forced them back.

Attempts at spreading the dispute in NSW were undermined by the state officials, through such tactics as refusing to distribute leaflets advertising a mass meeting, and referring stopwork decisions of mass meetings to delegates' meetings which voted against action.

The government escalated its response. On 4 December, a Friday afternoon, they announced that they would be standing down NSW workers from

Monday under the harsher CEEP regulations; this gave workers the weekend to worry. However, this escalation by the government meant that, under ACOA policy, the rest of the public sector had to be brought in. The policy stipulated a mass stopwork meeting, to be held within 48 hours of CEEP being used anywhere in the APS, and a 24-hour strike. APSA, for the first time, were bound to call stopwork meetings and be part of the campaign.

True to its word, the government began standing down DSS workers under CEEP provisions from Monday 7 December. This prompted mass walkouts from DSS and more workers 'CEEPed' the next day. The following Wednesday, Sydney Town Hall overflowed as 4,500 unionists carried the motion for a one-day stoppage. APSA members, denied a vote on this, forced their officials to grant them coverage to go out; but those officials reneged within hours and ordered their members back to work.

Straight after the meeting, over 3,000 striking public servants marched down Sydney CBD's George Street behind a Grey Collar banner, in what was clearly the high point of the campaign. There was a tremendous feeling of enthusiasm and strength.

It was left to the delegates to hastily organise pickets once the march and rally had finished. On that Friday, PSAG organised a mass picket outside DSS headquarters. Over 100 people chanted, sang *Solidarity Forever* and blocked both entrances with a circular marching picket.

But the action against CEEP was only one 24-hour stoppage. Over the weekend, the ACTU's Cliff Dolan met with Fraser and then with the ACOA. The union officials agreed to a joint staffing review as resolution of the dispute. It was a complete backdown, with DSS members left in the dark until five hours after the ACTU–ACOA press conference announced it. Members were left with no choice but to return to work, lift the bans and abandon any campaign; but it was not a completely devastating outcome. Harrison and Main note that later, apparently unconnected, increases in staff numbers could be viewed as vindication of workers' actions. They conclude:

> Although the 1981 dispute ended in a demoralising defeat,
> the experience was not lost on those who went through it
> … the high level of rank and file activity ensured that the
> basic union and delegates structure in NSW remained intact;

the limitations of a strategy based solely on bans, without a strong response to stand-downs, became obvious; and a base of militant opposition to the union officials was established[300]

The Public Sector Pay Dispute

The Fraser government imposed a total wages freeze in 1982, in its dying months. Union officials assured workers that a Labor victory in March1983 would restore wages; they opposed fighting Fraser's freeze – only to see the new Hawke government extend it for federal public sector workers to October 1983.[301]

The government made it clear that there was to be no post-freeze wages catch-up offer for government employees. They were expected to be satisfied with the small September CPI rise and drop demands for more. Job losses, attacks on other conditions and cuts to superannuation were heralded. But many APS workers had been involved in defiant industrial action against Fraser's anti-union attacks on the public sector. When the ALP gained power, these unionists weren't prepared to passively accept similar attacks, despite being 'bound' by the resurgent Labor Party to its new social contract with unions, the Accord.

For the unions and workers, there was a promise of industrial peace with improved standards of living; for the federal government – and the employers more generally – there was the commitment to increased productivity and union cooperation for workplace change. The leadership of the ACOA was firmly behind the Accord. APSA had opposed the pact, but eventually signed on. However, signing on hadn't meant that industrial action was over for either union in the federal public sector.

One of the promises made to workers by the incoming Hawke government was to restore wage comparability between private and public sector workers and regain wages lost in Fraser's wage freeze. It was even spelled out in the Accord: 'the government will ensure comparability of such conditions with the relevant State public sectors and the private sector fully consulting the industrial organisations concerned for their advice and guidance.' There was a get-out clause: 'The Australian Government employment sector will not be a pacesetter in established wage rates and cost-related conditions comparable in other public sector employment and in the private sector.'

As 1983 came to an end, it became increasingly clear that the government was reneging on its pre-election promises. Furious, the three public sector unions lodged an 8.3 percent pay claim in December 1983, using a little-known section in the Accord known as an 'anomalies' case. This was small recompense for the estimated 20 percent wage losses over the previous 10 years. The Arbitration Commission itself, comparing 26 public and private clerical occupations, noted: 'by March 1982 APS salary rates were next to last and in July 1982 they were last.'

The three unions had last run a serious industrial campaign for a wage rise in 1981, winning between 10 percent and 13 percent. In 1982, before Fraser's wage freeze, there was no industrial action, so the sector only picked up 6 percent, just half their claim.

The 1983 campaign did not begin militantly. The unions held three months of private meetings with IR Minister Ralph Willis, getting nowhere. ACOA told its members that the Labor government was 'behaving identically' to the Fraser government, 'forcing us into long arbitration processes with the aim of delaying and minimising any result.'[302] The Arbitration Commission confirmed this judgement by then further delaying hearings to haggle over when, why and how a 'market rates survey' of clerical wages – the basis for the wages claim – would occur. Only after this process would the Commission even begin to hear the log of claims, specifying that it would not be before June 1984.

The Victorian ACOA Reform Group and a group of APSA activists began agitating around the pay claim, putting out a leaflet demanding action: 'If we don't apply pressure the case could drag on till next year and the final result could be a very small pay increase, with no retrospective date of effect.' Victorian APSA and ACOA delegates met on 5 July 1984 to consider the state of the campaign. They called for joint mass meetings to plan industrial action. That night, the ACOA Branch Executive met and rejected the call. This left APSA alone to fight the campaign.

At the end of July, a Victorian APSA mass meeting voted overwhelmingly to launch a series of monthly 24-hour stoppages, beginning on 10 August. Victorian ACOA members met the next day, but a Reform Group motion to join the APSA stoppages was defeated by 12 votes.

On 2 August, the ACOA executive authorised ACOA members to go to work on 10 August, crossing APSA picket lines! *Alternative Viewpoint*, the ACOA Reform Group's journal, wrote: 'Friday, 10th August will go down in the history of public service unionism as "ACOA's Day of Shame".'

By November 1984, there had been no progress on the campaign. A joint ACOA–APSA mass meeting stayed out for the rest of the day and agreed to meet again in December. Having met in October and threatened industrial action, the FCU(TOB) finally called a 24-hour strike for 16 November, the same day as the ACOA–APSA meeting. They also imposed bans on some revenue collection.

Meanwhile, Willis promised support for the pay claim, but only if the ACTU could guarantee no flow-on of any increase to any other sector of the workforce.[303] He would not even wait for that guarantee, calling on the Arbitration Commission to hold off any wage rise until there was an inquiry to determine any flow-on effects.

Following the November stopwork, a series of mass meetings in December called on the Commission to hand down a rise by 18 January 1985. The meeting agreed to the officials' motion to take no further action and hold delegates' meetings in late January. Feeling isolated and under attack by Labor and the Commission, FCU(TOB) members lifted their bans – bans that had held up hundreds of millions of dollars in government revenue.

The Commission landed a bombshell on 10 January 1985, dismissing the claim. There would be no pay rise.

The decision provoked unprecedented anger and spontaneous walkouts across the country. National mass meetings – for the first time involving the FCU (TOB) – were held on 16 and 17 January, to plan future action. However, instead of a service-wide campaign, only a few departments – the so-called revenue departments – were called into action. The bans put on by Tax, Telecom, Customs and Social Security had a greater impact than anyone expected, but a total APS shutdown would have brought the government to the table more quickly.

In Victoria, members and APSA's branch officials made attempts at mass meetings to tap into a growing anti-Accord sentiment. An APSA anti-Accord motion was supported by about 40 percent of one mass meeting, but ACOA officials argued that it was more important than ever to stay in the Accord to pressure the government. ACOA produced badges with the slogan: 'The Accord says Pay Up!' – altered by activists to a more popular message: 'Stuff the Accord – Pay Up!'[304]

Rank and file members at the ACT ACOA mass meeting were openly hostile to National Assistant Secretary Peter Robson's statement that the union needed to 'stay within the Accord guidelines.' To loud acclaim from the meeting, one member replied, 'If it was a real Accord – an agreement – why do we have to fight for it?' The meeting resolved to set up a rank and file pay disputes committee to coordinate and conduct the campaign.

The government's response was to step up the attack. On 29 January, it took another feather out of Fraser's cap by applying for stand-down powers it had promised never to use. When bans continued, stand-downs began, 200 in all. ACOA did nothing to escalate the action, instead writing to federal MPs, calling on the government to 'honour the Accord' and seeking a continuation of the 'supportive and constructive relationship' which the union had with the Labor government.

Officials used this government attack to wave the white flag. ACOA National Secretary Paul Munro indicated that the union was prepared to negotiate a reduced claim of 2 to 3.8 percent for all, and a little more for the two lowest paid classifications.

Yet, the unions had the government over a barrel. The bans hit hard. David Bunn, Victorian ACOA Secretary, wrote: 'The campaign is of unprecedented strength ... Members in the front-line Departments have been heartened by support from others, including from waterfront unions.' By mid-February, Ralph Willis was complaining that about $41 million was held up in Telecom, $4 million in Australia Post and over $1 billion in the Tax Office. Customs alone was holding back $1.8 million, and its bans left goods piling up on the wharves. More generally, the bans disrupted government financing and the dollar's exchange rate.

To the last moment, the campaign kept ramping up. Just prior to the final mass meetings, hundreds of APS unionists had walked off the job in the Bureau of Customs in Fremantle and the Tax Office in Perth, in protest at stand-downs. In Melbourne, Tax unionists also walked out for the same reason – and walked back shortly thereafter, to sit at their desks but refuse to work.

All such action was summarily cut short as the officials rushed to close down the campaign. National ACOA delegates' meetings were held on 12 February to ratify the new claim. The meetings in Melbourne and Sydney rejected the sellout overwhelmingly and carried a motion framed by the ACOA Reform Group. This called for national, three-union stopwork meetings to consider the course of the campaign and more intensive action. Speakers from the Reform Group warned that, if industrial action was not kept up, it was unlikely that even the reduced claim would be granted in full.

These fears were realised when the final joint delegates' meetings of the campaign were held on 21 February and presented with a motion to end all industrial action, because: 'our campaign has been successful in obtaining the re-opening of the clerks' and clerical assistants' claim', adding that the ACTU 'supports and will argue on our behalf before the Commission.' Delegates carried the motion before sending it to small mass meetings of demoralised workers, who endorsed it by a clear majority.[305]

The ACTU gave no support to APS unions. Bill Kelty himself put the boot in from the beginning of the campaign to the end. In the Arbitration Commission, he repeatedly attacked the original wages claim and any attempt at wage parity:

> Let me make it absolutely clear, if it is not already clear, that the ACTU does not embrace and has never in fact embraced a claim for 8.3 percent across the board for all employees of the Australian Government employment sector.

Kelty went beyond attacking the APS workforce, slamming any form of 'comparative wage justice' and declaring that the ACTU, for the first time in its history, would not be supporting pay increases based on pay rises elsewhere: 'The concept of comparative wage justice is not a wage fixing principle and the ACTU will be saying that clearly to the courts and to its affiliates.' He even offered to intervene against any union bringing such a case to the Commission.

Three months later, on 25 May 1985, a decision was handed down: a mere 2 to 2.6 percent rise for the vast majority of workers, with a small group of keyboard operators gaining 4 percent, but no backdating for anyone.

It was a miserable result from a campaign that had such potential. Despite some determined rank and file activism and some influence by the ACOA Reform Group, the continued barrage of attacks from government, the press and the ACTU, coupled with a union leadership wedded to the Accord, prevailed. It could have been a major defeat for the Accord.

DSS Fight for Jobs

In the lead up to the 1988 dispute, workers in DSS had been through battles over staffing and occupational health and safety (OH&S) in 1984, the introduction of new technology (Stratplan), wages in 1984–85 (APS dispute), then departmental staffing in 1985 and again in 1986 and 1987.[306] For NSW ACOA Branch secretary, Trevor Deeming, the Hawke government was worse for the public sector than Liberal PM Fraser. Although the public sector unions had won some gains early in the Accord years, with a few promises kept: 'very quickly it turned sour.' And the union response – or lack of an effective response – meant that workers were getting frustrated and accusing the leadership of selling out. Deeming noted that members were critical of unions 'wandering around making submissions, talking about abstract concepts around the economy ... not really getting down to looking at the basic issues of pay and conditions.'[307]

The nature of industrial disputes began to change as Accord policies became more entrenched. Instead of mounting offensive campaigns, demanding more staffing or better wages and conditions, unions were increasingly in defensive struggles to keep what they had.

During the 1980s, public sector workers were under attack by state and federal, Labor and Liberal governments which embraced neoliberalism wholeheartedly. In July 1986, both WA and Tasmanian governments axed jobs and threatened pay cuts. The response of Tasmanian union officials was to help the government find $20 million in savings! Federally, PM Hawke swiftly confirmed rumours that he had a 'shopping list' of similar cuts, an immediate staffing freeze, and a promise of further job cuts or 'efficiency dividends' of 1.25 percent for the next three years. Hawke's list included abolition of flexitime and the 17.5 percent leave loading, cuts to superannuation and invalidity benefits, and dismantling of the promotion appeals system. Fraser's notorious anti-union CEEP Act, removed from the statutes by Labor in 1983, was to be revived.

APS workers threatened industrial action, and Hawke backed off somewhat; in DSS, Social Security Minister Brian Howe promised a staffing review, which was enough for the union leaderships to pull back.

In 1986, the federal Budget abolished 2,000 public sector positions. After beginning, and then scuttling, an industrial campaign, ACOA National Secretary Peter Robson announced that the union would help the government to make departments 'more efficient and cost effective.' The ACTU's Simon Crean's response was that the job losses did not matter given the high level of turnover.[308]

But the staffing issue didn't go away. Cutting staff is the white collar equivalent of speed-ups on process lines, while raising productivity means increasing workloads at the same time as cutting real wages and staffing levels. This push, begun under Whitlam and Fraser with the introduction of staff ceilings, was fine-tuned under Hawke with 'dollar budgeting' – setting staffing levels by arbitrary dollar allocation rather than workloads, along with a massive reorganisation of work under the second tier wage deal of 1987.

Up to the mid-1980s, despite Howe's staffing review, the government's only message was more job cuts through restructuring. ACOA rank and file militant and shop steward Eris Harrison explains: 'Governments are always restructuring. First thing you're decentralised, then you're all re-centralised. Every time, you saw staff disappearing in the name of efficiency.' In 1988, the government planned to shift much of the headquarters work to regional offices, cutting jobs in the central office but providing no extra staff to the regions to cover the extra work.

This was the third year DSS workers had fought for jobs – initially, claims for new jobs, but by 1988 simply opposing cuts. Unionists had won a small number of extra staff in the earlier campaigns, even taking four 24-hour strikes in 1987 to win 401 new positions nationally. Few workplaces actually saw these new staff, and those that did were inundated with new tasks, so members' anger over rising workloads grew.

Harrison and Main comment on the militant mood of the NSW workers at the end of 1987, describing the struggles of 1986 and 1987 as 'dress rehearsals' for the staffing campaign of 1988:

1987 included two pointers to what lay ahead. Firstly, there was overwhelming support at one point in NSW for a motion to stay out for a second day, turning a one day strike into two days. Secondly, there was a strong feeling among militants afterwards that one day strikes were not terribly effective. If we're going to strike for four days in future, they said, let's make it four consecutive days.

In 1988, the government announced the planned abolition of 3,000 jobs over several years – 1,271 in the first year. NSW would lose an immediate 303 positions, many more than they had won in 1987.

While the national union officials were prepared to wait for negotiations to kick in before any industrial response, workers in NSW state headquarters wanted immediate action. Given the struggles of the previous years, they were prepared for a campaign, as Harrison explains: 'We had a good bunch of active delegates whose skills had been honed over all these years. [In February] we got the members together and we walked out for the rest of the day.' Then the delegates put together a log of claims. Management has to be clear, she added at a conference session: 'Not just "we're really angry and we're going out". But "we're very angry, we're going out – and this is what we want [slaps demands down on table], so get thinking about it!"'[309]

NSW delegates pressured the ACOA national office into taking up the log of claims, including a firm rejection of any job cuts. The log of claims was then endorsed by state headquarters staff in other states and regional centres.

But nothing happened after the February walkout from NSW state headquarters (SHQ). On 14 March, delegates around NSW called for mass meetings to begin a joint campaign of all DSS ACOA members. There was another motion on 29 March and again on 12 April for action. After hesitating for two months, NSW State Secretary Trevor Deeming finally called it for 28 April. The city meeting voted massively in favour of a further meeting and united action against job cuts, only to be outvoted by the combined regions–country tally against action.

Militants in Sydney didn't pull back. They kept calling for meetings, and Deeming began to listen to the delegates rather than the national office. He called a Sydney-only meeting for 10 May. This meeting endorsed the delegates' motion for a statewide meeting in a week's time, then walked out for the rest of the day.

Persistent work by activists in that week saw regular statewide bulletins, direct calls to country members and a couple of flying visits to the Illawarra and Hunter regions, getting the message out about the issues across the rest of NSW. The result at statewide mass meetings on 18 May was strong support for a 48-hour strike for the following two days (Thursday and Friday), to meet again on Monday 23 May.

This next meeting was vital – would the union pause and wait for more negotiations or would they 'increase the shock value by piling one walkout on another'? At the preparatory delegates' meeting, the militants argued for and won the case to keep the momentum going. The 23 May meeting backed a further 48-hour stoppage and resolved to meet again on 26 May. They walked out for the rest of the day. Around the state, they were joined by some APSA members, although their union had refused to join the action officially.

For five days, almost every DSS ACOA member in the state was on strike – the longest stoppage the union had ever held!

Meanwhile NSW state union officials, even the RFA leadership, were keen to see an end to the industrial action and a return to negotiations. When the delegates' meeting recommended extending the five day stoppage, compromise motions recommended other options, such as a return to work with bans and a promised national stoppage to come.

The mass meeting on 26 May became a day of 'enormous contradictions.' The Sydney meeting was the largest yet, with over 500 packed into Trades Hall. Despite the confusion brought about by the conflicting motions to call off the strike and take partial action, or continue the strike, the mood remained high, and trust in the delegates swept the motion to stay out through. Union members poured into George Street and marched to DSS headquarters. It was a noisy, morale-boosting march, with some yelling at scabs, and it ended with speeches and street theatre.

Then came what could have been a devastating blow. The total state vote defeated the motion to stay out by 50 votes, while counting of votes for the compromise motions to take some action or end the strike was bogged down in debates about the validity of some votes and what the real result was. In the end, the delegates saw no option but to go back to work and see what happened. Demoralised, Sydney workers turned up to their workplaces on Friday morning. Confusion reigned as contradictory messages kept coming from the union offices. That afternoon, a meeting of the union State Executive determined that all motions had been lost; the strike was over.

Defiantly, SHQ delegates began ringing around other offices and convened a meeting where members agreed to walk out and call another mass meeting for the following Monday. Offices began walking out even before the vote was held at SHQ. Harrison and Main explain:

> This was the turning point of the strike. Members had gone back to work, the strike bureaucratically squashed. But the rank and file looked down the barrel of the gun and decided that this was defeat and that they wanted no part of it. The spontaneous walk-outs, although fragmented, were strong and effectively led. From being on the point of collapse, we rebuilt the strike with a new momentum.

RFA's Trevor Deeming again defied the other state and national officials by calling a mass meeting, which voted overwhelmingly to strike for another three days. The delegates' committee took the lead in organising to win the dispute. Together with a group of rank and file activists, they met frequently to discuss tactics, plan and organise the strike and set up a strike fund. They held mass meetings with report backs every three days, 13 altogether, to decide whether to stay out. Members voted to stay out each time, for a total of six weeks on strike. Harrison describes the mood during the industrial action:

> Quite a few people did get radicalised, that's inevitable in any strike. But there's such a wonderful feeling of solidarity when you go and stand in one of those big rooms, with all those other people and all the hands go up to stay out. There's nothing quite like it really.

Nor was it just a stay-at-home strike. Workers picketed every day at the departmental headquarters, to turn back any waverers and to show their determination to government and department heads. There were flying pickets, occupations and demonstrations, visits to backsliding offices, regular strike bulletins and collections for the strike fund outside government offices, at the union office and at mass meetings of other unions. And some DSS country offices began to pressure the union to bring them in.

Although there had been some initial one-day-a-week strikes by interstate members in their state headquarters, the national and state union leaderships quickly shut them down. They flatly refused to spread the dispute outside headquarters' offices and then restricted the action to NSW.

APSA officials continued to resist joining the strike until their members, sick of waiting, organised an invasion of their own Branch Office in Sydney on 2 June. About 40 of them bailed up their officials and demanded that APSA's involvement be formalised. APSA became part of the action.[310]

Unionists in some departments started carrying motions of support, and other unions stepped up to the mark. Having met some strikers during a national wage case rally in Sydney, Adelaide building workers donated money to the strike fund and, when they returned home, put bans on Commonwealth buildings in support of the DSS workers. There were even motions of support from workers overseas.

The government attacked the unionists savagely, playing on their worries about disadvantaging their clients, the poorest in society. The press ran such headlines as this in the *Sydney Morning Herald*: 'Strike has left needy to charities', and Brian Howe berated strikers at every negotiating session. He got some kickback after one such session, when he turned up for an ALP dinner in Sydney. He was met by a group of angry DSS protesters. One recalled:

> shouting and waving placards, we blocked the entrance to the Motor Boat Club so that he couldn't get in. He eventually pushed his way through the door, but the chants of 'Hands off DSS!' followed him inside.[311]

By standing firm, these union activists won ongoing improvements in the government's offer. Of course, Robson told workers at each meeting that the latest offer was the best they could do, and they should return to work. In fact, the momentum for protest began to build again. A call to country members to vote on action brought seven offices out on strike on 24 June, and Deeming announced that he would call out all NSW ACOA members for a union-wide mass meeting to discuss all threatened government cuts. The federal government now faced significant escalation of the dispute, and it rushed to offer a further compromise.

Continued undermining by national and some state union officials, a relentless barrage from the government and press and, finally, the government's compromise convinced Deeming that this offer was worth taking. He recommended it to the 28 June mass meeting, using his more left wing credentials to sell the final deal, as he had in other disputes. Because Deeming had 'been with us all the way', as one striker said, he had earned enough trust to get his motion through by a very small majority. The historic six-week strike was over, with a considerable reduction in staff cuts – from 1,271 to 486 nationwide, 303 to 99 in NSW – and a good redeployment package.

The win was made possible only by the rank and file control of the dispute. Even after it was over, workers were confident enough to keep watch and hold a couple more short walkouts to defend some members against victimisation. One striker concluded:

> Members did not return to work feeling beaten ... We'll be ready for the next attack, having shown that it's action and not the do-nothing methods of the officials which produces results.[312]

From its election in 1983, the Hawke government was relentless in its assault on the public sector. Intent on keeping wages down, it also used departmental amalgamations to cut staff and drive down conditions. As the government cut spending on health, welfare and education, among the first to be hit were departmental staff. The government heavily privatised sections of the public sector, selling off the Commonwealth Bank, Telstra, Qantas, the CES and Defence Services Homes.

The union leadership were all too often prepared to accept the government's rationale and quash members' resistance. On wages, they supported government demands for productivity trade-offs for increasingly small wage increases which fell far short of CPI rises. Consultation and industrial democracy became the buzz words as the union agreed to increased management control over the work process, at the same time restricting any industrial response. One report described how the department's industrial democracy processes 'tied them up with a diary full of elaborately titled committee meetings, mountains of agenda papers to read and an increasingly cynical membership.'[313]

Mass meetings became fewer and fewer. After losing one too many mass meeting decisions in DSS, the officials introduced a supposedly more democratic procedure: having meetings in each of the department's many decentralised offices. In the days before the internet, militants couldn't put their case as easily, and meetings didn't happen in offices with little union organisation. The result was that the number of people voting went down, the officials' position was usually carried, and the sense of being part of a department-wide struggle was lost.

The bruising campaigns, the continued undermining of rank and file activism, the constant degrading of conditions led inevitably to a decline in militancy and in union membership overall, mirroring exactly what was happening in the broader workforce. By 1988, the officials spent most of their time squabbling over union amalgamation. Except for a few brief displays of defiance, they allowed wages and conditions to be eroded.

But for a brief moment, the events in the NSW branch shone a light on what was possible in a union where the rank and file led the way.

CHAPTER 8
Pilot Unions – 'You go out and it's War'

The pilots' dispute was particularly controversial. A claim for a 30 percent wage rise quickly escalated into an all-out battle, with the Accord partners – the government and ACTU – and the airlines joined in crushing the pilots and their union. The dramatic use of the Royal Australian Air Force (RAAF) and local and international scab pilots finished the dispute.

The stakes were high. The end of the two-airlines policy was due in 1990, meaning cutthroat competition for the industry. There was no doubt among airline workers that cuts to wages and conditions were inevitable. The pilots viewed their claim as a last chance to shore up a higher base rate of wages and conditions before deregulation. The government, with an election scheduled for 1990 and the possibility of a historic fourth term for Labor and PM Bob Hawke, did not need a major industrial dispute, challenging the Accord, by a highly unionised group of workers.

Hawke was blunt in his warning to the pilots, 'It's a different game this time, boys. You go out and it's war.'[314] The pilots, the domestic airlines and Accord partners were on a collision course.

The Airlines and Government

Like industries such as steel and the waterfront, the airlines faced major structural change, facilitated by the government in the name of competition – part of the Accord agenda. Keating and Hawke drew up plans to end the long-standing two-airlines policy – shared by the government-owned Trans Australia Airlines (TAA) and the Peter Abeles–Rupert Murdoch owned Ansett

– by November 1990. In 1986, TAA was corporatised and prepared for privatisation. Both airlines were facing the huge expense of refitting their fleet of planes; needing to slash costs, they looked to employees' wages and conditions.[315] Alex Paterson, an AFAP member, argues that pilots' pay and conditions represented under 5 percent of operational expenditure. But removing the pilots from the equation would set an example for other workers and free up the airlines to tackle the key microeconomic reform of restructuring ground work without opposition from the other unions, especially the TWU.[316]

What were the airlines' strengths? They were extremely well prepared for a dispute and had regular tactics meetings with the government and the ACTU's Bill Kelty. They were expecting a short, sharp dispute. Abeles told a crucial 15 August 1989 meeting that the dispute 'will be short – we won't give them anything.'[317]

The publicly owned TAA had the resources of government behind it in the case of any confrontation or resistance from all its employees – pilots, flight attendants or ground staff. The government, at the urging of the ACTU and TWU, was prepared to prop up both airlines if the pilots held out. TAA had an experienced management team, including a number of former pilots and managers such as Ted Harris, a former CEO of Ampol petroleum, an old mate of Hawke's and good friend of Abeles.

Ansett also lined up a formidable team. Abeles ran Thomas Nationwide Transport – TNT, and Murdoch (News Corporation) had recently smashed the British printers and journalist unions in the 1986–87 Wapping dispute. Abeles had helped by directing TNT trucks from his British subsidiary to break the pickets and deliver the newspapers.[318] Murdoch and Abeles acquired the regional East-West airlines in 1983; this would give them flexibility in the event of industrial action.

Ansett had successfully employed a number of union officials from the Flight Attendants' Association of Australia (FAAA), Australian Transport Officers Federation (ATOF) and the AFAP on its management team. One ex-AFAP official was Len Coysh, an executive director of the Federation during the 1970s and 1980s, who resigned in 1986 to join Ansett. He was regarded as a turncoat by the pilots. On the other hand, John Raby, Vice-President of the AFAP during the 1980s, was in Ansett management for 10 years and went back to piloting and the union in 1986.[319]

Former pilot Ian Oldmeadow had become an official with Council of Australian Government Employees Organisations (CAGEO). On its merger with the ACTU, he became the Transport Industrial Officer. Ansett employed him in 1986 as an executive director for the Ansett Transport Industries complex. By the time of the pilots' dispute, Oldmeadow was Assistant General Manager and was quick to prove his worth, devising their hardline stance during the baggage handlers' strike in 1986. Abeles sacked the strikers, offering to rehire them on no-strike contracts. Within 24 hours, the TWU buckled. All the sacked employees signed the contracts to regain their jobs. Oldmeadow effectively ran Ansett's campaign during 1989, able to predict the AFAP strategy and plan countermeasures.

The Pilots and AFAP

Pilots covered by AFAP flew the domestic planes of Ansett, TAA and, until 1981, international flights for Qantas.[320]

The 1989 leadership team, President Brian McCarthy, Executive Director Terry O'Connell, Joint Vice-Presidents Noel Holt and John Raby and Industrial Officer Lawrie Cox, were following in the steps of leaders who had developed the Federation into a strong, militant union. Noteworthy was Dick Holt, President during the 1950s and 1960s, whose attitude was 'attack is the only defence.' In a 1954 speech to the AFAP Executive Committee, Holt declared:

> If all our conditions have not been met, we will simply go on strike and stay there until they are. Ha! Some of you will say, this is illegal, red, unprecedented, etc., we will be outside the court, we will be unpopular, we will throw people out of work and so on, but let me point out that ... almost no organisation ever got anywhere without one.[321]

The high-risk industrial move of mass resignations during the 1989 dispute would shock many, but the tactic had been used successfully before. In 1959, when the Australian Air Pilots Association (AAPA) found itself in contempt of an order of the Industrial Court over a seven-day strike of members at Qantas, they were fined £2,000. Frustrated with the arbitration system, the AAPA wanted to negotiate directly with the airlines but could not quit the system; every

APAA member resigned and joined a new, voluntary, unregistered organisation called the Australian Federation of Air Pilots. Outside the system, they negotiated an agreement with Qantas. Their industrial action was no longer subject to the penal powers (fines and other punishments) of the industrial relations laws. But in 1961, Qantas manoeuvred the Federation back into the arbitration system, despite a High Court challenge by one of the pilots.

In 1964, a three-day strike won an impressive victory on working conditions, despite threats of harsh penalties from PM Robert Menzies. When the pilots struck again in 1966, a bans clause was inserted in the award against each pilot, bringing them back into the system; the Commission added to the award a temporary clause which meant that, if the pilots took industrial action, they and their union would face fines and other punishments.[322]

The 1966 action was successful, winning the pilots a 35 percent wage rise, generous seniority and control over rostering. In 1974, under the Whitlam government and at the urging of then ACTU secretary Bob Hawke, TAA pilots won a 24 percent salary increase after a four-day strike, matching Ansett's offer. This rise was in contravention of the Arbitration Commission's ruling of a 17 percent general wage increase. Later, the pilots' wages win was linked to the start of the so-called 'wages explosion' that was blamed for destroying the Whitlam government.

Further stoppages in 1977 (Ansett) and 1978 (TAA) won pay rises, while East-West airline pilots stopped for a week in 1982, achieving a win over a contract provision relating to pay. Pilots' strike days only totalled 14 in 37 years, but they were very successful. The AFAP won several agreements between 1985 and 1988 for TAA, Ansett and East-West pilots. TAA pilots agreed not to negotiate a new agreement in 1987, because of the airline's poor economic position, but Ansett and East-West won pay rises after stopping work in August 1988, leaving TAA pilots well behind.

The Dispute

The Federation began 1989 in dramatic fashion by calling a snap 24-hour strike on 20 February over a new round of pay claims. The meeting gave *carte blanche* to the executive to run a pay campaign. It was the first total walkout of pilots since 1974, and it grounded the four main airlines.[323]

This disruptive action was triggered by Ansett's refusal to acknowledge the

AFAP as the pilots' representative in negotiations, a tactic not seen before in the airline industry. The pay claim itself had a longer history; pilots had fallen behind significantly through the Accord Mark III to V deals. In the 1987–1988 year (Accord Mark III), pilots, like other workers under the Accord guidelines, had been awarded a basic pay rise of just 3 percent and a further $10 per week for the following year. A 'second tier' productivity-based percentage rise could be capped at 4 percent. A complicated array of trade-offs – badged as improved career paths and changes in work value arising from improved skills or responsibility – was to be the basis for any wage rise.[324] Most workers found winning the second tier next to impossible. At meetings around the country –crucial at every stage of the 1989 dispute – members very reluctantly agreed to the leadership's recommendation to accept the deal, despite the fact that international pilots at Qantas had just signed a better agreement.[325]

The new Accord Mark V would cover 1989 to 1990. The deal was marginally higher than the 1988–89 agreement, promising a $30 or 6 percent rise, whichever was higher, with productivity trade-offs and a continuation of the 1988 'structural efficiency principle', now called award restructuring.[326] A $20 tax cut would come in July 1989. An earlier pledge to cut marginal tax rates from 60c to 49c had not yet been implemented; now the government was promising a further cut to 47c, but not until January 1990. Set against the backdrop of a 36 percent pay rise over three years for politicians, large salary increases received by top-end executives and record company profits, this was a slap in the face for workers.[327]

So the pilots enthusiastically supported a new wages claim. In May 1989, McCarthy announced that the union was preparing a log of claims with significant pay rises, including catch-up, inflation and future CPI increases, equating to a 29.7 percent increase. Pilots also wanted to be recompensed for unpaid overtime amassed during training for newly acquired planes. The AFAP gave airlines until 30 June to agree, or the union would deregister itself and take industrial action. Journalist Brad Norington, author of *Sky Pirates*, a history of the 1989 dispute, argued:

> The claim of 29 percent had no hope of being justified in the system and McCarthy knew this. His actions appeared a deliberate move to take pilots out of the system.[328]

The union set about informing its members of all contingencies in the lead up to action, at meetings and through the union's bulletin, *Deadline '89*. A *Countdown to D-Day* battle plan was mailed to pilots' homes from March onwards. They planned for industrial action if their claims weren't met, flagging initial actions, such as working 9am to 5pm with no overtime.

The pilots' log was a typical ambit claim, the sort most unions had used for decades. It was timed for the lead up to the October 1990 airline deregulation, to give pilots the best chance of winning a rise before the changes. A win would strengthen the union against the impact of deregulation and would set a benchmark for wages and conditions.[329]

The airlines refused to agree to any increase. Following negotiations on 11 July, Ansett management rejected the claim on 18 July. It was outside the Accord guidelines, said the airline, but now they wanted an industry-wide agreement, roping in the other airlines. The AFAP withdrew but promised their members they were 'prepared to look at anything to get your money.'

At a July meeting, Ansett's Abeles told the pilots, 'You do what you think you have got to do, but understand this – I have a deep commitment to the Accord.' Paterson notes, 'That was it. No beseeching speech. No dire threats. Just that one quietly spoken line. And Abeles then closed the meeting and left.'[330]

Not heeding that warning and undaunted by the airlines' rejection, the AFAP held a planning meeting over 24 to 25 July, to formulate an industry-wide claim. On 26 July, McCarthy served the claim on the airlines.

An important shift in the centralised wage fixing system happened next, with a crucial national wage case handed down on 6 August. The AIRC granted a maximum 6.5 percent, alongside an award restructuring process that effectively traded off conditions for a moderate wage rise (Accord Mark V). Knowing of the pilots' claim and a more generally restless workforce, the ACTU recognised that it had a major challenge in selling the new deal. Norington comments:

> This very fragile environment meant that Kelty was prepared to use all his resources to ensure that a highly publicised wage campaign by pilots, outside the system, did not succeed and encourage others.[331]

Negotiations recommenced on 1 August. Ansett's chief negotiator, Oldmeadow, announced that the airlines would neither pay 29.47 percent, nor backdate the claim, but they would offer another productivity–wage trade-off through the AIRC. McCarthy replied, negotiate outside the system, and we want an answer by 7 August.

On 4 August, the employers filed a dispute notice with the Commission, enabling them to bring the matter before the AIRC at any time. The road to compromise was now even more difficult. Could the Federation have won a better deal than the Accord was offering if they'd met with the ACTU leadership and agreed to stay in the system? It seems unlikely. The AFAP was not affiliated to the ACTU and had had a bitter relationship with the AIRC, which gave them no confidence in a fair deal.

For these reasons, Kelty and Crean's propositions about the flexibility of the Accord fell on deaf ears. Their insistence that Accord Mark IV had 'no ceiling' on wage rises, provided unions undertook genuine award restructuring, was undermined by Crean's suggestion of a limit of 12 percent. Other airline unions had gone down this path, but none had won as much as the pilots were claiming, and the wins were accompanied by significant trade-offs of conditions.

On 9 August, two days after the pilots' deadline, McCarthy suggested a compromise: they could take a deal to the AIRC, but, if it was rejected and only a lesser amount awarded (as had happened before), management would pay the difference as an over-award payment. Further negotiations produced no response.

ACTU Vice-President Martin Ferguson argued that pilots should not get any more than other workers, and any deal should contribute to increasing the productivity and efficiency of industry. The danger: 'If pilots are granted any more than six percent, every worker will be entitled to whatever they get.'

The AFAP planned another round of stopwork meetings from 11 to 14 August, to discuss the status of the dispute. The airlines appealed to the AIRC on 10 August for an immediate hearing. Justice Peter Coldham, who had adjudicated on earlier airlines matters, heard the case.[332] Lawrie Cox, Industrial Officer for the pilots, read a statement and accused the AIRC of interfering in the union's democratic rights. This drew an incensed response from Coldham. Directing that the meetings should be cancelled and a further hearing held on 11 August, he fumed:

> I find it somewhat incredible that a wage claim of these proportions can in the wildest of dreams be justified within the wage fixing principles – principles where wage increases and restructuring are inextricably intermixed.[333]

McCarthy reported to members' meetings that the AIRC was against the pilots from the start. At the next hearing, 15 August, the airlines tried to head off further industrial action with threats of 'a big stick' – the cancellation of the pilots' awards. That afternoon in parliament, Hawke, after a crucial meeting with Abeles, TAA's Ted Harris and Ansett's Graeme McMahon, reiterated the government's support for the companies. Coldham told the parties to go away and negotiate within the system. The talks failed. On 17 August, McCarthy repeated AFAP's refusal to commit to the Accord guidelines, flagging upcoming industrial action.

On 18 August, the pilots began their campaign, working 9am to 5pm as planned. Their press release put the pilots' case, adding:

> Our sole intention is to sit down across the table with our employers, negotiate an agreement, shake hands and know that the money will be in our pockets at the end of the month.

AFAP's strategy at this point reveals serious weakness. Norington blames it on the pilots themselves, arguing that their:

> simplistic approach, born out of arrogance harking back to the federation's militant past, ignored new realities. The heady days of maverick unions flexing their muscles were gone. Sheer industrial might was no longer sufficient against the force of Australia's modern corporate state.

It is true that AFAP underestimated the government and employers' determination to enforce the Accord. However, it was not arrogance to call on the union's militant past. It is incorrect to call a period of union militancy, which won major gains for workers, the 'heady days of maverick unions flexing their muscles.' Rather, the pilots' leadership was reflecting the highpoint of union strength in 1970s Australia, where workers had won improved wages and conditions before the ruling class turned the tide on them through the Accord.

Underestimating the Accord process and the widespread commitment to it was certainly a weakness in the strategy. The pilots should have taken into account the actions government and ACTU had already been prepared to take against other unions, including the BLF, FPU, AMIEU and PGEU. Significant warning signs were coming from Hawke, Kelty and the airlines.

Some obstacles they faced were unforeseeable. Hawke had convened a secret crisis conference with the airlines and the ACTU on 15 August, before the pilots' industrial action had begun. Compensation for the airlines, fast tracking foreign pilots into Australia, bringing in foreign charter planes and use of the RAAF were all discussed and agreed to by all parties at this meeting. Labor had only once before, during the 1949 coal miners' strike, used troops against striking workers.

A very real obstacle for AFAP was the pilots' fractious history with other unions in the airline industry, where they'd shown little or no solidarity for their fellow workers' industrial campaigns. In 1988, pilots did not support engineers during a crewing dispute with Ansett over the introduction of the new Airbus A320. Pilots had also ignored the pickets of other unions and had agreed to divert planes during earlier refuellers' strikes.[334] Kelty was more than prepared to use this hostility against the pilots, telling Hawke that the government should protect the other airline workers.

Nevertheless, the pilots were in a strong position industrially. They were effectively irreplaceable (or had been until 1989); they had a history of gains through militant action; and they knew that the airlines could afford their claim.

As soon as the pilots announced their 9-to-5 campaign, the airlines went to the Commission with an application under s.187 of the *Industrial Relations Act* to cancel the pilots' award. The hearing began at 3.30 the same day, under AIRC President, Justice Barry Maddern. Norington describes the Commission under Maddern as 'a silent partner to the Accord'; his decisions only 'deviated slightly from the ACTU's position.'[335] The pilots could not expect a favourable reception. Maddern directed the Federation to lift its 9-to-5 campaign by 4pm Monday, 21 August or lose their award.

The day before the deadline, with pilots continuing their campaign, Hawke and the airlines met again in Melbourne. The airlines, particularly Ansett, could not keep going through a sustained 9-to-5 campaign, although most passengers were eventually reaching their destinations. They would have to agree to the pilots' demands or find another way out.

The meeting decided that the pilots would be suspended if they refused to work outside 9am to 5pm; then the airlines would shut down their business while writs for damages against individual pilots and the Federation were issued. The pilots would be offered their jobs back, but only on terms which shut out the Federation. They developed plans for the use of foreign pilots and the RAAF or invoking s.45D or common law damages.

Hawke came out swinging and attacked the pilots. If they didn't lift the 9-to-5 bans, then, 'the Federation of Air Pilots doesn't exist' for the airlines. He hinted at deregistration, posing the question of 'whether ... they can have status at all within a system which they have deliberately said go to hell.'

The PM also returned to a common theme during the dispute, of privileged and overpaid pilots destroying the system for their own greedy ends. He played to public opinion, with polls indicating a three to one sentiment against the pilots. Infamously, he claimed on radio that flying was relatively easy, because he'd flown a small plane when he was at Oxford in 1954. Later that day, he stuck the boot in again, declaring that bus drivers had as much responsibility for passenger safety as pilots, it was simple to learn to fly, and 'the pilots have to understand that we will shut down the system if we have to. It's a different game this time, boys. You go out and it's war.'[336]

Monday 21 August, 4pm, came and went. The pilots did not lift the bans. Shortly after 4pm, Maddern signed the orders to cancel the pilots' 17 awards and agreements.[337]

On the evening of 23 August, with bans still in place, the airlines suspended pilots without pay and shut down the domestic airline system indefinitely. It was to be three weeks before these planes flew again.

Immediately, the government lifted the restrictions on international planes flying domestic routes, migration requirements for overseas pilots and the flight requirements for foreign aircraft. Qantas pilots refused to scab, agreeing only to take emergency or compassionate cases. The International Federation of Air Pilots Associations (IFAPA), covering 70,000 pilots in 75 countries, offered support that was mostly symbolic, because many overseas airlines employed non-union labour, but they did put some pressure on overseas pilots not to take Australian jobs. Paterson points to the international pilot shortage at the time and accuses the pilots who came to Australia of knowingly scabbing.[338]

While most of the RAAF planes were on a defence exercise in the NT (Kangaroo 1989) at the time, nine military planes were provided at heavily discounted prices for the airlines' use.[339] It was a stunning about face for Hawke, who, as ACTU leader just a decade before, had stopped Fraser's attempts to use the Airforce during an air traffic controllers' strike.

The first RAAF flight was at 9.30pm on 23 August. The first day, only 2,650 passengers flew, compared to the usual 30,000 per day. The flights were of symbolic importance, showing the Accord partners' resolve.

No planes could have got off the ground if the airlines' ground staff had refused to service them. But the unfortunate legacy of pilots' previous lack of solidarity, combined with Kelty's strategy of ensuring that other airline staff continued to get paid, kept the planes flying. The only support came from the TWU; members refused to refuel RAAF planes, forcing them to return to Richmond Airforce base for servicing. Flight engineer Jim McDonald's response was typical: 'Everyone felt uneasy about the arrangements, but in the end asked "what have the pilots ever done for us?"'

The choice before the pilots was to go back to the airlines and accept the Accord deal on offer, with the possibility of extra payments through 'special circumstances', or to try another tactic to force the airlines back to the negotiating table. In the first week of the dispute, following the threat to serve individual writs on pilots, some saw mass resignations as the only choice; this was not universally supported, because many feared that the pilots would lose control of the dispute. It was also not clear that resignation would protect pilots from threatened writs and other legal actions.[340] AFAP Executive Director Terry O'Connell thought that resignations were a bad tactic industrially and said so, but McCarthy was confident that it would force the airlines to negotiate.

Norington argues: 'To blindly act on the advice was a major deviation from the pilots' carefully thought-out campaign so far. A long-term strategy was supplanted by a mainly defensive move.' He suggests that waiting until they were sacked could have given the pilots the moral high ground; or a strategic return to work and selective work-to-rule campaign, rolling strikes and the like, would have had a better outcome. He does not take into account the determination of the airlines, government and ACTU, the fact that the 9-to-5 campaign had resulted in suspension without pay and the shutdown of the domestic airline system, nor the fact that the pilots' industrial action would have been declared illegal, incurring huge fines.

When the union realised that sackings were close, members were called in to sign the resignations. Only 37 notices were actually delivered by Ansett, but the AFAP believed that they had to lodge the forms.[341] For McCarthy:

> Today was the saddest day of my life when I saw 22 years of dedication to the aviation industry put in jeopardy because I wasn't prepared to submit to the rules of the ACTU.

McCarthy called an immediate press conference, condemning the ACTU, government, AIRC and employers:

> This dispute is not about 29.47 per cent; the outcome would have been exactly the same whatever the percentage. The dispute is about the legitimate right of employees, through their representative union, to directly negotiate with their employers. Pilots are being used by the Government and the ACTU to show the rest of the union movement and Australia what happens to any group which attempts to step out of line, regardless of the merits of our case.

IR Minister, Ralph Willis described the resignations as a 'rather kamikaze act', adding that the union had made itself irrelevant and the 'individual pilots cannot possibly win.' He wholeheartedly backed the government's use of the RAAF as strikebreakers and endorsed the airlines' non-union, individual contracts.

For the employers, the pilots' resignations were a gift. Ahead of industry deregulation, here was a golden opportunity to restructure the work process, get rid of conditions, slash pilot numbers and 'crush the invincible federation in one hit.' It would also send a strong message to other airline unions about the fate of those who bucked the Accord. While there would be some short-term financial pain, the airlines knew that the government was prepared to throw millions towards propping up the future of the industry. Much later, Ansett's Graeme McMahon gloated:

> I'll be perfectly honest. I couldn't believe my luck. Christ! Who would do that? Resign from what one of their own members described as the best contract any pilot in the world had!

Ansett and TAA quickly moved to the next stage. Arguing that the dispute was over, they were now recruiting both within Australia and overseas. Already, they had standard individual contracts to offer the new pilots – contracts with no union input, all okayed by the ACTU's Bill Kelty. The contract stripped away virtually all pilots' hard won conditions, effectively setting them back 30 years. TAA's James Strong expected productivity to rise by 100 percent under the new arrangements.

Negotiations did continue behind the scenes, but to no avail. Knowing that they would still have to deal with the pilots and their union at some stage in the future, airlines now focused on splitting the pilots away from AFAP or forcing the union to capitulate. Management engaged in a campaign of individual letters, advertisements, threats and offers, flying some routes with a few planes and reports of overseas pilots on the job; accompanying this were a media barrage and government opposition, including a personal 'Australian to Australian' letter from Bob Hawke. Abeles issued an ultimatum on *60 Minutes*: 'I won't give in … I'd rather close this airline forever.'

While things looked bad for the Federation, the government and airlines were in crisis. Three weeks into the dispute, only a few token flights were taking off. There were claims of losses of $30 million a week, $200 million cut from tourism revenue, up to 30,000 jobs lost across that sector, and no government compensation. Kelty pressured the airlines to keep the 20,000 other airline workers on the job or face retaliation from the unions; standing down these workers without pay would destroy the chances of defeating the pilots. The government had insisted that it would not pay compensation to the airlines, but a formal request for 'appropriate assistance' arrived at the

Cartoon satirising three key players in the pilots' strike: Bill Kelty, Bob Hawke, Sir Peter Abeles.

end of August. Ansett claimed to be losing $2 million per day, with a combined total loss of $50 million. On 6 September, Hawke announced that he was not compensating airlines, but was going to 'recompense' them for the 20,000 ground staff. This was confirmed by Cabinet on 12 September and backdated to 28 August.[342]

Despite the promise of 'recompense', the airlines did begin standing down ground staff and flight attendants without pay. Kelty managed to force the airlines to put workers on long service leave and pay them, but that was only for two weeks and covered just 60 percent of workers. The rest, including catering staff, were not covered at all. There were no deals for the thousands of workers or businesses in tourism.

Flight attendants were becoming increasing unhappy with the way they were being treated – particularly the use of overseas attendants to fly with the scab pilots. A meeting of FAAA members on 8 September saw motions that appeared to support the pilots, but nothing happened. Dissent within the ACTU and union movement more generally was rising. Two weeks before the biennial ACTU Congress in Sydney, eight unionists, including Martin Ferguson (the proposed successor to Simon Crean), issued a statement.[343] They declared that individual contracts, the refusal to recognise the Federation and the use of sanctions were in direct conflict with ACTU policy and had no place in Australia's industrial relations system. The AMWU's John Halfpenny described the use of the RAAF as a 'very dangerous thing' and refused to fly on the strike-breaking planes with scab pilots. All the unionists rejected the 29.47 percent claim, but they knew that others in the industry had won payouts well above the standard Accord deal.[344]

Even some on the right of the union movement, such as John Maynes from the Federated Clerks Union (FCU), criticised government use of the Airforce and opposed the encouragement of common law action by employers. Frank Belan, from the NSW FSPU, met with Kelty and wrote to the government, angry that employer reaction meant that: 'The pilots' strike has virtually ruled out industrial action. Every time we have some piddly little dispute we find ourselves in court.'[345]

Within the Labor Party, the Left issued a statement, signed by WA's Pat Giles and Victoria's Kim Carr, backing the eight unions in opposing individual contracts and sanctions against trade unions. None of these forces supported the pilots. The most they called for was a return to the AIRC to do deals 'consistent with other wage deals in the industry.' Neither the dissident unions nor the ALP Left was prepared to directly challenge the government, the ACTU leadership or the Accord itself. Hawke or Kelty dismissed the criticism, and Crean's opening address to the ACTU Congress began with an attack on the Federation. This was enough to cow Labor and union critics.

The question of pay and conditions for pilots in the industry was still in limbo. A case was finally heard on 29 September. The AIRC converted the airlines' individual contracts into legally binding awards. After minor changes, that was further ratified with an announced 6 percent pay rise, although the original contracts had stated the rise as 25 percent.[346] McCarthy's next move was to lodge a new log of claims on 4 October, expecting that the AIRC would find that a new dispute now existed. Maddern refused, dismissing AFAP's bid and telling them that, if they wanted to be part of the newly established award, they would have to drop their ban on pilots seeking re-employment, accept AIRC decisions and abide by national wage decisions. They could have no part in setting awards in the industry.

The ruling showed McCarthy the total failure of the AIRC process. The pilots still stood solidly behind the AFAP leadership and would not be going back. McCarthy was confident that the airlines would have to talk to them.

The companies weren't talking peace, hadn't let up on their legal threats and now prepared to go to court. While they dropped claims against 67 individual pilots charged at the beginning of the dispute, they sought from the Federation unspecified damages for the six days of the 9-to-5 campaign, inducing pilots to breach contracts, interference with trade and contractual relations and conspiracy to injure and intimidate. The government and airlines were sure that this would bankrupt the union and its leaders. McCarthy, though not optimistic, saw it as a way of swinging public opinion in AFAP's favour.

After a month of hearings in the Victorian Supreme Court, Judge Robert Brooking handed down a bombshell on 23 November. Brooking found for the airlines on interference of contractual relations, trade or business by unlawful means and conspiracy. He found that the Federation and six of its leaders were responsible for the 9-to-5 campaign, had set out to cause the airlines financial loss and knowingly induced breaches of contract and interference in trade. Irregularities in following union rules for stopwork meetings and other procedures were also charged against the union.

This shocking precedent was an attack on workers' ability to take industrial action. AFAP's Terry O'Connell described it as a 'horrendous day' for every trade unionist. He foreshadowed an immediate appeal.

The union movement was shocked to its core. It had comfortably stood aside and let the pilots fall on their sword, but this was a major threat to all unions. Kelty said:

> This is a matter of concern and about this issue the pilots have our support. That is, we are concerned to ensure that the use of damages is not used against any organisation, whether they be pilots, stewards or whatever.

The Victorian Trades Hall Council (VTHC) and a long line of officials, including the TWU's Ivan Hodgson, railed against the decision. These were unions that had done nothing to stand up for the pilots and even scabbed on the dispute. The ACTU had openly conspired to bring down the Federation. Now they were, rightly, opposing 'the provocative use' of common law and calling for a High Court challenge because the decision contravened various International Labour Organisation (ILO) conventions.

They would get no support from the government. IR Minister Morris appeared confused, claiming that all democratic countries had the right to strike, even though Australia did not! Hawke had never been confused, saying earlier:

> I say without equivocation, that when the airlines decided to initiate those legal processes with significantly very drastic financial penalties against individual pilots and their organisation, the airlines will be pursuing those legal processes with the full support of my Government.

Triumphant as the longest serving Prime Minister in his new, fourth term of office, Hawke did indicate some softening over the pilots – with breathtaking hypocrisy: 'At no point have I wanted to see the destruction of the AFAP. That would be anathema to my whole life, to talk about destroying a union.' His Cabinet vow to smash the BLF was clearly forgotten. Hawke claimed that, while it was okay for the airlines to seek damages from the union, he didn't want to see the airlines collect the money! Instead, it was a time for rebuilding, getting the airlines and union back together; he was, after all, a man of conciliation and consensus.

But the government, the ACTU and a number of unions had been totally complicit with the airlines in their attack on the AFAP, and now the union movement was to reap the whirlwind. On 12 February 1990, Brooking set damages of $6.5 million. Led by Ansett, the airlines showed some mercy, declaring that they would not recover damages from individuals. They did plan to collect $2 million in legal costs, and they reserved their decision on collecting the damages figure from the union. The strategy, drafted by Ansett, was again designed to maintain the pressure.

The AFAP was in dire straits. It represented no employed airline pilots, was in no position to secure jobs for any of its loyal followers and now faced bankruptcy as a union, with legal fees alone $1.5 million.

Meanwhile, the original wages and conditions case limped through the courts, with demands and counter-demands from both sides. The November hearings had revealed that the AIRC considered the new award, granted on 29 September, to be only an interim award that was open to amendment. McCarthy argued to re-establish many of the old conditions in the award as a condition of any union agreement with the airlines. Nothing was resolved; the employers refused to move, and the AFAP still had conditions on its return.

After the damages decision, the Federation had no choice but to go, cap in hand, to the AIRC. On 12 February 1990, O'Connell filed an application which sought to make the union a party to the industrial awards of all domestic pilots. There would be no demands, and they would accept the Commission's decision, regardless of the outcome.[347] It took until 15 May for the AFAP to be fully reinstated, but by then the union was ravaged. About 700 pilots remained unemployed, while 600 had found work overseas.

It was a bitter end to the dispute, made all the more so by seeing Qantas pilots win an 18 percent rise in January 1990 and flight engineers granted a 24 percent rise through the AIRC a month or two later. More galling was watching the ACTU abandon the centralised industrial relations system in September 1990, declare the AIRC irrelevant and begin the shift to Enterprise Bargaining – precisely what the pilots had been attempting.

It was a dark lesson for all unionists. Journalist Ross Gittins summed up the consequences for those stepping outside the system:

> The dark side of solidarism is that if you step out of line with your brothers, they look the other way while someone kicks you to death. First was the BLF; now it's the pilots. To Kelty, destruction of the pilots' union achieves two ends. It would avert a collapse of the centralised system as other powerful unions broke ranks. And it'd be an object lesson to any other union tempted to go for broke: Step outside the system and the tigers will devour you.[348]

CHAPTER 9

Then There Were Three

Three critical battles by workers were part of the ongoing resistance to the Accord: Cockatoo Island in 1989; CRA–Weipa in 1990; and the Australian Pulp and Paper Mill (APPM) in 1992. The Accord processes and Labor's anti-union laws gave the bosses weapons in the industrial battles, and union officials, wedded to the Accord, undermined workers' struggle at every point.

Workers at Cockatoo Island saw their struggle as inspiring others to resist. Claude Sandaljian, chair of the combined shop committee, reflected on the occupation 25 years later:

> Unless you get national strikes, you're not going to win; eventually they're going to get you. But the idea was, we're not the only ones, we're just the first ones – others are going to come ... Every time they announce a closure then they'll have a major strike against them. Unfortunately, it didn't happen, but that was the idea.[349]

Like the deregistration of the BLF, this defeat of militant maritime and manufacturing workers would have a chilling effect on worker militancy throughout the workforce. Union leaderships, who felt the chill winds of fines most and held to their Accord commitments, were crucial in policing and containing the militancy of their members.

The second example was an attack on workers at the CRA–Rio Tinto Weipa bauxite (aluminium) mining site. This large multinational company embarked on a clear union-busting strategy, engaging consultants to help it map out its tactics in its operations at its aluminium ore and smelting sites in NZ, Bell Bay and Weipa. Only at Weipa did workers make a stand.

Bruce Hearn Mackinnon delivered a damning assessment of the unions during these battles with CRA-Rio Tinto:

> Finally, in all cases under examination, management's strength and decisiveness was met by hesitant, disorganised and ultimately poor leadership from the unions. In all the Australian cases, the main union was the moderate AWU, which never at any stage demonstrated a coherent strategy of union resistance. Only at Weipa—and even there, far too late—did the union movement, in this case led by the CFMEU, mount a serious challenge to the company's agenda. In the coal industry, CRA–Rio Tinto attempted to implement its individual contracts system, but was largely stymied, by a more strategic, resilient and committed union, the CFMEU, demonstrating that unions' destiny does not have to be shaped by the state, the wider environment, or management strategy, but rather they can be masters, to some extent, of their own futures.[350]

Finally, the APPM dispute flared up in Tasmania. APPM's Burnie mill appeared in the news in April 1992, becoming the battleground over workers' so-called 'restrictive work practices', accused of holding up the company's competitiveness and survival. Actually, employers were using the Accord's industrial tools, such as non-union agreements, to re-establish managerial prerogative, break down conditions and sideline unions.

Despite its location in Australia's southernmost island, APPM was not some isolated company. It was a key part of the Peko-Wallsend stable – owners of Robe River mine and instigators of the attack on mine workers there in 1986. APPM management took the first step in its confrontationist strategy, but workers shared strategy and tactics too, building on the experience of Robe River workers.[351]

Cockatoo Island

'That's it, it's finished.' Bill Kelty delivered the grim news to the Cockatoo Island Dockyard workers in 1987. There would be no more ships built at what was once the largest and most important shipbuilding and repair site in Australia. The government's 'Two Oceans' policy, moving shipbuilding and repair to WA, meant that almost 2,000 workers would lose their jobs. Because of its prime position in Sydney Harbour, Packer and other moguls circled like vultures as the government slated Cockatoo Island (Aboriginal name 'Wareamah') for sale to private owners in 1992.[352]

Four years earlier, campaigning to win workers to the Accord and a Labor government, Bob Hawke promised that a new naval supply ship would be built at Cockatoo Island. Within months of the election, he reneged; there'd be no second ship after the *HMAS Success* was completed in 1984. One thousand dockyard workers marched on parliament in Canberra on 7 December 1983. They were met by a line of cops. They pushed through that barricade to find that no one from the ALP would come out and talk to them. Painters and Dockers' Bob Galleghan angrily commented: 'we got nothing, what's the point of coming down here?' With no concessions from Labor, unions believed that they had time to build a fight and gain support from other unions. The workforce had a militant history of industrial campaigns, and Cockatoo had been a dockyard since 1850, so history was on its side.[353]

Although closure seemed inevitable, the workforce took industrial action. Dockyards around the country had seen regular retrenchments, but the thinking at Cockatoo was always to get the jobs back when work increased again. Sandaljian, the Boilermakers' shop steward, explains:

> When they opened the books again, the priority was rehiring the people who'd been retrenched ... There were people who were old and couldn't do anything, but our position was that they had to come back. Only then could the company employ whoever else they wanted.

This time was different; everyone was going to be sacked. For the first time ever, the unions took action for severance pay. After a couple of weeks, they won a 26-week redundancy payout.

CFMEU national president John Maitland addresses Weipa strikers' meeting. Photo courtesy CFMEU.

The next shock came when one worker saw a real estate advertisement in the *Sydney Morning Herald* for the sale of Cockatoo Island in 1989. The workers had received no notice that a sale was imminent. The shop committee sent a delegation to see the minister responsible, Kim Beazley, who said: 'I've got dockyards coming out of my ears. You're finished.'

'That's when the idea of the fight for the jobs started', Sandaljian says. 'You fight anybody who's going to cut your jobs.' They decided that the only option was an industrial dispute to keep the shipyard open. Cockatoo had had plenty of strikes before, but a strike alone would not be enough this time:

> I said that the only way we're going to stop every bastard working is to occupy the island. We can't put picket lines and all that rubbish ... It's a war; we took it as a war, that's it.

Everyone had to be on side, including the Island's white-collar workers, who had never struck before. Sandaljian had the job of getting them in this one. He said to their delegate:

> All of our jobs are on the line; you can't fight on your own,
> and if you stay here there's going to be a lot of shemozzles …
> Try to convince your people to come to the mass meeting.

The meeting was the key; he had the numbers, and the white-collar workers would be bound by any decision the meeting took if he could get them there. They came down the hill to the shipyard hangar at the island's edge, where mass meetings were held. The vote to occupy was carried, but the occupation didn't start immediately. The time to move came in May.[354] A routine navy manoeuvre in north Queensland meant that a ship and three submarines would be in dock at Cockatoo Island. On 10 May, Sandaljian went to see the Painter and Dockers' delegate and said: 'Today we're going to call a mass meeting and occupy.'

After the mass meeting, they explained the changed situation to the bosses: 'Your Island is under occupation.' When Sandaljian rang his union organiser, telling him: 'Listen Pat [Johnson], we've occupied the island', Johnson exploded. The ACTU and NSW TLC carried token motions of support, but no one from the ACTU visited. 'The only people who came were the Trades and Labour Council, and after two weeks they told us to go back to work and we tossed them out.'

That night was the first of a strike and occupation that lasted 14 weeks. It was organised entirely by the island's rank and file through the shop committee. One worker recalled that they:

> first seized the administration block and fanned out across
> the island to take control of the entire installation. By the
> end of the process the workers not only held sway over
> the workshops and dry docks but were in control of two
> submarines and a navy supply vessel *Jervis Bay*. For the first
> time in Australian history 300 armed forces personnel were
> forced to evacuate a defence installation on Australian soil.[355]

Weipa strikers' picket line. Photo courtesy CFMEU.

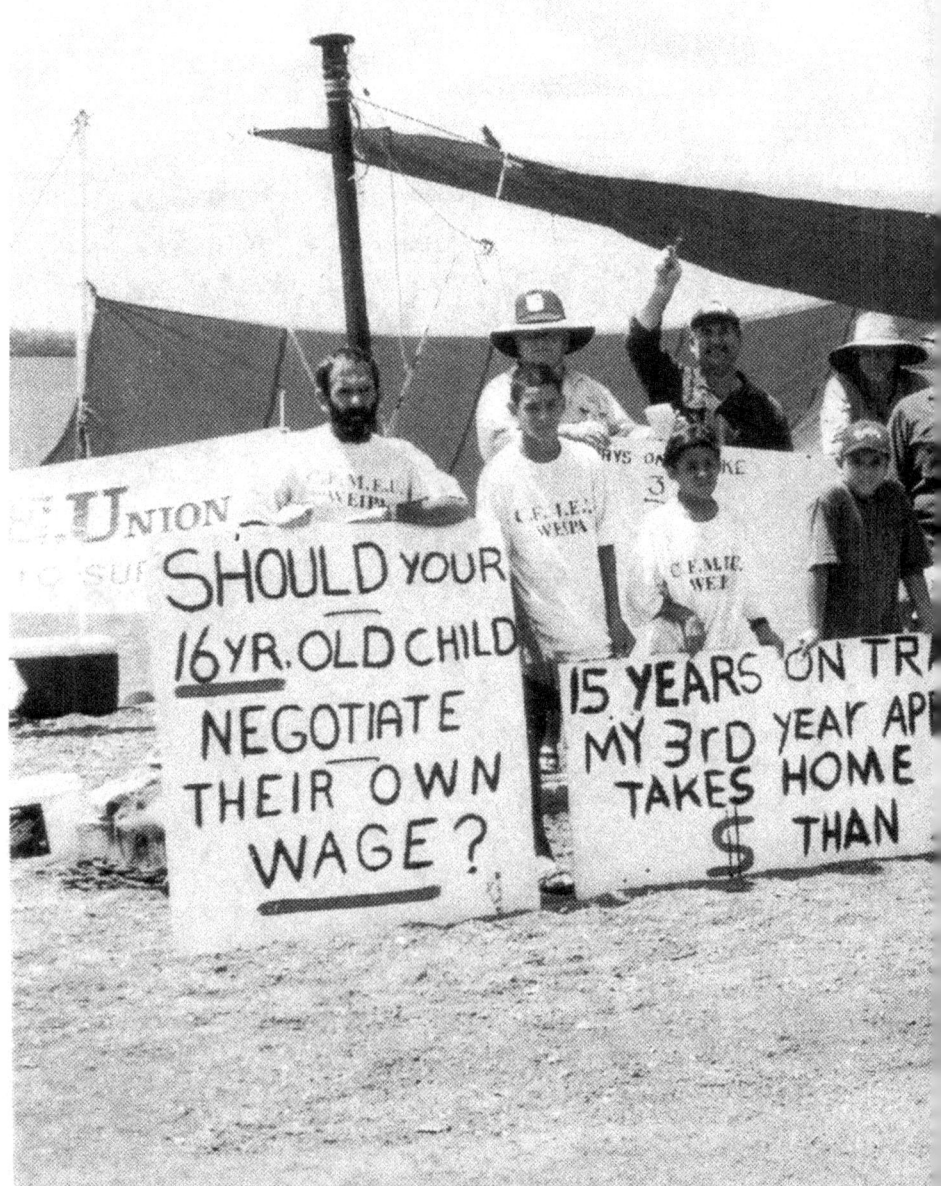

Weipa strikers at Evans Landing picket. Photo courtesy CFMEU.

The full workforce of 1,600 couldn't be maintained on the Island, so a roster ensured that at least 100–150 were always there. They slept on the floor of the island's offices: 'It wasn't a five star hotel, it's very cold … we survived just like everyone else.' Important gestures, from day one, were to keep a fire burning on the island – a beacon for those onshore and passing ships – and to fly the Eureka and Aboriginal flags as reminders for everyone that the fight continued.

Sandaljian describes the organisation that was required, including basics like keeping the fire alight and the site clean: 'There were people to provide food, people to provide the booze, people who went around giving speeches, people in the office answering the phone, talking to people who need their rent paid.' Musicians and entertainers kept morale up, showing solidarity, and a goat called Beazley served as a mascot.

Workers went out collecting:

> We started spreading around asking for contributions to the strike. We organised what we called the bucket collection. Twenty people used to go around the city with signs that said 'Cockatoo' and collect support. We got it.

The TLC was targeted too. Sandaljian told them, 'You go downstairs of the Labour Council and every time some bastard comes down you get some money off them.'

Money to support the occupation came from workplaces across the country, mostly 'big shops' in the mines and on the waterfront. 'Wherever we went, they'd give us money.' In week 10, a $25,000 cheque from Queensland miners significantly extended the life of the strike. Collecting on the streets brought financial and moral support from passers-by. On one collection outside NSW Parliament House, a worker noted:

> It's not only Cockatoo we're fighting for, we're fighting for everybody's job, everybody's right to have a job, where they want to … They're [people in the street] telling us 'Don't give up. Stick it up the bastards.'

Weipa strikers launch a floating picket. Photo courtesy CFMEU.

Protests in the city often included members of other unions, from the BLF (even though deregistered) to public sector workers. All recognised that, if Cockatoo workers lost their jobs, many more would 'go down the gurgler' too.

Union officials and the NSW TLC regularly tried to undermine and stop the occupation. Initially, the ACTU and the TLC backed the workers, but that became open opposition, while the Hawke government threatened fines and deregistration.

Towards the end of the dispute, a 'Day of Outrage' was called after the TLC voted down an attempt to call a 24-hour general strike. While dockyard workers and their supporters were out the front, TLC officials locked themselves on the top floor of the Sussex Street headquarters. On the street, workers heard speakers condemning Hawke, Defence Minister Kim Beazley, the ACTU and the TLC. Workers found an open fire door and marched up to the floor below the TLC officials; meanwhile, police attacked those remaining in Sussex Street, where a fight started by a plain clothes police provocateur gave uniformed police an excuse to move in. Targeted arrests saw six leaders of the strike committee pulled away by police, to face trial later on trumped up charges.

At the last mass meeting, the 93rd day 'on the grass', union leaders warned strikers that they were open to fines under section 45D of the *Trade Practices*

Weipa picketers celebrate CRA backdown. Photo courtesy CFMEU.

Act. Bob Galleghan defiantly replied that anyone with a s.45D fine could stand on the end of the line with all the other creditors to the union.[356]

Lacking industrial support from NSW union leaders, Cockatoo Island workers were forced to end the occupation. Sandaljian knew early on that they couldn't save the dockyard, but hoped that the strike would spread. 'The decision to go back was not very nice, but what are you going to do, you're finished.' Nonetheless, workers won a better deal than they had at the start of the strike. And the land was turned into a public park and historic site, now enjoyed by many, not exclusively by rich buyers. Politically, the workers exposed the true ruthlessness of Hawke and his mates. One worker commented: 'We've got a Labor government federally and in some states and the capitalist class is not one jot concerned … The Labor government simply runs the system in the interests of the capitalist class.'

At the end, the shop committee wrote a statement to be published in union newsletters. Union leaders rejected it, as they had all material during the occupation. The last paragraphs read:

We will leave Cockatoo Island with our heads held high
and we will continue to struggle in other workplaces to
bring about better working conditions and a better union
which is accountable to its members and not to the
Labor government.

One striking feature of the occupation was the combined shop stewards' committee. There were 22 unions altogether, but most were covered by the FIA, Federated Ship Painters and Dockers (FSP&D), Boilermakers and Engineering sections of the AMWU and the WWF. During the whole dispute, the combined shop stewards' Committee ran their own militant campaign, often defying their leaders. They won support from passers-by on the street, from the deregistered BLF and from fellow unionists. But in the face of opposition from government, the ACTU, the NSW TLC and many of the union leaders (their own and others), without mass industrial action from the rest of the country's workers, they could not win. While they went down fighting, extracting concessions such as a better redundancy deal, many never worked again despite promises of jobs at the Garden Island facility.[357]

Cockatoo workers could not save their jobs. They are remembered for keeping Cockatoo public, for showing how to fight and for clearly identifying their enemies.

CRA–Rio Tinto

Quietly watching Robe River's union-busting endeavours, CRA–Rio Tinto was gearing up to do the same thing. From the mid-1970s, under chair Sir Roderick Carnegie, management consciously developed specific strategies and tactics to deunionise its operations, while insisting that they considered all workers the same and were not union-busters. At Rio Tinto's bauxite and aluminium arm, Comalco, Tony Filmer asserted: 'Union membership is a private issue of no concern to us. I presume that some of our employees are union members. That's their right.'[358]

Management nonetheless argued that individual contracting was the only way to increase productivity and cut costs. Comalco managing director Karl Stewart made it clear, as early as the mid-1980s, that 'the real gains in cost competitiveness would come when the entire workforce of the organisation was behaving in a way which was demonstrably much more committed to the objectives of the organisation.' Under collective agreements, said the company, workers were paid for their time; with contracts, they were paid for their work. Management was enthusiastic about contract workers: 'it is both expected and demonstrated that people seek to – wherever they can – in fact work themselves out of work.' That the workforce did seek this is highly unlikely, but the company certainly helped by regularly sacking workers while amassing significant profits from individual contracting.

Rio Tinto enacted these strategies – and won each time – at its NZ Aluminium Smelter (NZAS), Hamersley Iron mine and Bell Bay smelter. Workers at Weipa, however, would win a war of attrition, forcing the company to accommodate collective bargaining.

The company launched its deunionisation campaign in a supportive climate. A new right wing government, new legislation which seriously weakened union rights, and falling commodity prices enabled the company to move on its Tiwai Point smelter workforce in NZ. A five-year restructuring program began in 1986. The site had a 20-year history of collective bargaining, negotiated through a single union bargaining unit, but the company reversed previous practice in 1988 by offering staff higher wages than the union workforce, considerably weakening the union position. By 1990, divisions within the unions, the loss of local union leadership and a refusal to take industrial action in the face of management intransigence led to acceptance of this second-rate deal. The national *Employment Contracts Act 1991* abolished awards and compulsory unionism. Over that year, NZAS bypassed the union to bring in contractors, offering individual contracts and voluntary redundancies. Refusing to take industrial action, despite members' initial rejection of management offers, the union lost all legitimacy and effectively collapsed.

At Hamersley Iron, in WA's Pilbara region, a change in management attitudes was largely economic. Japan's steel industry was then Australia's major iron ore market. When it forecast easing, which was likely to drive down commodity prices, every resource company tried to lower costs. Mackinnon explains that CRA, Hamersley Iron and Comalco stressed the economic imperatives driving CRA's strategy across its operations: 'The only means of gaining a competitive advantage in the resource sector is through cost effectiveness and reliability ... Our competitiveness depends almost exclusively on controlling costs.'

This would involve a major restructure, job cuts, and lower wages and conditions – as it had in NZ. The workforce was fully unionised, with compulsory unionism, or closed shops, built into collective agreements from the 1970s throughout the Pilbara. Even the election of the conservative Court government in 1979, which removed many union rights and banned compulsory unionism clauses, did not stop Hamersley Iron effectively honouring the closed shop throughout the 1980s.

Things changed suddenly in 1992. Phillip Beales, a mechanical fitter, was not a member of the Metal and Engineering Workers' Union (MEWU). The company would not force Beales to join the union or dismiss him. The union called a strike for 17 June; Beales and two others scabbed. Unsurprisingly, the WA Industrial Commission ordered the union back to work on 18 June, but a mass meeting on 20 June voted to stay on strike. In the following week, 14 crossed the picket line at the Tom Price mine, while 2,000 stayed out.

Hamersley hand delivered a letter on 26 June, informing the unions[359] that they and the striking workers would be liable for damages over the loss of sales of 1,465 million tonnes of iron ore and incurred shipping penalties, a total cost of $45 million.

Union officials recommended a return to work on 29 June, and the 2,000 went back. But on the day they returned, Hamersley filed a writ against the unions and their officials in the Supreme Court, seeking damages of almost $49 million and unspecified damages – the largest common law action ever taken against a union at the time. Hamersley also sought an injunction against future strikes over Beales' continuing employment on site, a move strongly opposed by the unions. Undermining the unions' case that there was no precedent for such action, the employers found that Victorian courts in 1976 had successfully stopped workers' action over a similar incident.[360] The WA judge used it to rule in favour of Hamersley's injunction.

The company swiftly sacked several union militants – claiming that they had harassed scabs. They refused all but formal contact with unions and abolished staff-award distinctions allowing management and professional staff to do award employees' work. Undermining the unions further, management then agreed to an enterprise-based wage increase for all workers.

On 7 December, the company announced a 13 percent job cuts program, to get rid of the 'hard men' in the unions. If 'voluntary' redundancy failed, the unions were told, these workers would be retrenched anyway. The backbone of union militancy was broken; by the end of 1993, Hamersley was effectively deunionised.

Any remaining protection workers had in collective agreements was wiped out in February 1993, when a new Liberal government in WA introduced the option of individual agreements for all workers in its *Workplace Agreements Act*. By the end of 1993, around 90 percent of Hamersley workers had signed individual agreements, with the promise of a wage increase, improved security, and access to the company's health care scheme and its staff superannuation scheme.

At the same time, CRA–Rio Tinto targeted its aluminium smelter at Bell Bay in Tasmania. A low-key announcement by management that it would no longer enable payroll deductions for union membership started the attack The company then refused to negotiate an enterprise agreement with the union throughout 1992, even after the union agreed to withdraw its officials and installed union members as their negotiating team. In 1993, the company jumped onto the bandwagon of non-union enterprise agreements introduced by federal Labor – the Enterprise Flexibility Agreement. The company deal included some conditions available to 'staff', with an option of going straight onto individual agreements. Workers rejected the deal, 83 percent voting against. During 1993 and 1994, the company constantly told the AIRC that only direct negotiations with workers was an option. These tactics successfully delayed a new enterprise agreement for two and a half years. Faced with individual agreements as the only option, all but 22 of the company's 430 workers had signed up and left the union by 1 July 1994. Despite union appeals to the Commission and hearings in the Federal Industrial Relations Court and High Court, the decision finally handed down in May 1996 gave the case to the employer. The unions had taken no industrial action!

CRA (as Comalco) was now ready to act at the huge bauxite mine in Weipa, the third biggest in the world. In the face of CRA–Rio Tinto's three earlier victories, the ACTU's Bill Kelty famously drew a 'line in the sand' in a desperate bid to hold Weipa as a union site, after 78 members of one union finally went on strike in 1995.

Comalco had already started to act against the unions in 1991, cutting training and overtime pay and undermining conditions. The company and the AWU then did a deal which gave that union primary membership rights at the site, effectively shutting out the more militant CFMEU.[361] In mid-1992, the Weipa Industrial Site Committee (WISC) began negotiations with management at the nearby Kaolin operations. At the same time, management was directly contacting the blue-collar workforce and offering clerical staff individual contracts. By January 1993, all staff had switched over to contracts. Now the precedent had been set and the employer's hand strengthened.

Initially, blue-collar workers at Kaolin approved a draft agreement, subject to union acceptance. The AWU took from April to September 1993 to reject the deal, but had no plan to tackle the company's preferred option of individual contracts. The company began offering these in October. In November, when most Kaolin workers rejected individual contracts, the unions struck for six days. The company response was to delay responding to the unions and continue to offer slightly amended individual contracts directly to the workforce.

Instead of taking further industrial action, the unions applied to the Commission in May 1994 for a paid rates award that would be higher than the individual contracts. Comalco outmanoeuvred them, winning approval for two minimum rates awards for Kaolin and Weipa instead of a paid rates award. The unions agreed, and the Commission approved the new awards on 4 August 1994. Comalco was now free to offer workers the individual contracts because they were higher – up to $20,000 more – than the awards. Realising their blunder, the unions went back to the Commission, led by the AWU. Their appeal failed. The court-based campaign had been a total disaster; union membership fell dramatically, most workers were on contracts, and those few still on awards received lower pay and conditions. The employer had the upper hand.

Seventy-five die-hard CFMEU members who had refused to accept individual contracts and were on the 1994 minimum rates award, doing exactly the same work, turned the situation around. On 13 October 1995, they launched strike action. 'It was all to do with equal pay for equal work', explained Nigel Gould, CFMEU Weipa lodge secretary.[362] Workers were attempting to defend their conditions, he added: 'Those conditions were hard fought for by unionists, our forefathers and we weren't gonna let them down.' The strikers set up Weipa's first ever picket, a vehicle blockade on Mission River bridge, which linked the town to the mine. When management ferried non-union workers across the river to the mine, the unionists devised another strategy:

> Well, the WISC – that's all the unions combined – we had our think tank there ... working out where are the company's weak spots, where are their vulnerabilities? And where was our expertise? And of course, we love our fishing up here! So we decided to hit their hip pocket. Of course, if they can't get the ore out, they can't make any money!

Shifting the focus squarely onto the company's revenue, they set up a blockade of small boats, a floating picket aimed at the tugs and pilot boats servicing the huge ore freighters docked at Weipa's port. For weeks, the strikers risked not only arrest but their lives, ducking and weaving their small, aluminium boats ('tinnies') around the colossal bulk carriers. Comalco went to the courts, seeking writs for damages, but the dispute was taken out of the company's hands when maritime and coal workers around the country answered Weipa's union calls for solidarity. 'They were inspirational', according to Nigel. 'The coal workers were the ones that led ... They were the ones who said, right, we're not gonna let our comrades be screwed.'

More than 2,000 unionists at Blair Athol and Tarong coal mines in Queensland, along with the Dalrymple Bay coal-loading terminal, walked out on 8 November for 24 hours. Next day, maritime workers aboard the *River Embley*, a bulk carrier stuck at the Weipa port, stopped work for 24 hours. By 10 November, 3,000 workers at CRA's coal and coke works throughout Queensland and NSW were on the grass.

Disregarding company threats, the unions were 'as determined as ever', said WISC secretary Wayne Holmquist. Port workers refused to handle any CRA export coal, and the union launched a three-day general strike on 15 November. The CFMEU announced a seven-day nationwide coal strike on the same day, to begin the following week. Other support flooded in. From Bougainville, where CRA had the huge Freeport Copper Mine, the

Bougainville Freedom Movement sent a solidarity message. Local Aboriginal people whose land stolen had been stolen by CRA also backed the strikers. Ordinary people around the country, even pensioners, sent money and poems, and one interstate supporter videoed himself singing a song he'd written for the strikers.[363] The ACTU announced that unions were ready to take action against CRA in other industries – including manufacturing, power, oil, gas and transport. Nigel was thrilled by this unexpected level of support: 'Even the not so active unions said, OK, this is the line in the sand, we're all gonna get behind you.'

Weipa was national news. With the mining and maritime unions ramping up their actions, and the shipping and stevedoring employers heading to the courts, the ACTU was forced to get behind them. On 13 November, Secretary Bill Kelty said, 'These are heroes these people at Weipa … because they have said … on behalf of working people in this country, we won't have a bar of individual contracts.'[364]

Kelty, backed by the MUA and CFMEU officials, hypocritically expressed desperation after the numerous union defeats (many engineered by Kelty himself), insisting: 'We won't be beaten, we can't be beaten. For us to be beaten is for the Union Movement to lose its heart, its soul and its purpose.'

On 17 November – day 36 of the Weipa workers' strike – there was a national maritime strike, an approaching national coal strike and a slated ACTU meeting to discuss spreading the campaign to other industries. By 19 November, 25,000 coal miners were out across the country, costing the bosses an estimated $20 million per day. Enthusiasm for the strike was so great that 2,000 coal miners across six mines walked off the job 30 hours early.

All this was soon dissipated, the momentum lost, as the ACTU ordered maritime workers back to work and put all other actions on hold from 19 November. They returned to the disastrous court strategy, the one that had weakened the unions, caused two years of delay and returned the advantage to Comalco. ACTU Assistant Secretary Tim Pallas had earlier appealed to the Labor government to 'abide by its Accord commitments to stop the use of non-union agreements which de-unionise existing workplaces.'[365] The government did intervene, persuading the company to drop the millions of dollars in damages claims, but the parties returned to a compulsory AIRC conference on 20 November with former Prime Minister Bob Hawke as the ACTU advocate.

In the end, the Weipa workers did win what they were after – 'equal pay for equal work', back pay and the right to negotiate collective agreements through the unions – but at a cost. The award and contract conditions were equalised, enforcing 12-hour contracts; within a year, Comalco was again trying to compel workers to sign individual enterprise agreements. This time, unionists went out immediately, leaving management no option but to withdraw the demand within two days and negotiate a collective enterprise agreement.[366]

The Weipa workers revived union militancy across the country for a moment in time, with a return to 'old school' unionism. They struck, setting up pickets and calling for solidarity – and getting it. In 2015, at a reunion marking the twentieth anniversary of the strike, one recalled: 'It was the best seven weeks of my life. The unity … having control over something. It wasn't just about us, it was about the future generation.'

Within two years, union membership had doubled from 78 to 150. One of those rejoining was Mal Loftes, a truck driver who had been praised by John Howard for being the voice of the future. In 1997, facing the insecurity of yearly renewals, six-monthly assessments and no guarantee of pay rises for those on contracts, Loftes admitted: 'Without the backing of the union, then you really are heads in the chopper.'[367]

Australian Pulp and Paper Mill

The APPM dispute was a 'microcosm of 1990s industrial conflict with large companies attempting to re-establish managerial prerogative through litigation and unions seeing the fight as one of survival.'[368]

APPM began the confrontation, arming itself with some of the most ideological of North Broken Hill–Peko's managers. In 1991, former Robe River CEO Herb Larratt was brought in; this was the man who told a Mining Conference that 'every worker should go to work each day expecting to be sacked.'[369] With La Rat – as the workers called him – were other management hit men, including Chris Oldfield, publicity agent and member of the HR Nicholls Society, to whose audience he boasted in March 1992 about the company's ambitions, long-term planning to achieve change in a hurry and determination to do whatever it took to increase profitability in a tightening market:

We spent about a year going around all our sites, having a look at where we believe we could do better ... we then took a legal look and decided what things we could do legally and what we couldn't do, and what was discretionary. The decision was made that we would give 30 days' notice to our unions on 3rd March this year [1992] that we would withdraw from all over-award agreements with four exceptions.

Although confident that the workforce would sign over, Oldfield effectively admitted that they didn't dare drop the industry standards of a 25 percent over-award payment, the 35-hour week, superannuation and redundancy payments.[370]

After announcing their non-negotiable changes, management refused to meet with the ACTU. When President Martin Ferguson came down to address two-hour stopwork meetings at the end of March, the company threatened workers with loss of pay and disciplinary action if they attended them. They threatened to take damages action against the ACTU for any signs on site advertising the meetings.

Oldfield held multiple onsite meetings and used the media to put the company case. He had reason to think that workers would accept the deal. Chris Northover, the pulp and paper workers' federal secretary, described the union role in APPM before the dispute erupted: 'In the past five years the most radical work changes in the company's history have occurred – demarcation, flexibility, training, multi-skilling and manning levels have been or are being addressed.' Since 1987, 300 jobs had gone – with the cooperation of the union leadership. The CFMEU's Shane Murphy admitted that unions were prepared to accept the shutdown of two of APPM's three mills, if the company would sit down and 'be bloody honest.'[371]

This time, however, the unions' first response was to oppose APPM, taking the company to the AIRC on 6 March 1992. The unions' application to retain conditions was dismissed, then revived later in the month, seemingly as a result of intervention by federal IR Minister Peter Cook.

On the eve of the notice period's end, Oldfield flatly denied any provocation on the part of the company, insisting that their pronouncements 'are honest and we have told people what we are doing and then individual workers can make up their own minds as to what they want to do tomorrow.' CEO Peter Wade emphasised the problems APPM was facing: falling paper prices, tariff cuts and rising labour costs. 'We must change the culture. We want to give management and employees the freedom to work together.'[372]

The unions were not persuaded. Bob Richardson, ACTU organiser, responded: 'What it's about is that they want to run the place as they see fit whether workers agree or not.'

The first flare-up came on 9 April 1992. Management directed boiler operators to train staff to operate the boilers, effectively enabling future strike breaking. The 11 FEDFA members refused, citing safety issues, and were sacked on the spot. Other unionists refused to work until the FEDFA workers were reinstated, and safety pickets were set up outside the plant.[373]

Oldfield freely admitted to the HR Nicholls Society that APPM had ordered 6,000 tonnes of paper from the USA to back up their inventory in preparation for prolonged industrial action. When it arrived on 16 April, pulp mill workers rallied at the wharves but were unsuccessful in preventing its unloading. Eight were arrested for trespass. In a rare victory for workers, the AIRC directed the company to reinstate FEDFA members, but they also ordered an end to the strike.

After weeks of provocation and in contravention of AIRC orders, on 11 May the company directed FEDFA boiler operators to attend a 'train the trainer' TAFE course. The operators refused and occupied the boiler room. APPM called the police to end the occupation. Five workers were arrested for trespass on 12 May, causing the rest of the workforce to strike and establish a 24-hour picket line at the site's thirteen gates.[374]

Life on the picket lines in Burnie's winter was cold and wet, but support was growing. Strikers were determined to stay because, one striker noted, more and more people were realising that this was about the right to have a trade union. They also organised several noisy rallies and marches through the town. Throughout May, APPM orchestrated a number of attempts to break the picket line: managers driving trucks up to the line, ordering apprentices to work, and threatening others with the sack. Far from being intimidated by APPM's provocative attacks, including bringing in six karate-trained security guards, workers became more determined. Unionist Eric

Robertson, 30 years in the mill, said: 'It's all or nothing. But we will stay out as long as it takes.'[375]

Workers at APPM had been expecting such a move by the company, and they were more prepared to fight this time. Over 1988 and 1989, reciprocal visits occurred between WA unionists involved with the Robe River dispute, NBH–Peko workers at Pasminco and APPM in Tasmania. Robe River workers gave invaluable advice about building support, based on their own experience – in particular, how to involve the wives and families of the striking unionists.

So, on the first day of the dispute, Mike Grey (FEDFA) and shop stewards Norm Britton and Ken Fraser spoke with Helen Britton and Julie Fraser about the urgency for the families' participation. The following day, 40 women came together to discuss action. Some joined the Relief Fund Committee, distributing food and money to those in need. The Support Pulp Employees Committee (SPEC) involved 16 wives of striking mill workers, producing a regular newsletter, *SPEC NEWS*, to spread information about the strike and unions and raise general community awareness. It also provided support for women, encouraged women's involvement in the pickets, organised child care and delivered morale-boosting entertainment to the picketers and their families.[376]

The picket lines usually involved around 300 unionists and up to 60 women during the day. Some women attended for five to eight hours a day, picketing for at least six days each week. Mike Grey referred to the picketers as a 'community of families', and picketer Bruce Roberts penned a poem including women's lines: 'and when you strike, we strike together, and when they sack you, they sack me.'

Burnie Police Inspector Roy Fox commented:

> generally speaking, the women were more strongly opposed to the entry of the strike-breakers than the men. The men were still determined but were not as vocal … The women's input into the picket lines far outweighed their numbers.

Within Burnie, widespread support came from shop owners and other local businesses for the women's support groups. Around the country, support came from unionists. The ACTU set up a $6 million fighting fund, and even the local branch of the police union donated $10,000, indicating the close community ties in Burnie and the dilemma for management and the government. This was also a potential danger for workers; if they became too reliant on the police support, they would not be prepared for the government to bring in police from other jurisdictions.

The federal and state governments supported the workers initially, with federal Labor seeing the company's moves as a 'New Right' threat to the Accord. Tasmania's Liberals were more concerned about an electoral backlash if they were seen as too close to APPM.

However, Premier Ray Groom withdrew support on 4 June, after the Supreme Court ruled the picket lines illegal and ordered police to break them up. The picket line stood firm against two police attempts to break through, but at the 3pm afternoon shift changeover, another 50 police from Launceston and other regions arrived. What followed became known as the Battle of Burnie. *Age* reporter Andrew Darby described the roar as strikers pushed against police:

> Their roar was mixed with screams and cries of people being trodden on, being squashed and infuriated. Burly strikers were flung away from a police wedge protecting a handful of strike-breakers. Push came to shove in the APPM dispute.[377]

Charges of assault, striking, spitting and obstruction were laid against 41 arrested unionists but were later dropped because the Burnie police refused to proceed with what they considered 'minor' infractions.

Undeterred, even more picketers turned up for the next 24 hours. The few scabs who got through the gates were sent home 'sick' after only two hours on the job. Other unions began turning up the heat on APPM. The TWU banned shipment of paper from the company's mainland depots, and the miners' union declared a 24-hour solidarity strike. Christmas trees began appearing on picket lines, an indication of the mill workers' resolve.

At the instigation of Premier Ray Groom and federal IR Minister Peter Cook, the AIRC called a compulsory conference. The industrial relations machine began to grind out a secret deal. Amid Commissioner Paul Munro's threats of penal sanctions, massive fines and deregistration, the full terms of the settlement were concealed for three days until a six-page document was handed to strikers at their final meeting on 9 June.[378] Workers had two hours to decipher and vote on the agreement, an agreement that in the end contained little joy for the workforce. APPM Burnie's manager Ken Henderson boasted: 'the sky's the limit!' He claimed that the deal was better for the company than earlier rejected deals and assured the company of 'a demarcation-free workplace, employees are to work as directed, staff can operate the plant, set manning levels, freely use contractors and there will be no union veto of management decisions.'[379]

Unbelievably, the ACTU also claimed victory. As union bureaucrats focused on their role as brokers of labour, as the go-between agents of labour and capital, they claimed a win because the company was forced to negotiate with the unions. In the end, that was all the ACTU officials wanted. For them, the dispute was less about defending workers' rights and conditions, although the company's actions forced them to do more than just mouth platitudes; it was – as for all disputes and industrial issues since the 1983 signing of the Accord – about the best way to reform Australian capitalism to make it internationally competitive.

Bill Kelty argued that the deregulated NZ road was not the way forward. It would result in low wages rather than increased productivity and skills and higher wages, leading New Zealanders to a vicious downward economic spiral:

> All of this is not the real source of competition. The real source of what make countries comparatively stronger is basically how skilled their workforce is, how fast they adapt to technological change, how competitive they are in marketing.

According to the ACTU, this can only be achieved by consultation and cooperation between unions and management. Martin Ferguson made this quite clear at the beginning of the APPM dispute, when he called off the first solidarity action:

> efficiency of operation needs cooperation and goodwill ...
> Our strategy will not be about confrontation ... It is about a

new industrial relations culture, a culture based on changes in attitudes and a requirement by all of us to discuss matters rather than seek to provoke one another into confrontation.

The comment from one of the workers is more telling:

> What's the point of having discussions when they go behind your back and set the rules to suit themselves? The consultations, touted by the ACTU as a victory following the strike, are just window dressing. APPM tolerates them just to win back some of the damaging public relations it lost during the picket.[380]

CHAPTER 10

Workers' Capital? Superannuation and the Accord

The BWIU's Tom McDonald proudly proclaimed that, by winning superannuation for workers through the Accord processes, unions had created the biggest workers' cooperative in Australia's history.[381] Indeed, he thought: 'We might really have outdone Lenin.'[382]

It is doubtful that Lenin would have claimed superannuation for the workers' cause, given how thoroughly superannuation is enmeshed in the capitalist market. One of superannuation's strongest supporters, Treasurer Paul Keating, identified superannuation as a booster for capitalism. 'The real wealth is made in stockmarkets … We created a new model. Super was the flag carrier of the new turbo-charged capital markets.'[383]

Superannuation was not new to Australia, but it was not universal and only compulsory in the public sector. Private retirement funds were established by companies to reward employees, mostly white collar and management, for long periods of service. The employer usually paid. The first schemes were set up in the mid-1800s, predating the 1908 establishment of the national Age Pension.[384] Employer contributions to superannuation schemes were made tax deductible in 1915. Two federal Labor government attempts, in 1928 and 1938, to introduce a national superannuation scheme for all workers failed. The federal government did succeed in awarding its own employees superannuation in 1922, with contributions from both the public sector workers and government. The Chifley government made plans to introduce a national superannuation scheme, also bolstering the Age Pension through a National Welfare Fund. On succeeding Chifley, Liberal

PM Menzies used the Fund for other purposes and delayed any moves to set up national superannuation.[385] The 1890s Depression forced the closure of the NSW state scheme, but it was relaunched in 1916. Other states followed, with state teachers, railway, local government and utilities workers often having separate funds. Coal miners' funds, which covered retirement and disability, were standouts in terms of benefits.[386]

In the face of almost poverty level Age Pension rates and no Labor or union campaign to fundamentally lift the rate, some in the union movement saw industry-related superannuation as a way to secure a fairer retirement. The WWF reacted to the unstoppable shift to containerisation on the wharves and the resulting job losses in 1969, with National secretary Charlie Fitzgibbon arguing for superannuation and permanency, among other demands, in exchange for accepting containerisation. The union won, but not until their industrial power forced the employers' hand.

Winning superannuation for blue-collar workers was slow. By 1974, only 32 percent of all workers were covered.[387] Resistance came not only from employers; Tom McDonald found that workers in the 1970s had their reservations. Members at one meeting told him that they couldn't afford the 5 percent effective pay cut. Still, support grew. A survey in 1979 showed that

78 percent of workers considered retirement plans the most important of a range of extra employee conditions. At that time, 56 percent of all workers were covered, and 68 percent supported industrial action in this area, although union leaderships were reluctant to back the demand. In the 1970s, the ACTU saw superannuation as an economic right for all workers and supported campaigning for a national scheme.

The Whitlam government started the ball rolling with the Hancock National Superannuation Committee of Inquiry in 1973. Fraser refused to implement the Report's findings when it was handed down in 1976. By 1979, the ACTU had set up its own superannuation committee to coordinate and assist unions in their campaigns and to develop ACTU policy.[388]

The Accord changed the status of superannuation from a mainly professional and management benefit to a general workers' right, but for reasons other than protection of workers in retirement. Part of the neoliberal agenda of the Accord partners was the creation of a pool of funds for the country's 'nation building' projects, reducing reliance on local and overseas capital, and a shift to privatising retirement, placing retirement savings at the mercy of the market. For the Labor Party, Keating said: 'this involved an intellectual transition from retirement welfarism to a compulsory self-provision through the share market.'[389] For workers, it was a repudiation of their earlier victory, winning the Age Pension in 1908. The ACTU and unions led the move away from the demand for a universal, government-funded pension scheme, providing a decent retirement income for all.

Treasurer Keating and ACTU leader Bill Kelty single-mindedly pursued superannuation, with both still singing its praises today. According to Ian Silk, CEO of Australian Super, it:

> wasn't just visionary, it was incredibly courageous of Kelty because there were so many people in the union movement that said 'this is a load of bullshit' and he relentlessly pushed it through.'

Kelty was abetted by influential unionists Garry Weaven, Greg Sword and Simon Crean.[390] Australia Reconstructed, the ACTU and Trade department study tour of Western Europe in 1987, provided the economic and international case for the Accord partners to expand superannuation. The report noted that the overseas funds 'are channelled into domestic productive activity which creates not only current economic stability but builds on infrastructure capable of supporting a socially adequate standard of living.'[391] Others, such as the AMWU's Greg Harrison, saw universal superannuation as giving greater flexibility to industry, by encouraging employee mobility in a technology-driven, rapidly changing workplace. Easson, in her history of superannuation, comments favourably on Harrison's 'compelling economic reasons for reform':

> This was the kind of argument an economist inspired by the principles of 'economic liberalism' might be expected to support. Yet the view was being articulated by a unionist marshalling every argument for the cause.[392]

Quite!

Although it would be of long-term benefit to Australian employers, who had run superannuation schemes since the 1800s, there was some opposition to the Accord's superannuation plans. It focused on control, with employers trenchantly opposing any union role in funds' management. Ken Lovell, head of the National Industrial Construction Council, agreed that superannuation would be positive for building workers. But he hit out at the prospect that 'unions would be able to determine the future of the scheme, make all decisions about the way in which the scheme could be altered and have control over its investment policies,' thereby opening the way for large amounts of money to be directed to political or social objectives. Peter Costello, former Howard government Treasurer, put it more crudely, saying that unions viewed the prospective funds 'like rats eyeing a grain silo.'[393]

Superannuation for All

After the bruising experience of the Fraser years, ending in the 1981–82 recession where unemployment rose and inflation spiralled, workers became less confident. The AMWU's Laurie Carmichael saw thousands of metal and manufacturing workers losing their jobs. The union did little to build a fightback. The ACTU supported the argument that workers' demands for wage rises had led to this crisis, so it was workers' responsibility to fix it. Kelty told Carmichael: 'Laurie, you can never let that happen again!' and argued that the union should adopt superannuation as a goal for the future. In other words: adopt a deferred wages scheme which would protect them against such 'wage-profitability' driven crises. Reluctant at first, Carmichael backed the ACTU plan, much to Kelty's relief.[394]

Kelty and Crean held out a glittering prize. Replace wage demands with superannuation claims and be 'a part of the wealth-creation thrust ... active participants in the big social change'; a vision of a golden age of plenty with more jobs, higher wages and conditions and a comfortable retirement. This proposal was incorporated as one of the key recommendations of the 1987 report, *Australia Reconstructed*. The report also recommended socially responsible investment by the funds, such as national development projects and social housing, through a publicly controlled National Development Fund.[395] Keating told the ACTU Congress in 1989 that unions could also use their control over the funds to add 'institutional muscle' to their industrial muscle. In a hostile political environment, unions could flex their institutional muscle in the financial sector instead of passing resolutions in the trades halls. There has actually been little sign of this institutional muscle being used, and recent Coalition governments have attempted to abolish any union involvement in industry funds.[396]

Not every union was a fan of superannuation. Some, mostly on the left, opposed any deferral of wages. Public sector workers were also aware that having superannuation was a common excuse for governments to resist wage increases. There were concerns about a loss of union independence and cooption into the capitalist system through the privately owned funds.

The left-leaning leader of the Miscellaneous Workers' Union (FMWU), Ray Gietzelt, considered superannuation bad for his members, with payouts only going to those who had long-term employment. The building industry was divided, with the BLF and Plumbers lukewarm about the scheme. Norm Wallace from the BLF explained: 'We were opposed to superannuation as the worker was the one who paid for his own pension.'[397] Even right wing unions had reservations. At the 1985 ACTU Congress, the AWU, the FCU, the Shop, Distributive and Allied Employees Association (SDAEA) and the Clothing and Allied Trades Union feared that it meant abandoning the upcoming wages claim. Public sector workers, already holding superannuation, understood that they would not receive the 3 percent, potentially losing both wage and superannuation increases.

Those unions were right to be concerned. From the beginning of the Accord, there were warning signs that the promise of maintenance of real wages 'over time' was more illusory than real, and superannuation had to be fought for every step of the way. Hawke and Keating's first year in government extended Fraser's pay freeze, and the Arbitration Commission delayed the wages case, so most workers got their first wage rise in 1984 rather than 1983. The government also introduced some precursor steps to push more into superannuation. This came as a tax on previously untaxed retirement lump sum payments, unless the money was rolled over into funds not accessible until retirement age.

After the first year, the delays and discounting of wages continued. In September 1983, wages rose by 4.3 percent; in April 1984 by 4.1 percent; and over 1985–87 by 2.6 percent. Treasury indicated that real earnings declined by 2.4 percent in 1985–86. Public Sector wages lagged by up to 4 percent in the year to August 1986.

Before the Accord, unions had the ability to bargain for extra wages and conditions outside the agreement period. Many improvements in wages (often as allowances) and conditions were won in this way. But at the very first national wage case under Labor, unions had to accept a no-extra-claims clause for the length of the agreement in order to be awarded a wage rise. Any attempts to go outside the system would – and did – face concerted attacks and legal threats from the ALP and ACTU. Other unions remained silent or openly backed these moves, complicit in the attacks on fellow workers.

With delays, discounting and no-extra-claims commitments, unions had their hands tied. When promised superannuation was delayed, workers naturally became angry, At this early stage, such anger could turn into industrial action, posing a real threat to the Accord.

The ACTU scrambled to contain the situation, promising that they would accept further wage discounting, if the Labor government delivered on superannuation. They then had to sell the deal to workers, focusing on prospective social wage gains (Medicare, family benefits) and, of course, superannuation. Convincing workers was one step; actually getting runs on the board, as workers battled intransigent employers and the industrial relations umpire, the AIRC, was harder.

Kelty explained to Easson:

> I said, 'fine. I'll get the unions together – the key unions – the bargaining unions' … We got the unions at the ACTU wage negotiating committee and we said, 'we've got the chance in history. This is your great chance. This is a night I think you'll remember. This is the night that we are going to create national superannuation for everybody.' And a couple said 'no.' And all the really tough unions that Carmichael set the course for, every real bargaining union said 'of course.'[398]

The ACTU needed a breakthrough win to save the Accord and the superannuation deal itself.

Get your Boss on the BUSS

Initially, the ACTU planned to use the AMWU as the test case, but the employers' organisation, the MTIA, was implacably opposed.[399] Union members themselves were ambivalent. Greg Harrison admitted: 'Super is a very complex issue and it's not something the membership has picked up and run with.'[400] So the ACTU turned to the construction industry. Again, they ran into trouble; not all building unions were in favour of superannuation. Many members considered it pie in the sky.

Superannuation was not a priority for the BLF and the Plumbers. Their main goal was a promised $9 wage rise, part of the BIA made in 1983. ACTU Building Industry Convener Garry Weaven got union agreement to camouflage the claim as a BIRP and went to the Commission, where it was summarily rejected.

Weaven and the unions were unaware that Kelty had already ensured that rejection. When the BWIU's Tom McDonald began to waver on superannuation, saying that the union wanted the wage rise now, Kelty told him: 'I will do my utmost to make sure you are not getting the money.' He did not mention that he had spoken to AIRC Commissioner Justice John Ludeke: 'I said, "in no way is the BIRP allowance going to flow through the industrial system's wages...I don't want you to give it. I want you to reject it... We will transfer this into superannuation".' Ludeke rejected the extra $9 on the grounds that it increased pay beyond the 4.3 percent increase allowable under the national wage guidelines.[401]

The BLF rejected the Commission's ruling, telling Kelty and employers that this decision had short-changed building workers: 'One way or another the $9 has to be fixed.' Superannuation was not one of the ways. Instead, they lodged another wage claim for the $9 from February 1984.

After McDonald's meeting with Kelty and the Commission's rejection of the claim, McDonald went back to Weaven and agreed to back superannuation. They planned how to present superannuation to workers as more militant than the BLF's $9 claim. So they made it an $11 demand – $9 superannuation, plus $1 for administration and $1 for death and disability insurance.[402]

The BLF was presented with a fait accompli. They'd faced this sort of situation before and stayed on course. But, with deregistration hanging over its head, the union was forced to accept the superannuation deal on the basis of an ACTU promise to head off deregistration. In fact, the ACTU needed the Federation to head up the campaign if they were going to win; Weaven admitted that the BLF: 'added further immense weight to the militancy and effectiveness of the campaign.'[403]

With the employers stalling, a meeting of building unions convened by the ACTU on 28 February 1984 decided to present the builders' organisations with a demand to commit to superannuation by 1 April. Tom McDonald explained:

> While building workers supported the wage increase being paid as super they were not prepared to forgo that payment for years, waiting for the superannuation scheme to be established. So we had only months, not years, to set up such a scheme. It was mind boggling.

In Melbourne during March, representatives from all unions went round the jobs in 'flying squads', less flatteringly called 'rat packs' by the employers, talking to building employers about signing up and putting on bans when they wouldn't come good. When the employers hadn't met the 1 April 1984 deadline, the union campaign began again with bans in South Australia and a rally of 1,400 in Sydney.

The campaign temporarily derailed while the national wage case was dealt with, and July came and went with no progress. By September 1984, only 4,000 of the country's 80,000 building workers were in the BUSS (now Cbus; the superannuation scheme); even then, few builders were actually paying the contributions. Negotiations floundered. The Queensland Confederation of Industry advised member companies: 'Procrastinate, argue, complain, defer a decision, but don't sign up!!! ... You must stop this dreaded BUS Scheme!!!' Queensland Premier Joh Bjelke-Petersen introduced special legislation to stop the BUSS operating in Queensland but was stymied by unions setting up 'independent' BUSSQ.

The Plumbers reimposed bans; the BLs followed. The bans brought results, with the Plumbers winning changes they wanted in their Agreement, including the right to claim a 36-hour week on shopping centre sites. By September 27, all unions except the BLF had signed on. The final obstacle for the BLF was over the right to take industrial action against any builder who would not register with the superannuation scheme. They argued that unions should treat BUSS like No Ticket No Start to have any hope of making it work. Gallagher warned, 'our enemies will use this to whip up a lot of public feeling against the union.' Indeed, Victorian Labor Premier John Cain threatened a 'concerted attack' from state and federal governments and the ACTU. Cain said that they had been discussing 'for some months' how to take on the Federation. The result was a dramatic eleventh-hour move on 4 October, when Gallagher flew to Canberra and made a joint announcement with the Master Builders Federation (MBF): the BLF had signed the Agreement. The union had got everything the Plumbers had won, plus the right to take action over BUSS.

The deal was to be implemented in two phases – from 1 July 1984 for big construction firms and from 1 January 1985 for subcontractors. It came with a warning from the AIRC to the ACTU not to let this deal flow on to any other sectors.

Finalisation of the agreement brought an end to a potential threat to the Accord, which was critical ahead of December 1984 elections.

Superannuation and Accord Mark II

Unions still had a fight on their hands. Superannuation had only been won by a small percentage of the workforce, and the government's aim was to funnel all other claims through the 1986 Accord Mark II, in exchange for trade-offs.

Before the case could be heard, employers fought a rearguard legal battle to stop any further deals through the award system. Arguing that superannuation could not be a federal industrial issue under the terms of existing industrial relations laws, employer groups took their case as far as the High Court. The ACTU was furious; it wasn't the High Court's role to determine whether superannuation was an industrial issue, it was a worker's right. 'They can say whatever they like,' Kelty argued. 'We want it.'[404] In May 1986, the Court rejected it, as they did a second case raised in 1992.[405]

Unionists in transport, on the waterfront, in coal mining, BHP, building and metal workers, journalists, glass workers, breweries, pilots and textile workers embarked on a series of campaigns, including bans and strikes, to win or improve superannuation entitlements.

The Business Council took out a full page advertisement in September 1986. An open letter to unions bellowed: 'AUSTRALIA NEEDS YOU TO BACK OFF THIS STUPIDITY NOW.' But the BCA was divided; despite its call for a moratorium, many of its members continued to negotiate with unions.[406]

Transport unions broke through this employer resistance, setting the example for others. Bans by TWU members on major transport companies in February led to two adjournments of the national wage case but had the effect the unions were seeking. Although forced by the ACTU, Labor and the Commission to lift the bans at TNT and Mayne Nickless, the TWU persisted and won a general deal with the transport employers' peak body, ARTIO, giving workers in the industry the first 3 percent from 1 July 1986.

Seven days of strikes by the WWF in June and July saw improvements in their fund, the Stevedoring Employees Retirement Fund, but only from 1 January, 1987. Women workers in the Textile, Clothing and Footwear Union of Australia (TCFUA) brokered an agreement on 23 December 1986. The first major win for women affected 120,000 workers.

By this stage, the national wage case –Accord Mark II – had already been finalised. Starting deliberations in February 1986, the Commission delayed

a decision until June 1986. The delay cost workers an estimated $250–$400 million. A union call for backdating the payments was refused, and superannuation was delayed for many more months. The unions agreed to a 2.3 percent wage rise – a 2 percent discount – from 1 July 1986. Citing concerns about negative effects on the economy and orderly implementation, Justice Maddern granted a further 3 percent to be paid as superannuation, delayed until 1 January 1987.

Even this was not guaranteed. The AMWU's difficulties illustrate the problems even strong unions had in getting the 1986 Accord Mark II implemented. As the economy weakened in the second half of 1986, employers were reviving their opposition and demanding trade-offs, and unions were concerned that the momentum was being lost.

Firstly, the union leadership had a hard time convincing the members of the value of superannuation. Alan Morrison from the AMWU Victorian branch commented:

> At the time, a lot of the blokes had mixed feeling about ... super because they moved from state to state and job to job with different employers and they reckoned it would be all stuffed up somewhere along the line and they'd rather have the money in the hand at the time.

MTIA chief Bert Evans reportedly 'simply refused to play ball. He won't discuss it with unions and when pressed about it ... proudly pronounced it a "dead issue".' Not until 1988 was agreement reached to establish and start payments to the industry fund Superannuation Trust of Australia. Even then, the union conceded an unprecedented number of conditions, including voluntary employer contributions and choice of funds (rather than the nominated industry fund).[407]

One of the superannuation goals of unions was for funds to invest in projects that would help workers, such as social housing and saving jobs. The MTIA was having none of this; Bert Evans told the AMWU:

> Very early in the piece there was a suggestion to buy an apple-packing factory at Batlow to save 40 jobs ... and I said, 'pig's arse!' ... Could you imagine it if we owned every darn factory in Australia?

Easson praises this intervention as indicating the invaluable contribution employers made in the development of the superannuation industry! As for any claims that the industry funds were in any way controlled by the union members, she concluded that they were not in any sense union funds after 1986: 'They were bipartite in their board composition and nearly as one on most issues.'[408]

Another union that looked strong but ended up being hammered was the PGEU.[409] By the end of July1986, they were fed up with the Accord. 'We tried two and a half years of restraint. We've been underpaid $70 per week because of it,' claimed Victorian assistant secretary Bill Davis. Members complained that it was 'costing them heaps in tax, heaps at the supermarket ... Now we're going back to the traditional means of fighting.' SA and WA employers called for the union to be deregistered and the Master Plumbers Association took out ads accusing the union of 'taking on the mantle of the BLF.' Victorian IR Minister Steve Crabb dismissed this, insisting that the Plumbers were doing 'the traditional thing of pursuing a quid ... in the field and they've got the right to do that.' He then called on the MBA to have some 'discipline' to resist such demands!⁴¹⁰

The Plumbers went ahead with their claim – $70, shorter hours, 2.3 percent national wage rise and 3 percent superannuation without a restrictive no-extra-claims commitment. Members, except in Newcastle, overwhelmingly supported it. The (deregistered) BLF backed the PGEU, doing what they could on the jobs. John Cummins told members that the Plumbers were 'challenging the Accord on behalf of all workers.'⁴¹¹

The campaign continued through into 1987 but faced a wall of opposition from government, the ACTU and employers. Clive Bubb from the MBAV said that builders had learned from the BLF and were united; the Plumbers' campaign would end in a humiliating backdown. He had reason to be confident. Fewer builders directly employed workers, instead using subcontractors so that any bans were technically secondary boycotts. The employers could then lodge punitive s.45D applications, as they had at Mudginberri, threatening huge fines and jail. That was the outcome for the PGEU.⁴¹²

The day Bubb forecast the end of the Plumbers' campaign, the union was fined $280,000 in the Supreme Court, with an additional $140,000 for every day bans continued. The PGEU lifted the bans but refused to pay the fines. Ten days later, the employers accused the union of keeping the bans on; they threatened to cancel the award and charge the union with contempt of court. Minister Willis backed the bosses, warning them that they risked penalties themselves if they backed off from their tough stance. The ACTU and building unions railed against this 'threat to the very essence of trade unionism', but, except for the BLF, did nothing. The Plumbers paid the fines. Secretary George Crawford insisted that he had no regrets; they had won the $70 on many of the jobs, although the 'existence of 45D would have an effect in the future' on activities of the union.⁴¹³

The builders continued to threaten court action. At the end of June, the PGEU was forced into the Accord straitjacket, without back pay and with a three-month good behaviour bond. The national wage rises due from July 1986 and March 1987 were only paid from July 1987, and they were told that, if there was any more industrial action 'outside the wage fixing system', the bosses would be allowed to go back to Arbitration to take even this pittance away. In December 1987, the union withdrew the $70 log of claims, reaffirmed the no-extra-claims commitment given in March and agreed to adhere to no-strike clauses in the severance pay deal. It was only then that the employers actually withdrew the legal threats.[414]

Superannuation and the Accord 1987–1992

Accord Mark III delivered the end of wage indexation, entrenched the practice of trading off conditions for wage rises, and included no superannuation increases. The two-tier wages deal produced more delays, a miserly 2 percent/$10 flat increase, paid in two tranches, and a further 4 percent to be negotiated sector by sector and dependent on significant trade-offs of conditions. Unions with few extra conditions or little industrial strength were hit hard, sometimes unable to gain any of the second tier rises. Even some of the stronger unions experienced a drawn out process, costly to members.

Unions were constricted in following up earlier claims, such as the 3 percent superannuation from earlier Accord agreements. The government withdrew support. IR Minister Willis slammed the unions' industrial action, citing the 55,000 working days lost across 17 industries.

Superannuation was not increased between 1987 and 1990, and every delay in wage increases, every trade-off of wages against conditions, kept earnings lower than they otherwise would have been. This also impacted superannuation, which was calculated against AWOTE.

Accord Mark VI, in 1990, finally considered the next tranche of superannuation – coupled with a wage freeze, tax reductions and improvements in the social wage. The whole process heralded a significant shift in industrial relations with the introduction of enterprise bargaining, earlier described by unions as a New Right policy. The superannuation employer contribution was to be raised by another 3 percent to 6 percent, but phased in over a three-year period from 1 May 1991 to 1 May 1993. The deal cemented ACTU support for superannuation as integral to, and inseparable from, any wage fixing package.

Before agreement was reached, there were changes in the ACTU which signalled some changes in tactics and some rejigging of the superannuation claim, but no change in support for the Accord itself. Crean left in 1990, winning a seat in parliament, and Weaven departed to carve out a career in the superannuation industry. Assistant secretary Martin Ferguson, then described as being on the left, stepped into Crean's shoes. Ferguson adopted a different strategy, bypassing the Commission and focusing more on industry or workplace campaigning as a step towards a new enterprise bargaining model for determining wages and conditions. This ACTU was not prepared to wait for employers or for lengthy AIRC processes, instead preparing for industrial action on the job.

From August, the ACTU launched its field campaign, targeting a wide range of industries – building, furniture, metals, transport, airline and aerospace, mining, photographic, pulp and paper, health and brewing. Industrial action began with a protracted dispute in oil, rolling strikes in transport and a national port closure. Agreements were reached in the car industry in mid-October. In metals and manufacturing, the Manufacturing Trades Federation of Unions (MTFU) and the MTIA settled in late November, with a guarantee for the first 1 percent and 'a mechanism' for deciding further action over the remaining 2 percent.

Nonetheless, progress remained slow. Despite attempts to avoid the AIRC, the unions were forced into it when the Commission rejected all Accord partners' claims in the national wage case in April 1991, knocking back the shift to enterprise bargaining and supporting the employers' submission that a rise in superannuation was premature. Enraging unions and government, the AIRC condescended: 'the parties to industrial relations have still to develop the maturity necessary for the further shift of emphasis now proposed.'[415]

In October 1991, the AIRC finally agreed to enterprise bargaining but still refused to grant the superannuation rise, further propelling the unions away from the Commission in the fight for superannuation. This time it was harder, with only BHP, building, manufacturing and meat industries implementing the 3 percent increase. Attempts to spread this to other areas proved difficult.

With the unions' capacity to engage in industrial action waning, and employers resisting, the Accord partners considered legislation the only path to universal superannuation. Hawke and Keating were prepared to oblige. In 1992, when the AIRC again refused to lift superannuation contributions, parliament passed two bills, the *Superannuation Guarantee (Administration) Act* and the *Superannuation Guarantee Charge Act*. These implemented the government's 1991–92 Budget commitment to tax employers a Superannuation Guarantee

Charge (SGC) to bring superannuation contributions up to 6 percent by 1993.

Laws were no guarantee that employers would pay the SGC, nor that a Coalition government would honour the commitment. In 1993, John Hewson campaigned for the Coalition with his Fightback! Agenda, pledging to halt compulsory superannuation contributions. His government would rely on choice and incentive to encourage payments. Although that hadn't worked in the past, there was nothing in Hewson's rhetoric that explained how it would work in the future. The *Financial Review*'s Gerard Noonan revealed the uncomfortable fact that no country in the world had financed a universal pension or superannuation scheme through non-compulsory contributions.[416]

Keating again spelled out Labor's real motive for compulsory superannuation, telling parliament in May 1992: 'This government has encouraged the organised workforce to agree to take 10 percent of its income as savings rather than cash. It has never been done before.' He added that it would be a significant factor in Australia's investment future in terms of savings; indeed, in 2019, Australia was fourth in the world in the value of superannuation, at nearly $3 trillion. Keating also forecast better living standards and a better retirement, neither of which has actually materialised; the 2017 Retire Ready Index reported that 47 percent of the workforce were unlikely to have enough money in their superannuation accounts to retire comfortably.[417]

After 1993, Keating legislated for a rise to 12 percent, promising 15 percent if he won the 1996 election. He lost. The Howard government immediately deferred the 12 percent rises in the SGC to the 2021–22 to 2025–26 financial years, with 15 percent not even on the radar. In 2019, the Morrison government, right wing think tanks and business moved to defer the 12 percent indefinitely, warning of a catastrophic impact on business.[418] Since superannuation was expanded, the Coalition and their business backers have been seeking ways to strip superannuation funds of any union involvement at all. Given the fact that industry funds regularly outperform the others, this should be seen for what it is: a naked grab for money.

One of the much touted aims of the union superannuation funds was to invest in socially sustainable projects. Attempts to set up specialised funds, financed by the superannuation institutions, mostly collapsed. One fund with these aims, financed by the AMP Staff Superannuation Plan and four of the larger industry funds, soon divested from low-cost housing to hold pure development capital and infrastructure projects. Faced with the logic of the market, the aim of the funds had to be the best return for members' retirement. Losing money by investing below market rates, no matter the social value of a project in a capitalist economy, was simply not in the best interests of members.

The superannuation funds themselves, thoroughly enmeshed in the logic of the market, capitalised on the changing investment market in the 1990s by playing a role in government privatisation of key businesses such as Qantas and the Commonwealth Bank. Such decisions were dressed up by some as 'infrastructure mutualisation', rather than privatisation. Some funds did reconsider their investment profiles and took some ethically-based decisions in the 2000s, withdrawing from firms which sold tobacco products or ran migrant detention centres in Australia and investing in more 'green' projects. Again, company profitability became key, as they sifted from a declining market to profitable new sources.[419]

The Unlucky Lottery?

Has the Accord commitment to superannuation left a positive legacy for workers, or have they gone backwards? Is superannuation the 'unseen revolution' or 'pension-fund socialism'? Is it a new mutualism, a new kind of 'third way', as popularised by Labour's Tony Blair in England, a third way between capitalism and socialism?[420] What are the facts?

Superannuation is decidedly not pension-fund socialism or some third way between capitalism and socialism, and it has generally not been positive for workers. Financial advisers estimate that a retiring couple would need their superannuation account(s) to contain between $600,000 and $1.2 million to live comfortably. A single person would need between $406,000 and $545,000 in their account. The same experts reported that, in 2016, the estimated average male account was between $290,000 and $320,000, and women held between $138,000 and $180,000 – far short of providing for retirement.[421]

For people in the better managed industry funds, those ranked in the top ten in recent reviews, superannuation will provide a more comfortable retirement than if they had simply banked the money during their working lives. Workers in this situation will have had a history of relatively stable, well-paid, full-time work, covering most of their working lives. Many workers, however, have next to nothing to show for their hours of work; exposés in retail, hospitality and agriculture, in particular, reveal the stark reality that having the legal right to superannuation is no guarantee of employers paying into the funds. An estimated $2.85 billion – or $17 billion over the past seven years – was stolen from workers by employers' non-payment of the superannuation levy, possibly up to 30 percent of the workforce.[422]

Karen Chester, lead author of the 2018 Productivity Commission Report on superannuation, called superannuation the 'unlucky lottery.'[423] A combination of lower pay, intermittent working history and part-time or casualised employment has left many still reliant on the Age Pension to survive retirement.

Some funds have also performed poorly. The Productivity Commission estimated that $2.6 billion every year is lost to workers with multiple jobs, where their small superannuation accounts lose money from fee gouging or poor fund management (a scandalous one in four). The Productivity Commission and the Hayne Royal Commission into the banking, insurance and superannuation industries uncovered many other illegal and corrupt practices, whose goal seemed to be to deliver profits to the companies and their boards and trustees, rather than future retirees.

The funds themselves are not struggling. Industry funds held a massive $155 billion in assets in 2019, predicted to rise to $300 billion by 2024. The combined total for all superannuation funds had reached nearly $3 trillion by July 2019, eclipsing the Australian GDP and the entire market capitalisation of all the companies listed on the Australian Stock Exchange. Superannuation created a whole new growth sector in the finance industry, with a bevy of financial advisers, new firms and boards of management. Many at the highest levels are ex-union bureaucrats, running the funds while rank and file workers have no direct say. Investment in socially responsible projects is pathetically low.

Beyond the pitfalls of superannuation are the wages traded off against an employer-funded contribution to superannuation. Because superannuation is calculated against AWOTE, when wages stay lower, so do the employers' contributions and, of course, the final retirement fund amount.

What is the actual cost to employers of superannuation? Between 1992 and 2002, during the phase-in of the SGC, fears that it would be prohibitively expensive for employers were not realised. Keating later told Easson:

in every year the Superannuation Guarantee Charge grew
by a further one percentage point ... unit labour costs fell
markedly. This meant that the cost of superannuation was
never borne by employers. It was absorbed into the overall
wages cost. Indeed, in each year of the SGC growth between
1992 and 2002, the profit share in the economy rose. The
growth in trend productivity over the period was so large it
paid for generous wage settlements [generous according to
Keating], including superannuation, while accommodating a
higher and higher share of national income going to profit.

Wages growth at the time was around 2.5 percent. In other words, employees paid the Superannuation Guarantee Charge, not the employers.

Astonishingly, Easson goes on to say:

It might seem odd to say that this was a triumph for the
labour movement as the victory was associated with a
drop in workers' real wages and that the drop was only
partly compensated or offset by concomitant occupational
superannuation arrangements; with company profit share
on the rise. The argument here, however, is that this was
the labour movement's singular commitment to getting the
Australian economy on track, growing GDP and employment
and encouraging the repair of the damage done in the decade
before Hawke's election as prime minister in 1983.[424]

As the 2000s enter the third decade, welfare payments are being squeezed or frozen well below the poverty line and eligibility tightened. Workers are continually pressured to pay for all their services and welfare – education, health, employment or retirement. With a concomitant downward pressure on wages, the changing nature of work, increased casualisation and 'self-employment', retirement savings will suffer.

But for Bill Kelty, 'Keating was our champion ... We accepted real wage cuts and he delivered on super.'[425]

Socialist Action August 1986.

CHAPTER 11

Enterprise bargaining – Accord Mark VII

Unions were at a crossroads in 1990. The government and the ACTU pushed for a fundamental change to the way all wages were determined, a shift from a centralised, award-based system to enterprise by enterprise bargaining.[426] Accord Mark VII was framed around the concept of a wage–productivity trade-off at the enterprise level. This would decentralise the wage system, with the AIRC relinquishing responsibility for determining wage rises and only now concerned with safety net issues and arbitrating disagreements. Enterprise Bargaining Agreements (EBAs) would be registered by the AIRC or state equivalent and become enforceable documents, replacing awards. This was necessary, said Kelty, because:

> By 1991 Australia was going into an open economy. The productivity growth of some industries was going to be six percent and others minus two percent. You can't sustain a centralised system in an open economy like that, even with all the good will in the world. We knew we had to change the system.[427]

Enterprise bargaining was not new, but the political climate and state of the unions had changed significantly, and enterprise bargaining played a new role. Throughout Australia's industrial history, many blue-collar unions, particularly the AMWU, had successfully won over-award increases enterprise by enterprise. In the past, says researcher John Buchanan, such collective bargaining meant that 'a gain in one industry or occupation eventually flowed through to the [whole] workforce' – commonly known as comparative wage justice or flow-ons. Accord Mark VII was designed to bring in enterprise bargaining for everyone and to quarantine each deal, preventing any flow-on of wages or conditions. In 1994, Buchanan concluded that it had already succeeded.[428]

The first moves towards more 'flexible' work, as allowed by Accord-style enterprise bargaining, followed the 1985 Hancock Review recommendation of a total overhaul of the industrial relations system. The new *Industrial Relations Act 1988* introduced Certified Agreements under s.115, allowing firms to reach fixed term arrangements with unions independently of the centralised system. It was to have unwelcome repercussions for unions. Again, it was the ALP introducing anti-union, pro-business provisions in the Accord process which led to non-union agreements. Julia Fellows, consultant to then IR Minister Ralph Willis and contributor to framing the new legislation, later wrote:

> It is a testimony to the adaptability of the Accord, the robustness of the Accord relationships and the pragmatism of the industrial partners, that, within six years, this first cautious legislative initiative for union-based, non-variable agreements had materialised into readily accessible non-union Enterprise Flexibility Agreements, capable of overriding specific Award provisions.[429]

There was a similar provision in NSW to the federal Enterprise Flexibility Agreements (EFA), s.170 NC. They were a gift to employers, who had the sole right to apply for an EFA; unions only had to be notified, and could make a submission.[430]

By 1991, this 'flexibility' was incorporated into enterprise bargaining for everyone. At the national wage case hearings in April 1991, the AIRC refused any further wage increases until the end of 1993 but rejected the Accord partners' enterprise bargaining submission. The ACTU was furious and endorsed industrial action to pressure the Commission. To head off any return to militancy, the Commission waved Accord Mark VII through with minor changes in October. An 'enterprise bargaining principle' was established;

agreements had to comply with 'public interest and traditional wage fixing principles', although the new agreements rarely transferred over all the award conditions. Industrial action around an EBA would be allowed, but in strictly controlled situations which made it harder to take than before. To guarantee the employers' picnic, the AIRC pared down basic 'safety net' conditions to four – annual leave, long service leave, standard hours of work and ordinary time earnings. Everything else was up for grabs at each EBA negotiation. Amendments to the Act in 1992, 1993 and 1994 weakened scrutiny of the various agreements.

The shift to enterprise bargaining and individual contract agreements began in 1991 in most Australian states, as Coalition governments swept into power in the years to 1994. Because some states' legislative moves were more radically against workers' interests, union leaderships swung behind the federal government's push for the new Accord, citing it as protection against the states' regimes. In the states themselves, rather than fighting against the new laws, many unions chose to shift their registration to federal coverage, a move which backfired spectacularly when the Coalition won national government in 1996. In 1992, the *Industrial Relations Act* was amended to require the AIRC to ratify workplace agreements between unions and employers, extended in 1993 to agreements between non-unionised workers and employers. New IR Minister Laurie Brereton, supported by PM Keating, wanted the non-union legislative changes to break the 'monopoly power' of unions over enterprise bargaining, to create 'fresh opportunities in the non-union sector.'[431] Under the 'recession we had to have' in 1990, Keating saw the key role for enterprise bargaining as forcing up productivity. Paul Kelly identifies two consequences for wages from the recession: 'it destroyed the market power of unions and provided a "safety zone" to create enterprise bargaining' and, with unemployment rising to 10 percent, entrenched low wage rises.[432]

A pessimistic scenario faced the unions, including the near certainty of a conservative government at the next election. The ACTU leadership, keen for the wage–productivity trade-off, was also anxious 'to get muscle into individual unions for certain combat against a new Liberal government likely to abolish awards and shut down the Commission in a "no prisoners" assault.' But Kelty knew that union power had been seriously weakened under the Accord. Challenged by Keating to hold the line on wage rises, he answered,

'To be honest Paul, some of our unions are incapable of bargaining anything, let alone a four percent wage increase, so I wouldn't worry much about it.'[433]

Some in the union movement were aware that enterprise bargaining could be more of a tool for employers, that 'organised labour is being transformed in the image allowed for it by employers, at the cost of its autonomy and vibrancy', but others saw some positives.[434] Approaching Accord Mark VII, TCFUA federal organiser Susan Gray spoke of the opportunities enterprise bargaining could provide. Workers could win 'work-based childcare, occupational health and safety, special purpose leave, job redesign and work organisation, job sharing and training, promotion and career opportunities.'[435] Gray did not explain why these could not be won collectively and inserted into general awards, but she did warn that the consultative aspect of negotiating enterprise bargains risked being turned into a sham by employers and argued that members had to be educated. The TCFUA had trained 1,000 members in the necessary consultative skills and examined the impact of the Textile, Clothing and Footwear industry plan – a totally wasted exercise when major tariff cuts undermined the TCFUA plan, ravaged the industry and left thousands jobless. Training in traditional trade union industrial action and fighting for jobs would have been a better option. In 2013, ACTU President Ged Kearney continued the positivity, arguing that 'the centralised system had become a yoke and shackled the unions and the movement fought for and won direct collective bargaining.'[436]

The transition was relatively rapid. By 1993, fewer than one in eight workers were covered by EBAs, with the rest on AIRC-endorsed national rises and awards. In July 1994, roughly 1.2 million people, 20 percent of the workforce, were covered by 3,730 registered EBAs; of those, 1.1 million workers were under federal jurisdiction, with Queensland, NSW and WA making up 145,000 under state laws. Victorian Premier Jeff Kennett had transferred state industrial relations to the federal sphere, so Victorian workers' EBAs were registered federally. By the end of 1999, EBAs applied to more than 3.5 million workers (48 percent), while those reliant on awards amounted to just 23 percent. By 2012, only 16 percent were covered solely by awards; 42 percent had collective agreements; and 38 percent were on individual contracts. Almost 40 percent of enterprise agreements were made without unions.[437]

Some stand-out industry sectors still did not transition quickly to enterprise bargaining. Liberalisation of the labour market, said Buchanan, had allowed 'massive surgery' on awards, 'to make most of their provisions subject to being over-ruled with a simple agreement of the workforce concerned.' There was no need for firms to bargain workplace by workplace; they had everything they wanted under the award system. The federal award covering the thousands of employees in the motor trades was one example.[438] Other impacts came from this Accord's continuing 'efficiency' requirements, which drove down staff numbers in government-owned enterprises by 24 percent, while productivity rose by 100 percent.

All this was achieved without major industrial action by the unions. Unsurprisingly, union membership plummeted, falling to 35 percent by 1994, with the fall between August 1992 and 1994 from 2.5 million to 2.25 million in a workforce of 8.2 million.[439] The ACTU tried various strategies to win back workers. In 1993, their *Future Directions* and the Evatt Foundation's *Unions 2001* reports proposed introducing new non-work services to members; union amalgamations; union call centres; and publicity and recruitment campaigns. An ACTU-led Organising Works program recruited and trained 'flying squads of highly motivated young recruiters who will go out and sell our message to key groups of younger workers.' It misfired, writes Tom Bramble, because:

> they failed to address the obvious factor – that the Accord with its decline in real wages in the 1980s, followed by the trading away of working conditions, made trade unionism less attractive for workers seeking to defend their conditions of employment.

Bramble notes that ACTU President Martin Ferguson promised a more 'active, democratic responsible and flexible union movement but not one that would fight or seek to reverse the damage' of the Accord. The strike rate fell to a postwar low.[440]

Enterprise agreements initially raised wages and won improved conditions in stronger workplaces, but those who had no power to bargain or had nothing to give away saw their wages fall. Those whose wages rose lost significant conditions. Employers succeeded in increasing the standard work

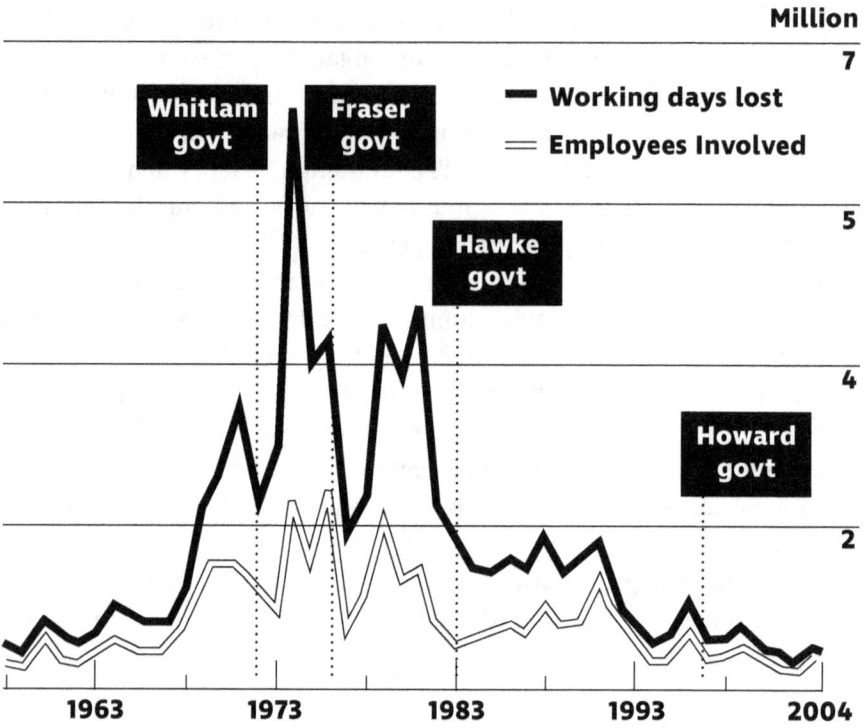

Figure 3. Industrial disputes 1958 to 2004. Source ABS. After The Australian Financial Review 22 July 2004.

day, cutting into penalty time and reducing penalty rates, introducing 24-hour operations and extending overall working hours. Agreements entailed increases in the percentage of part-time, contract and casual workers, at management's discretion, while the promise of career paths and upskilling commonly manifested as work intensification and loss of jobs. Companies and government departments were divided and subdivided into smaller and smaller isolated 'bargaining units', eliminating the capacity of workers to take a united stand against their employers. It was one more factor in smashing solidarity, pitting workers in one workplace against another, dividing unions against each other, succeeding only in weakening the whole union movement. And the unions, right down to the shop steward level, were seen as complicit with management in cutting workers' conditions.[441] Naturally, workers started to shun unions (see figure 3).

The government's 1993 industrial relations legislation was promoted as a win for unions, because it allowed for 'protected' industrial action after an enterprise agreement ended, during bargaining for a new deal. Limiting industrial action to this short time frame and imposing requirements such as seven days' notice of planned action rendered action at any other time illegal, with workers and their unions risking significant fines. Companies were able to ask the Commission for an end to the bargaining period, which was usually granted. This left workers either without a deal and forbidden to take industrial action to win one; or having to accept the employers' offer; or, in some cases, returning to the AIRC to have it force an agreement – usually favouring the employer – on the parties. It became evident that employers often stalled negotiations, leading to delays of months or even years, wearing down workers' resistance, before a new, worse, agreement was reached.

More damaging for the union movement was the change in attitudes that enterprise bargaining introduced. Qantas negotiator Julia Fellows was angered by union officials who baulked at company insistence that wages be considered in the light of company profits. Several years on, she found the same officials 'quite relaxed about profitability being the appropriate determinant of the size of the pool available for additional wage adjustments.' Fellows didn't experience the same relaxed attitude from Qantas's TWU baggage handlers, so she:

> triggered a lock out, until individual employees were prepared to sign an undertaking that they recognised that their employment would be terminated if they again breached the dispute settlement procedures and took industrial action.[442]

Workers' Experience

The last phase of the Accord was very damaging for workers in both public and private sectors.

Media Entertainment and Arts Association (MEAA) National Secretary Anne Britton observed that most employers adopted a negative cost-cutting agenda. Those with substandard awards were reluctant to risk bargaining, because an EBA might improve pay and conditions. Many registered existing over-award agreements, containing nothing new for the workforce. For example, the MEAA had been running a five-year battle with Hoyts theatre chain, originally to have the relevant award adhered to. Under the new legislation, Hoyts refused to engage the union in EBA negotiations, instead transporting non-union representatives around Australia to win support for non-union EFAs. To survive under this less regulated regime, Britton acknowledged, unions had to abandon the complacency that came from relying on regular AIRC decisions. They needed to stay in touch with their members. The MEAA has survived, but it suffers the general malaise of Australian unions in the 21st century and has failed to run successful campaigns against media job losses.[443]

In the rapidly expanding communications industry, new carrier Optus negotiated its first union EFA in 1992. In 1994, in the second round of negotiations, they squeezed out the union. Employees voted for a non-union agreement with significant wage increases (not guaranteed), longer working hours, more flexible work practices and a performance-based bonus system. The union later reported that the bonuses never eventuated, and not everyone received a wage rise. Rival telecom Telstra soon began to offer non-union contracts, mainly at management and professional level. Optus, meanwhile, won the praise of IR Minister Laurie Brereton for its 1994 agreement; his office actually offered financial support to any company interested in following Optus' lead.

Metal manufacturing firm ASAHI responded. In 1995, Brereton backed ASAHI's successful bid in the AIRC to keep unions out of negotiations over new working arrangements.[444] The AMWU had failed in a bid to recruit workers at ASAHI but went to the AIRC seeking an order to force the company to negotiate with the union anyway. In December 1994, Commissioner Hodder ordered ASAHI to negotiate in good faith with the AMWU. ASAHI appealed, and a full bench of the AIRC ruled on 1 March 1995 that:

> The industrial relations system envisaged by the Act is one designed to facilitate and encourage direct bargaining underpinned by an effective award safety net. However, this is not a system of compulsory negotiation.[445]

The case alerted those unions who'd cooperated with Accord Mark VII, expecting that it would encourage union membership. Unions believed that they could recruit workers in non-unionised or poorly unionised workplaces and offer them better pay and conditions under a certified EBA. This would protect them from adverse decisions, because the AIRC, which had to register all agreements, could knock them back if they didn't adhere to basic conditions or result in 'genuine' productivity improvements. The *Industrial Relations Reform Act 1993* had given them hope that an unwilling employer would be obliged to negotiate an enterprise agreement 'in good faith.' The ASAHI decision quashed that interpretation.

THE PUBLIC SECTOR

Agency by agency bargaining was ushered into the APS with some fanfare in November 1992. Its objective was to rip away the long-standing sector-wide wages and conditions determinations, leaving departments to negotiate on their own; quarantining the stronger, more militant areas would ultimately weaken them all. The IR Minister wrote that the service-wide framework agreement for the initial two-year period:

> reflects the biggest change ever in the way the APS ... will work ... the framework provides direct incentives for management and unions in individual Public Service departments and agencies to negotiate positive workplace reforms that will boost productivity, efficiency and flexibility in their organisations.[446]

It did that – at enormous cost to the unionised workforce.
Although the Commonwealth Public Sector Union (CPSU) had failed

to win any pay rises for public sector workers over the previous two years, no Agency Bargaining Agreements were signed off by workers until March 1994 – the Department of Veterans' Affairs (DVA), the Australian Tax Office (ATO) and the Department of Employment, Education and Training (DEET). Across departments, members frequently rejected the deals on offer because of lack of consultation with workers and a generally undemocratic process. In DSS, a workplace delegate reported that consultation consisted of a couple of seminars headed up by the union. Delegates furiously attacked the proposal put to them at meetings and became even angrier when they discovered that it was not a management offer, but the union's position!

In DSS, management offered Saturday and public holiday morning openings on ordinary time with a morning off during the week, a more rigid flexitime arrangement and more management-initiated part-time and temporary jobs. They intended to develop a joint union–management approach to absenteeism, expansion of competency-based training, assessment and pay.[447] The department proposed, in exchange, a miserable 1 percent pay rise and a further 2 percent a year later. Research showed that public sector workers were 8 percent behind those in the private sector. The offer was rejected out of hand. But the CPSU's pro-EBA strategy undermined any attempt by members to seriously challenge for a better deal.

The CPSU nominated 'pay activists', delegates who were meant to be involved in determining the agreements. 'I don't think I did anything different', recalled one. 'I certainly didn't stand up with a red nose on my face, which was suggested by one union official … I think it was a symbol of their dithering because they really didn't know what to do.' The union call for volunteers was viewed as an attempt to 'get a few suckers in to do their dirty work.'

In August 1993, when bargaining stalled, CPSU called members out to fight for agency bargaining, including stopworks and strikes. Many local offices carried resolutions wanting nothing to do with agency bargaining. They certainly did not want to take industrial action to win it: 'Who needs a boss when you've got the union officials?' said one.

The agreement was forced through with some management backdowns on Saturday and public holiday openings and flexitime, coupled with a slightly higher pay offer. Final acceptance came from a workforce demoralised by union officials' continued refusal to accept members' votes through the undemocratic shutting down of mass meetings, where agency by agency bargaining was consistently rejected.

LATROBE VALLEY

Luke van der Meulen, a power station worker and later union official, summed up the cocktail of events that hit his Latrobe Valley community hard: the Accord in its various stages, including structural efficiency, union rationalisation, outsourcing and privatisation, a wave of voluntary redundancies, and deep divisions between the main unions at the Valley's power stations.[448] By 1995, the workforce had dropped from 10,800 to 3,000. The region was in crisis, but union officials branded anyone who had raised concerns or predicted the crisis as 'knuckle draggers or Neanderthals' who didn't understand the 'big picture' of the Accord. Luke says:

> It's a history of an Australian community that was smashed by [a betrayal of trust] and was, in 1999, recognised by the Industry Commission as the hardest hit region in Australia as a result.

In Victoria, the Cain Labor government undertook the restructuring, corporatisation and privatisation of the government-run State Electricity Commission of Victoria (SECV). The process began innocently enough in September 1987, when the government set up the Natural Resources and Environment Committee, involving the peak union bodies, the SECV and mining companies, BHP and CRA. This, ultimately sham, consultation process ended when the government unilaterally announced its plans for restructuring the industry.

The Loy Yang Cost Study (LYCS) was established in 1989 to inform the first stage of the privatisation process at Loy Yang A power station, with restructuring then to flow on through the rest of the SECV. The LYCS was a high-level government, ACTU, VTHC and union leadership-driven process, launched by PM Bob Hawke. It had little support among workers, given the earlier sham consultation process. Rank and file resistance, both at the power station and the mine, grew as the workforce rebelled against their union officials' role, some even refusing to act as workplace delegates. Within months, the LYCS collapsed.

SECV General Manager Jim Smith released a report in April 1989 targeting jobs, classifications, career paths, work practices (conditions) and rosters. In June, management announced their intention to shed 20 percent of the SECV's 22,000 workforce. By 1997, 70 percent of jobs would disappear. A three-year target for a Voluntary Departure Package was reached within months, and the strong unity between the unions fractured. In October, while the local Loy Yang unions were working out a common SECV award, the ASU, NUW and ETU national branch secretly approached management with a special EBA (an EEEE Award) to go to the AIRC. The application for a new award failed, but the attempt fostered deep divisions among the unions. The Latrobe Valley union branches of the AMWU, FEDFA, ETU and AWU then pledged to stick together and fight the job cuts.

Despite action by local TWU and FEDFA members and officials, their state leaderships and the Victorian THC okayed the sell-off of the SECV Transport Workshops and the Brooklyn Stores (warehouses) to private operator Linfox. The deal cut jobs and delivered the TWU coverage of the remaining staff for 12 months. No guarantees were given about job numbers. This deal 'set the scene for many rotten deals that were to follow.' Luke van der Meulen explains:

> We understood the 'golden rule' and knew the Accord could not be flexible when it comes to workers. We understood the Accord. We knew that its three primary functions were to firstly apply restraint on wages growth, then to lower real wages, lessen then eliminate industrial disputation, particularly in relation to declining wages and thirdly and probably most importantly, dupe the workers into believing the Accord and enterprise bargaining was there for them.

So much disquiet remained in the Valley during 1990 that the Gippsland and Victorian THCs and union secretaries organised a 'Rally in the Valley' for 18 December 1990. Little was done to build the protest, but 4,000 turned up to hear speeches from union leaders and march sedately through Morwell; instead, led by van der Meulen, angry workers marched to the SECV main gate, gaining significant media coverage.

Socialist Action September 1986.

Workers in the Valley still had some real power in their hands – if they chose to fight. The SECV approached the first EBA by going straight to the state union officials, bypassing the local sub-branch, to get an agreement to an Operations Review – to become a Heads of Agreement between two unions, FEDFA and ASU, and SECV management when finalised. Important issues such as staffing, skills, rosters, classifications, roles and responsibilities were either predetermined or left up to management. The strong Latrobe Valley FEDFA Mining and Energy sub-branch (FEDFA M&E) rejected it as conditioning the workforce for privatisation, especially after the bitter experience of the earlier privatisations and later outsourcing of the maintenance section to private company Fluor Daniels, with very limited job guarantees and the scrapping of a day-labour contract agreement. The national and state officials finalised the agreement in May 1993, virtually unchanged.[449]

Strong resistance made the Heads of Agreement unenforceable. Union betrayals left 500 maintenance workers at Fluor Daniels stranded in three 'redeployee pools' (known as 'vegi patches') without work, unless they signed the contracts. Maintenance workers set up the Latrobe Valley Maintenance Forum, but they could not stop the relentless march of privatisation.

EBA negotiations in the Latrobe Valley were in lock step with the union amalgamation process that was being introduced across Australia. In the Valley, the process would have seen the effective elimination of the M&E sub-branch, giving their work – and members – to the 'principal' union, the newly amalgamated ASU.[450] Because M&E members refused to budge on the amalgamation or the Heads of Agreement, the SECV, with the full cooperation of the ACTU and ASU, raised a s.118A case in the AIRC to force the transfer of M&E members to the ASU. During negotiations over the EBA, management offered to drop the transfer case if the members would accept the Heads of Agreement. Members rejected the offer, believing that they had 'nothing to lose.' The forced amalgamation failed. The M&E became the major union in the industry in the Valley, with the ASU relegated to minor status. ASU members flocked to join the FEDFA M&E branch and escape the union so deeply part of management and ACTU–state government plans.

Partial privatisation of the Loy Yang B plant in 1992, followed by separation from Loy Yang A, was agreed to by the ACTU and ASU. The split seriously weakened the workforce. More damagingly, Loy Yang B was designated as a 'greenfield' site: the new private company recognised no existing agreements or rights, including the decades-old award. Sole coverage at Loy Yang B was given to the ASU.[451] The complicity of the ASU leadership with the new owners, Mission Energy, was such a blow that the ASU never recovered in the Latrobe Valley and eventually lost their entire membership on many sites, including Loy Yang B.

The M&E sub-branch set up a Jobs Action Campaign in February 1995. Funded by a levy on members, it organised marches outside parliament in Melbourne and a range of actions in the Valley itself. There was little official support, including from the FEDFA Victorian branch, but their actions won them a better EBA, including improved job security, pay and superannuation. It came too late to stop privatisation; by 1997, all power generation in the Valley had been sold.

Even the option of involving unions in enterprise bargaining was to be stripped away next. The 1999 round of enterprise bargaining at Yallourn Energy saw management demanding their 'seven principles' – or 'seven deadly sins', according to unionists. The company would have the right to carry out compulsory retrenchments and control shift rosters and the number of casual workers on site; unions would give up their control over structures and staffing levels, the number of contractors and the right to veto new technology; and union members would be required to do whatever work they had the skills and training for, regardless of union demarcation. Giving up these core conditions would earn a 12 percent pay rise. The company refused to negotiate on anything other than the full acceptance of their seven principles. In November 1999, they set a damaging precedent by applying to the AIRC to have the existing EBA terminated.

Mass meetings of members followed. In January 2000, the CFMEU, AMWU and ETU agreed on industrial action. AMWU maintenance workers imposed bans on 4 January and found themselves locked out. Yallourn Energy bought back-up power, enabling it to avoid a shutdown, the unions' strongest bargaining chip, and stymie the campaign. A *force majeure* agreement with the state government compensated them in the event of industrial action and also allowed them to perform essential maintenance. The AMWU and ETU withdrew from the action after a few days and agreed to the seven principles in exchange for a redundancy deal, hailing it as a victory.[452] For the CFMEU, the dispute continued to November, when CFMEU M&E workers across the Valley called a snap strike. The Labor government attacked the union, and their own state secretary, John van Camp, called them 'rebels, rogues and knuckleheads', but a deal was worked out with the government to end the strike and protect workers from being sued. Within hours of the return to work, the government and the SECV reneged on the agreement, going on to sue the unionists for tens of millions of dollars. Yallourn Energy dropped the writs, but the union was forced into arbitration, ending up with possibly the worst enterprise agreement in Australia's power generation industry. It took another 13 years and a 100-day lockout for workers to rebuild the union sub-branch and claw back these losses.[453]

Thirty Years Later

The same year that the Latrobe Valley workers won their improved EBA, 2013, the Accord partners, academics and business people were celebrating the thirtieth anniversary of the 1983 launch of the Accord. Part of Bill Kelty's assessment was a comment on enterprise bargaining and its negative impact on union membership. For Kelty, it was not the Accord's enterprise bargaining model that transferred power from workers to employers; it was the fault of unions, in failing to 'adequately embrace the shift to enterprise bargaining.' Employers, as this history shows, 'embraced' enterprise bargaining wholeheartedly, going on a cost cutting, conditions busting spree. Under that Accord, unions sacrificed power, further diminished by the debilitating enterprise bargaining process. Few were in any position to push back against the Howard-led onslaught.

Kelty argued that the ACTU should have acted earlier to restructure unions, presumably to reduce the number of unions bargaining with any one employer. But the Latrobe Valley experience showed that the ACTU attempt to enforce the establishment of the ASU as the single union for workers in the Valley had disastrous results, especially at Loy Yang B. Kelty offered SDAEA as one example of a union that embraced enterprise bargaining and thrived. SDA members are very familiar with the kind of sweetheart deals done by their union with big supermarkets and the cuts in pay and conditions that follow minimal pay rises for some. Challenges by activists and a new Retail and Fast Foods Workers Union have more recently forced companies and a reluctant SDA back into the Commission to extract a deal that actually benefits the workforce.[454]

Responsibility for the results of the Accord, Kelty suggests, lies with all of us. 'Who's to blame?' he asks, answering: 'we are all to blame, including me.' He went on to blame everyone but the ACTU. Centralising the power of the unions in the ACTU to drive the Accord gave the peak body 'unprecedented authority'; but: 'essentially the decline in unionism occurred from the point that [the ACTU] gave the authority back' [to the unions] under Accord Mark VII. It was then up to the unions, and they failed!

This chapter, and this history, refute Kelty's blame shifting. The ACTU continued to control the unions, to stymie any attempt to build strong independent unionism, to prevent any attempt to take on the employers (except through the Commission) and to advocate openly for anti-union laws to smash unions that dared to defy the Accord. With the ALP and the Accord-backers among the union bureaucracy, the ACTU bears responsibility for the dire state of unionism at the end of the Accord years – and through to today.[455] The workers who fought back, who tried to break through the Accord strictures, are the only ones who left Australian workers any guidelines, any legacy on how to rebuild the union movement from the wreckage left by the Accord and reinforced by both Labor and Coalition governments since.

CHAPTER 12

'The Accord Gospel: Profits, more Profits'

In 1984, Mark Burford wrote a glowing prospectus for the Accord:

> It is necessary to break out of the circle of mobilisation followed by containment and frustration. The Prices and Incomes agreement can help to do that by extending the role of workers' organisations beyond that of defence against the reaction to the employing class and giving them an expanded and creative economic and political role. It can, if carried out to the level of union/government/employer negotiations and discussions, bring unions into the economic policy planning areas as well. Unions would then have a much expanded responsibility and potentially creative role.[456]

As late as 1991, then IR Minister Peter Cook enthused:

> A crucial consequence of all the economic, industrial and social progress that the Accord achieved has been what could be called the empowerment of the union movement … For more than eight years, the union movement has been pivotal in designing, developing and carrying out a range of economic and social policies.[457]

This history illustrates how far this was from the truth. The reality of the Accord years is assessed more accurately by *Financial Review* journalist Michael Stutchbury in 1989, a full six years before enterprise bargaining became Labor's last assault on the working class:

> The bottom line is that the Accord has kept the line on wage inflation during what has been Australia's biggest economic boom since at least the early 70s. Under the Accord, the ACTU has deliberately facilitated the biggest redistribution of national income from wages to profits.[458]

The Accord still has its supporters, denying that it was a fundamentally class collaborationist project against workers' interests. Some argue that it was poorly implemented, that workers did not understand it, or that workers did not back it as strongly as they should have. The Communist Party's *Tribune* of August 1984 reached a new low, blaming everyone but the ruling class and labour leaders for the failure of Accord policies: 'The Accord is as yet far from an effective instrument because of insufficient support from inside the union movement and from the disadvantaged outside unions including pensioners.'[459] The end results certainly give the lie to any positive interpretation, and a reading of the Accord document itself, along with pronouncements from the government and union leaders at the time, shows clearly that a return to profitability was its primary goal. In 1986, Bob Hawke boasted:

> You don't need a wages policy in times of recession because the recession will do the job for you. But we had to get into place a policy and habits which would stick in times of recovery. Now we have delivered the goods.[460]

That year, a work practices summit was held at the instigation of the BCA. There, representatives of the ACTU, CAI and BCA agreed on the need to remove 'restrictive work and management practices' to enhance productivity, most effectively at the enterprise level. The pronouncement showcased the award restructuring and enterprise bargaining stages of the Accord, just as business – and labour movement leaders – wanted.[461]

The constraints on workers became more apparent over the Accord years: workers' wages were to be maintained 'over time'; equal pay was 'outside the guidelines'; the social wage was subject to 'economic circumstances.' At the thirtieth anniversary forum in 2013, Kelty admitted that the Accord partners had lied about wages when he said, 'What do you think – everybody said "That's a nice idea – a real wage reduction would be good, can I have another one next year please"?' Kelty ruthlessly enforced a decline in real wages and never backed away from taking credit for it. He and Simon Crean, he says, were 'prepared to get the economy refocused and stabilised and accepted for a period of time that there had to be real wage concessions.'[462]

When support for the Accord began to wane, the officials brandished threats from 'New Right' employers or a Howard-led neoliberal government, turning those threats into its own 'catalyst for a campaign of sustainable change in the labour market', to implement deregulation. The *Financial Review* acknowledged that Labor and the ACTU would have to push more rapidly than the unions wanted and 'side with the employers against union recalcitrance.'[463] The threats were real, but when Labor itself offered up policies that attacked and undermined unions, workers were hard pressed to distinguish between the two. Lindsay Tanner, a member of parliament on Labor's left, admitted in a 1997 ABC *Four Corners* program:

> We have done so many things through enterprise bargaining through to competition policy, through to privatisation and deregulation that would be typically associated with a Liberal government, that it is difficult for the Liberals to differentiate themselves from what Labor in office did or for Labor to differentiate itself from the Liberals.[464]

Small wonder, then, that Simon Crean could say in his 1989 ACTU Presidential Address:

> We are not provocatively threatening industrial action against or refusing to work with a non-Labor government in the future … We have demonstrated an ability to work with government and make tough decisions. The question is not

can we work with government, but whether government is prepared to develop a constructive relationship with us.[465]

It was Labor, the ACTU and Left union officials who brought in neoliberalism and launched an offensive against workers through the Accord. Treasurer Paul Keating intended building on the government's approach 'of deregulation, of removing the meddling hands of bureaucracy from the operation of markets, of forcing our businesses and our workers to confront the realities of world markets and international opportunities.'[466] Elizabeth Humphrys makes a strong case for the neoliberal nature of the ALP–ACTU social contract and adds a warning for those who argue that 'the Accord model should not be written off for all time because it failed in inauspicious conditions.' Rather, she and other critics argue that such social contracts as the Accord's class collaborationist project, whether part of a neoliberal or reformist Keynesian program, should never be revived.[467]

The Accord was a disaster for the Australian working class, cutting wages and conditions, undermining and seriously weakening union organisation and driving down unionisation. Union membership collapsed from 50 percent in 1982 to 40 percent in 1992 and at twice that rate from 1992 to 1996. It stagnated below 25 percent in the 2000s and hovered around 9 percent in the 2010s.

The Accord bastardised the notion of solidarity, one of the real strengths of unions. Solidarity was called for and built by workers struggling against the Accord. Queensland ETU delegate Bernie Neville addressed SEQEB and other protesters outside the 1985 ACTU conference, warning against Hawke, Keating and IR Minister Willis:

> Watch out for their kind of unity … of defeat … of the sellout, instead we must demand the kind of unity that comes from organisation, solidarity and struggle … the kind of unity that will lead the working class to victory.[468]

With the support of the ACTU and key Left union leaders, Labor used the police, the Air Force and legislation to smash two unions. They supported the employers' use of anti-union laws to penalise any union who dared to fight back. The ACTU claimed to oppose penalties against workers and strike breaking by employers, but it wholeheartedly backed government and employer moves against unions such as the pilots and the BLF. Any union which did face the system's penalties was accused of bringing it on themselves. Simon Crean slammed the AFAP: 'Having chosen to go outside the system with its obligations and discipline, the Pilots can't expect to enjoy the benefits, protection and support … [It] has jeopardised its future.'[469]

Profits soared, and the ruling class won battle after battle against organised labour. In 1998, one of the Accord's authors, the BWIU's Tom McDonald, finally admitted the failings of the Accord. He took no responsibility for his role in it, including the smashing of the BLF – directly benefiting his union. In his and wife's biography, *Intimate Union*, he concluded that the great weakness of the Accord:

> was that it disempowered workers to the extent that it took away from them the right to struggle for higher wages and better conditions of employment. Everything associated with the Accord was decided at the top echelons of power.[470]

By then, the Accord had left organised labour with few weapons to fight new state-based industrial laws. The Coalition won government around Australia and then federally in the 1990s, introducing laws which stripped workers of their rights and enforcing enterprise-based agreements which squeezed unions out of the picture.[471]

Marxists Rosa Luxemburg and Antonio Gramsci explain why such class collaborationist, reformist programs appeal to the trade union leaders. Gramsci wrote:

> Under capitalism, when individuals are only valued as owners of commodities, which they trade as property, the workers too are forced to obey the iron laws of general necessity; they become traders in their sole property – their labour power and professional skills.

Exposed to ruthless capitalist competition, hoping to protect themselves, workers combine 'their property' – their labour – 'in ever broader

TWU banner Mayday Parade 1992. Photographer unknown.

and more comprehensive "firms"... and impose prices and hours and discipline the market.' These 'firms' – unions – can strengthen the workers' hand with their ability to act collectively against the employer and build solidarity with workers in other unions. Ultimately, however, they are part of the capitalist system. They adopt the features of the capitalist company, with 'a trusted administrative staff ... able to dominate market conditions, to lay down contracts, to evaluate commercial risks and to initiate profitable economic operations.' Their officers, the union bureaucracy, quite logically emerge as protagonists of capitalism and defenders of the capitalist system, forever seeking theories or programs which, as Luxemburg said, 'would open up an illimitable vista of economic progress ... within the capitalist system.'[472]

Gramsci also explained that disciplining workers flows logically from the officials' role. The union bureaucrat:

'THE ACCORD GOSPEL: PROFITS, MORE PROFITS' 253

> sees only chaos and willfulness in everything that arises from the working masses. He does not understand the workers' act of rebellion against capitalist discipline ... in these conditions union discipline can only be a service to capital.

So it was with the Accord, where any 'unruly rebellion' threatened the wage restraint that was essential to restoring capitalist profitability.[473]

A grim picture; but it is important not to keep a one-sided view of the Accord years. Certainly, workers' losses were legion and our victories small, but resistance was there from the beginning to the end.

We must tell the story from our side, the story of rank and file workers who stood up against the Accord's strictures. Among the few workers who actually got to vote on the Accord – albeit after the ALP, ACTU and union leaders had signed off on it – was ETU shop steward Dean Mighell. He understood that the deal being promoted was wrong. At an MTFU meeting at the Victorian Trades Hall early in 1983, Mighell heard AMWU state secretary John Halfpenny giving one of his 'brilliant' speeches recommending that delegates vote for the Accord. Although he'd never spoken in such a forum before, Dean felt concerned enough to stand up and call for a vote against the Accord:

> To me something was fundamentally wrong. Workers tied their wages to CPI yet bosses had no cap on profits. I just couldn't understand why we agreed to that as it was against all I had come to understand.

An AMWU steward from Hawker de Haviland supported Mighell and was roasted during Halfpenny's fire and brimstone right of reply, which asserted that opposing the Accord was the work of the bosses and against the interests of workers. Both shop stewards stuck to their guns, the only two voting against the Accord.[474]

Resistance to the Accord was evident during the big battles during 1984 and 1985, detailed earlier, and also in some smaller struggles, such as those of the FPU, which won deals outside the Accord in about 80 percent of the industry through successful bans and strikes. Food Preservers' organiser

Denis Evans insists that: 'we weren't going to become industrial policemen.' If members said they couldn't live on what they were getting:

> what right does a union official have to say, 'you can't improve your wages and conditions because the Accord says you can't.' It takes away the freedom from the people who are actually the union itself ... Members fuelled the anti-Accord position.[475]

After listening to the rank and file, the FPU had 'decided to bite the bullet' and keep fighting.

The invective and the attacks heaped by government upon such successful resistors included accusations of selfishness, denial of unemployment benefits, exclusion from national wage cases and legislation to cancel awards or deregister unions.

By mid-1986, many union members were restive about falling wages. The Communist Party National Executive observed:

> Rank and file feeling in some industries (metals, teaching, public sector, building and construction) ... indicated a growing level of discontent over the drop in workers' purchasing power and an increasing wish for the union movement to take effective action on wages.[476]

By Accord Mark III in 1987, the two-tier system was being rejected by many unions, all demanding a full CPI rise with no trade-offs. Some unions were starting to threaten to withdraw from the social contract, so Accord Mark IV was quickly negotiated, promising fulfilling career paths and training opportunities through award restructuring. Approaching the 1988 national wage case, there were left wing challenges in the Vehicle Builders Union, the Federated Clerks and the leadership of the Victorian THC, and a general strike was held in Victoria on 6 July.

Within a year of the Accord's implementation, early 1984 in Victoria, there was an attempt to develop a political and industrial response to the Accord. Begun as the Social Rights Campaign by left wing unions and some

Left parties, it later became the Fightback Campaign, holding two Fightback Conferences during 1987. On 28 October 1986, 200 delegates from 20 left wing unions met to form a Workers Campaign Committee. The meeting resolved to resist the two-tier system, opposed Work for the Dole programs and voted solidarity with the BLF, nurses and plumbers. Its first action was to call a rally for higher wages on 11 November – the day sacked SEQEB workers were rallying in Brisbane, and public sector workers were demonstrating around Australia against cuts to their conditions. Apart from the long running 'Defend the BLF, Defend the Unions' campaign, neither Fightback nor the Workers Campaign Committee lasted, primarily because there wasn't a clear political position or party, with links to union officials and rank and file unionists, which could hold opponents of the Accord together politically and industrially and build more than very modest solidarity actions.[477]

The level – and the potential – of resistance within the working class is attested to by how far the government had to go. They publicly backed extreme right wing employers at workplaces like Robe River and Dollar Sweets; they relied on the policing role of the union leadership and the ACTU; they used the full force of the law and the police, bringing in the armed forces and spending millions in the battles against workers over 13 years.

Tom Bramble writes that, in the later years of the Accord and its aftermath, the working class:

> battered and bruised and having lost the networks of militants that could have organised a fightback ... was at the same time, increasingly bitter towards government and employer attacks and the sacrifices expected in the name of international competitiveness ... Many workers were experiencing a joyless recovery in the 1990s and understood the effects of the ongoing employer and government offensive. This class antagonism meant that, when a call to fight was given by their leaders, workers responded enthusiastically.

There are two legacies of the Accord years. One is a working class movement wearied and weakened by years of defeat in the workplace, the whittling away of union organisation, a timid union leadership with no strategy to rebuild, a tiny revolutionary left and a shrinking reformist left that has continued to move to the right.

The other is more positive: we can look to the struggles that did take place during the Accord years, detailed in this history, and those that followed – the anti-WorkChoices campaign that ended Howard's government, the strikes against Kennett in the 1990s that effectively killed his industrial laws, and the many others detailed by Tom Bramble in *Trade Unionism in Australia*. Many of our earlier industrial struggles – particularly the highpoints such as Clarrie O'Shea in 1969, the International Workers of the World (IWW) in the 1910s, the BLF in the 1970s or waterfront workers against apartheid – had a common feature: the presence of socialists. Socialists, belonging to left wing parties, stood for class struggle, were prepared to break the laws, fought for solidarity both internationally and locally and brought with them a vision of a better world beyond capitalism.[478]

The labour movement was distancing itself from an Accord-type program in 2000, when the ALP's Arch Bevis admitted: 'Many people in the trade union movement don't look on the Accord with fondness.' In 2013, however, ACTU president Ged Kearney told the thirtieth anniversary forum that 'the spirit of the Accord must be revived, a modern-day version is now needed.'[479] Reviving these reformist ideas and programs show that our labour movement leaders have learned only right wing answers from the past. They have no answers to the current crises or to the problems of capitalism itself: wars and recession, repression and exploitation, environmental destruction and oppression. The idea of socialism is growing in popularity around the world. Climate strikes and near-revolutionary uprisings are sweeping the planet; but we also see the rise of far-right and fascist forces and the election of increasingly repressive governments. In this polarising situation, we need a different solution today, one that looks to the organised working class with the socialist politics to challenge the system.

Over 175 years ago, Karl Marx presciently wrote in an article about Chartism:

> In order to rightly appreciate the value of strikes and combinations, we must not allow ourselves to be blinded by the apparent insignificance of their economical results,

but hold, above all things, in view, their moral and political consequences. Without the great alternative phases of dullness, prosperity, over-excitement, crisis and distress, which modern industry traverses in periodically recurring cycles, with the up and down of wages resulting from them, as with the constant warfare between masters and men closely corresponding with those variations in wages and profits, the working-classes of Great Britain, and of all Europe, would be a heart-broken, a weak-minded, a worn-out, unresisting mass, whose self-emancipation would prove as impossible as that of the slaves of Ancient Greece and Rome[480]

The Australian working class has not become that unresisting mass, heartbroken or worn out. Time and time again, this working class has been defeated and rebuilt. Each rise in militancy relies on the value of 'strikes and combinations', informed by socialist politics of implacable opposition to the ruling class. This book, detailing and celebrating the history of working class resistance during the Accord years, is a contribution to that renewal.

ACRONYMS

A

ACM	Australian Chamber of Manufacturers
ACOA	Administrative and Clerical Officers' Association (now CPSU)
ACT	Australian Capital Territory
ACTU	Australian Council of Trade Unions
ADSTE	Association of Draughting, Supervisory and Technical Employees (now AMWU)
AFAP	Australian Federation of Airline Pilots
AFCC	Australian Federation of Construction Contractors
AiG	Australian Industry Group (now Ai Group)
AIPA	Australian and International Pilots Association
AIRC	Australian Industrial Relations Commission (also IRC, earlier the Conciliation and Arbitration Commission)
AJA	Australian Journalists Association (now MEAA)
ALP	Australian Labor Party
AMIEU	Australasian Meat Industry Employees Union
ANMF	Australian Nursing and Midwifery Federation
AMWU	Australian Manufacturing Workers Union
APRA	Australian Prudential Regulation Authority
APS	Australian Public Service
APSA	Australian Public Service Association (now CPSU)
ARTIO	Australian Road Transport Industrial Organisation
ASC&J	Amalgamated Society of Carpenters and Joiners of Australia
ASIC	Australian Securities and Investments Commission

ASU	Australian Services Union
ATEA	Australian Telecommunications Employees Association (now CWU)
ATF	Australian Teachers Federation
ATOF	Australian Transport Officers Federation
AWA	Australian Workplace Agreement (1996)
AWOTE	Average Weekly Ordinary Time Earnings
AWU	Australian Workers Union

B

BCA	Business Council of Australia
BLF	Builders Labourers Federation (also ABCEBLF – Australian Building and Construction Employees and Builders Labourers Federation)
BUSS	Building Unions Superannuation Scheme (now Cbus)
BWIU	Building Workers Industrial Union (now CFMMEU)

C

CAA	Civil Aviation Authority
CAEP	Council of Action for Equal Pay
CAGEO	Councils of Australian Government Employees Organisation (merged with ACTU)
CAI	Confederation of Australian Industry
CAOOAA	Civil Air Operations Officers' Association of Australia
Cbus	Construction and Building Unions Superannuation
CFMEU	Construction, Forestry, Mining and Energy Union (now CFMMEU) Construction, Forestry, Mining, Maritime and Energy Union)
CPA	Communist Party of Australia (1920–1991)
CPI	Consumer Price Index
CPSU	Community and Public Sector Union
CWU	Communication Workers Union of Australia
CWUA	Confectionary Workers Union of Australia (1925–1992) This name from 1986. (Now part of AMWU)

D

DEET	Department of Employment, Education and Training
DSS	Department of Social Security (now Centrelink and Services Australia)

DTU	Defend the Unions, Defend the BLF Committee
DVA	Department of Veterans Affairs

E

EFA	Enterprise Flexibility Agreement (1993)
ETU	Electrical Trades Union

F

FAAA	Flight Attendants' Association of Australia
FCA	Federated Confectioners Association of Australia
FCU	Federated Clerks Union (now part of ASU)
FCU(TOB)	Federated Clerks Union, Tax Officers Branch (now part of CPSU)
FEDFA	Federated Engine Drivers and Firemen's Union (now part of CFMMEU)
FEDFU	Federated Engine Drivers and Firemen's Union – WA branch of FEDFA
FIA	Federated Iron Workers Association of Australia (now part of AWU)
FIMEE	Federation of Industrial, Manufacturing and Engineering Employees (was the FIA and then part of the AWU)
FMWU	Federated Miscellaneous Workers' Union of Australia (now UWU)
FPU	Food Preservers' Union of Australia (now part of AMWU)
FSP&D	Federated Ships Painters and Dockers
FSPU	Federated Storemen and Packers Union (now UWU)

G

GTLC	Gippsland Trades and Labour Council

H

HEF	Hospital Employees Federation (now HSU)
HSU	Health Services Union

I

IAC	Industry Assistance Commission
IFAPA	International Federation of Air Pilots Associations
IPA	Institute of Public Affairs
IRC	see AIRC

M

MATFA	Meat and Allied Trades Federation of Australia
MBA	Master Builders Association (branches in every state)
MBF	Master Builders Federation – peak body of MBAs
MEAA	Media, Entertainment and Arts Association
MEWU	Metal and Engineering Workers Union (WA, now AMWU)
MIA	Meat Inspectors Association
MLA	Member of the Legislative Assembly, Victoria
MOA	Municipal Officers Association (now ASU)
MTFU	Metal Trades Federation of Unions [peak body]
MTIA	Metal Trades Industry Association (became AIG)
MUA	Maritime Union of Australia (now a division of CFMMEU)

N

NFF	National Farmers Federation
NSW NA	NSW Nurses' Association
NSW TLC	New South Wales Trades and Labour Council
NT	Northern Territory
NUW	National Union of Workers (now UWU)
NZAS	New Zealand Aluminium Smelter

O

OH&S	Occupational health and safety
OSPDU	Operative Ships Painters and Dockers Union

P

PGEU	Plumbers and Gasfitters Employees' Union
PM	Prime Minister
POA	Professional Officers' Association (now CPSU)
PPWF	Pulp and Paper Workers Federation of Australia (now part of CFMMEU)
PSAG	Public Servants Action Group

Q

QEC	Queensland Electricity Commission
QIC	Queensland Industrial Commission

QTLC	Queensland Trades and Labour Council

R

RAAF	Royal Australian Air Force
RANF	Royal Australian Nurses' Federation (became ANMF)
RFA	Rank and File Action (NSW)

S

SDAEA	Shop, Distributive and Allied Employees Association. Also known as SDA
SEN	State Enrolled Nurses
SEQEB	South East Queensland Electricity Board
SGC	Superannuation Guarantee Charge
SPA	Socialist Party of Australia (1972 to 1991 then became the CPA)
SUA	Seamen's Union of Australia (now part of CFMMEU)

T

TAA	Trans Australia Airlines (merged with Qantas)
TCFUA	Textile, Clothing and Footwear Union of Australia
TNT	Thomas Nationwide Transport
TUSG	Trade Union Support Group Queensland
TWU	Transport Workers Union

U

UV	United Voice (now UWU)
UWU	United Workers Union

V

VTHC	Victorian Trades Hall Council

W

WIRA	Waterfront Industry Reform Authority
WISC	Weipa Industrial Site Committee
WPA	Workplace Agreements
WWF	Waterside Workers Federation (now MUA division of the CFMMEU)

ENDNOTES

Abbreviations

AGPS	Australian Government Publishing Service
AFR	*Australian Financial Review*
AIPP	Australian Institute for Public Policy
ALR	*Australian Left Review*
GLW	*Green Left Weekly*
JAPE	*Journal of Australian Political Economy*
JIGS	*Journal of Interdisciplinary Gender Studies*
JIR	*Journal of Industrial Relations*
MLR	*Marxist Left Review*
NZJIR	*New Zealand Journal of Industrial Relations*
SMH	*Sydney Morning Herald*

Introduction

1 I T Henderson, Queensland MP for the seat of Mt Gravatt, 1984, as quoted in B. Russell 1992

2 Full title: 'The Statement of Accord by the Australian Labor Party (ALP) and the Australian Council of Trade Unions (ACTU) regarding economic policy'

3 Bill Kelty was an industrial advocate and research officer for the Federated Storemen and Packers' Union during the period 1970–1974 and then at the Australian Council of Trade Unions [ACTU] 1974–1977. He was a member of the ACTU Executive and Assistant Secretary from 1977 to 1983, then Secretary until

2000. At the 2013 thirtieth anniversary forum, Kelty recounted Hawke's comment, dating it as being on 12 November 1975, the day after the dismissal of the Whitlam government.

4   In some countries, these social contracts included employers specifically.

5   Ross et al. 1986

6   Accord thirtieth anniversary http://www.youtube.com/playlist?list=PLRl3LQExZ1f1ABfME8VZfYrVkw0wFdhWc

7   Accord thirtieth Anniversary

8   Ewer et al. 1991 p.xiii. The authors are critical of the Accord, but their analysis of the nature and history of the union movement is flawed.

9   Accord thirtieth Anniversary

10 Haines reported to the union journal, *The Lamp*: 'I did not feel ... that I had the right to cast my vote as an elected representative of the Nurses' Association for a document that I conscientiously believe, may, in some circumstances work against the interests of nurses.' Quoted in Schofield 1990, p.9

Chapter 1

11 Carmichael claimed this at the 1985 ACTU Congress; quoted in Ross et al. 1986 p.13

12 Lavelle p.37

13 O'Lincoln 1993 p.23. In 1973, Clyde Cameron as Minister for Labour claimed to have presided over 'the greatest redistribution in the favour of wage earners ever to be recorded in any one year by any country in the world.' But by 1974, the year of the greatest number of strike days since 1919, he was complaining that the general public were sick and tired of unions' industrial action. 'It is this bloody-mindedness on the part of a small section of the trade union movement that is slowly, but surely, pricing thousands of Australian workers out of employment.' Bramble 2008 p.80

14 For detail on the Whitlam and Fraser years, see O'Lincoln 1985, 1993; Bramble 2008; Bramble and Kuhn 2011.

15 Armstrong 2012; Archer 2006

16 Lavelle p.163

17 These arguments had surfaced earlier when Fraser first came to power. 'A VBEF demo in Geelong in October 1975 cheered Malcolm Fraser and hoisted him aloft

after he promised to reverse Whitlam's tariff cuts.' Bramble, 2008 p.85

18   O'Lincoln, 1985(a), 1993

19   This and Willis quote from Langmore in Wilson et al. 2000 p.20

20   Bill Hayden, Ralph Willis, Bob Hawke from the ALP, Charlie Fitzgibbon, Bill Kelty and Jan Marsh from the ACTU. Langmore characterises Hayden as uneasy about the Accord. Hayden lost the argument and then the leadership. Paul Keating was also sceptical of the value and feasibility of the Accord but kept his unease in check during the 1983 election campaign. Langmore in Wilson et al. 2000 pp.21, 24

21   Kuhn 1986(a) See also Kuhn 1981–82, 1982, 1987

22   Ross et al. 1986 p.13

23   Bramble 2008 p.86

24   Burford points to some bitter arguments between Hawke and Hayden and much of the Left of the labour movement, including the AMWU, who strongly opposed Ralph Willis' 1979 proposals for a form of social contract. The spectre of the UK's failed social contract was uppermost in their mind; quoted in Bramble 2008 p.119

25   MTIA became the Australian Industry Group – AiG. Easson p.134

26   Easson 2017 p.134. Evans told the Australian that he and Carmichael made the deal, without shaking hands, in a back lane in Sydney's Darlinghurst. Hannan, 'Union peace deal set scene', *The Australian*, 31 May 2013

27   Accord: thirtieth anniversary.

28   Easson 2017 p.225

29   Ross et al. 1986. By this time Bernie Taft had left the CPA and joined some ex-CPA members, ALP and unionists in a new group, Socialist Forum, which began in 1984 and included, amongst others, one-time Labor Prime Minister, Julia Gillard. http://gallery.its.unimelb.edu.au/imu/imu.php?request=multimedia&irn=4992

30   Ewer et al. 1991 p.26

31   Bramble 2008 p.119

32   Ewer et al. 1991 p.28

33   Green and Wilson in Wilson et al. 2000 p.115. Under the *Fair Work Act*, these are known as Individual Flexibility Agreements.

34   Ewer et al. 1991 p.32

35   Ewer et al. 1991 p.33-36; Ross et al. p.11

36 Bramble p.178; Frijters and Gregory 2006. These authors outline in more detail how workers' wages, employment and welfare suffered under the Accord with little recovery of lost entitlements.

37 Former Ralph Willis consultant, Julia Fellows, in Wilson et al. 2000 p.29

38 Don Rawson in Crosby and Easson 1992 p.7

39 O'Neill 1994–95

40 Ewer et al. 1991 pp.75-76; Bramble pp.153-154; Beazley federal House of Representatives Hansard 8.4.1998 – 2729. This sort of 'industry planning' was one of the underlying causes of the Mudginberri dispute, see Ch.3

41 Federal Senate Hansard, 24 October 1984 p.2312

42 Statement 3 May1983, quoted in Easson 2017, p.59

43 Dabscheck, in Wilson et al. 2000, p.100

44 Margaret Gardner as quoted in Easson pp.67, 114. On 11 June 1986, Hawke called for a real wage cut to match a 3 percent reduction in GDP, only one pay rise in 1986, discounting of up to 3 precent in next wage cut, further cuts in government expenditure, delays in tax cuts and lengthier implementation of superannuation.

45 Green and Wilson in Wilson et al. 2000 p.114

46 Bramble p.151, quoting 1989 research by Rimmer and Zappala. At a VTHC delegates meeting I attended, Simon Crean was met with heckling when he announced the ACTU was giving up biscuits with morning tea for their 2nd tier payment. Many pointed out they didn't even get a morning tea break, let alone free biscuits.

47 Quotes in this section from Strauss 2011, pp.155, 156 and 162.

48 Peter Cook in Crosby and Easson 1992 p. 157

49 McCreadie and Booth 1991

50 Unpublished talk

51 Dabscheck in Wilson et al. 2000 p.100

52 Ewer et al. 1991 pp.56–7

53 Brewer and Boyle p.10

54 Bramble p.174–5; Peetz 1998 p.133; Rafferty pp.100–1; Ewer et al. 1991 pp.98–9

55 Ewer et al. 1991 p.98

56 Ewer et al. 1991 p.1

57   *AFR* 15.8.1991

58   For a highly critical commentary on increases in the superannuation levy, see Mike Seccombe, 'Super Costly', *The Saturday Paper*, 5–11 October 2019, p.9

59   Forsyth 2014

Chapter 2

60   The H R Nicholls Society was established at a seminar at the CWA Hostel in Toorak, Victoria, in February– March 1986, in response to the 1985 Hancock Report, recommending a centralised IR system, and the Mudginberri dispute. Young barrister Peter Costello was one of the founding members. He represented Dollar Sweets, Seymour and Wagga Wagga Abattoirs, Peko-Wallsend/Robe River and Odco-Troubleshooters and went on to become Treasurer and key architect of IR policies in the Howard Coalition Government.

61   McLachlan 1988 pp.30–31

62   Kitay and Powe 1987 pp.386, 387

63   Albrechtson, 'An antidote to union sob stories', *Australian* 4.1.2006. Her column was a suggestion to the Film Finance Corporation to fund a film about the clash, something different to such films as *Rabbit Proof Fence* or *Priscilla, Queen of the Desert*.

64   The decision in the Dollar Sweets court case was applied against meatworkers at the Oakleigh Abattoir in 1988, forcing the AMIEU to lift the picket line. The August 1988 *Meat Worker* wrote: 'The threat of legal action contained in the Solicitor's letters had great substance. The law did allow the companies to seek rapid relief by way of injunction. It did afford them an action for damages. The picket line was lifted.'

65   Kelly 1992 p.255. Costello, 'Fred's place in political history' *Sydney Morning Herald* 26.7.2006. Mcallum and Cameron, 'It's there in WorkChoices where the whole notion is to make strikes so formulated, so prescribed, so lacking in surprise, that they become almost token' *Sydney Morning Herald* 26.7.2006.

66   The Federated Confectioners Association of Australia (FCAA) changed its name to the Confectionary Workers Union of Australia (CWU) in 1986. It is now part of the AMWU.

67   Passant 1986 p.11

68   Telecommunication cables were cut to the factory on one occasion. Telecom workers refused to cross the picket lines, so in the dead of night a Telecom

management team snuck in and repaired the cables. Claims of violence on the picket line continue to be aired every time the Dollar Sweets dispute is mentioned, even as late as 2006 in tributes to Stauder on his death.

69 Costello says the guards cost the company $70,000. Costello 1988

70 Costello 1985 p.51

71 As a rookie lawyer employed by Stauder's Kroger-Costello legal team, future Coalition MP Eric Abetz found one employer who, unlike others, responded, 'Why should I worry if Dollar Sweets goes down? It will mean more business for me.' Coleman 2014 https://www.spectator.co.uk/2014/02/australian-noties/ O'Malley, 2006, claims it was Kroger who briefed Alan Goldberg who then retained Costello as his junior.

72 Costello noted that, before December 1985, there was considerable doubt that the Supreme Court 'would exercise common law jurisdiction to grant injunctive relief against unions involved in industrial disputes'. This was primarily because the Arbitration Commission was set up explicitly to deal with industrial disputes as a separate matter. The CWU argued this case in court – and lost. Costello, 1988

73 Quotes in this section from Petersen

74 Costello, 2006. http://workers.labor.net.au/features/200602/b_tradeunion_costello.html

75 *Age* 26.7. 2006 http://www.smh.com.au/news/national/the-sweets-of-a-famous-victory/2006/07/25/1153816182414.html?page=fullpage#contentSwap2

76 Costello and Coleman 2009 p.36

77 The NFF only became involved in the dispute from 1983 when the AMIEU served its log of claims on all NT abattoirs. Some farmers had abattoirs on their properties; if they were members of an association affiliated with the NFF, the NFF became eligible to be a party to award negotiations.

78 In 1983, the NFF had another victory against an AWU $14 pay claim for pastoral workers, convincing the Commission to defer the rise on the grounds of employer incapacity to pay. Kitay and Powe p.373

79 David Trebick, http://archive.hrnicholls.com.au/archives/vol6/vol6-7.php Kitay and others also see the two earlier disputes as being game changers. Trebick is spelt as Trebeck in some publications.

80 Ian McLachlan http://archive.hrnicholls.com.au/archives/vol28/vol28-1.php

81 Kitay and Powe 1987 pp.365–6

ENDNOTES

82. Jerrard 2017
83. Trebick
84. Trebick added, 'One of the great advantages the farmers had, of course, was that they could go home and no-one could find them. A là, the Boer War.'
85. Houlihan http://archive.hrnicholls.com.au/archives/vol1/vol1-4.php
86. Brian 2001 p.119
87. Kitay and Powe 1987 p.372
88. There were some serious doubts about the viability of the industry in the Territory, some seeing it as overcapitalised. Brian 1999 p.110
89. An earlier attempt by MATFA in 1977 to establish an award for the non-award NT abattoirs was resisted by the union and it was dropped. Kitay and Powe 1987 p.374
90. Kitay and Powe 1987 p.375
91. Houlihan
92. 'Tally' simply refers to the minimum output a workers could be expected to produce in a normal day's work. Head tally – number of animals slaughtered. Unit tally – equivalent units of labour required to process 100 animals. Brian, 1999 p.112; Kitay and Powe 1987 pp.366–8
93. Brian 1999 pp.114–5
94. As quoted by Brian 1999 p.114
95. Commissioner Gough was excluded from arbitrating the case because he had earlier conciliated the award, invoking a never-before used passage in the Conciliation and Arbitration Act. Anderson, 1996.
96. Brian 1999 p.124 fn 62
97. Westpac had recently refused a $200,000 loan to Pendarvis. Kitay and Powe 1987 p.390
98. Kitay and Powe 1987, p.390. Jim Baird claims that, once domestic production began at Mudginberri, the NT government bought and stored the meat; after the dispute, they sold it back to the abattoir at half the price so that it could be on-sold for export. There was a significant upside for Westpac as well: the NT government soon afterwards transferred all its banking to it from the Reserve Bank.
99. Brian 1999 p.116
100. Alice Springs maintained their picket lines in 1984 and 1985. Victoria River continued to work despite the picket line. Brian 1999 p.110

101 The federal Meat Inspectors went back to work on July 14, but stopped again until August 7, forcing Mudginberri to close down again. Kitay and Powe 1987 p.375

102 Brian, 1999 p.123 Fn 37. In 1987 the High Court weakened the defence of managerial prerogative with its judgment that industrial tribunals should have wide powers to impose current community standards on industry.

103 Brian 1999 p.116

104 Surplice. Personal interview with Brian. 1999 p.116; Houlihan

105 Clause 33(c) states 'The terms of any system of payment by results ... shall be established by negotiation and agreement between employer and the majority of employees concerned or their nominated representatives.' Clause 33(a) stated that pieceworkers should get at least 20 percent more than minimum rates, and 33(d) that piecework rates would be registered with the Arbitration Commission and be legally binding.

106 Kitay and Powe 1987 p.379

107 Brian 1999 p.119

108 At Victoria River, meatworkers continued working despite the picket line. In Alice Springs, the picket held for two seasons, 1984 and 1985. Brian 1999 p.110. Point Stuart did not open in 1985.

109 Brian 2001 p.198; 1999 p.111

110 Kitay 2001 p.192. 'Had Mudginberri been on a standard award-based tally system and maintained the same throughput, their incomes would have increased, but Pendarvis considered this to be economically non-viable.'

111 Anderson 1996–97. Quote from Surplice in Kitay 2001 p.192. Brian 1999 p.121

112 Brian 2001 p.198. Claimed to be due to stock unavailability, the *National Farmer* reported that cattle producers had voted to boycott the Katherine meatworks, a claim that farmers later denied. Brian 1999 p.117

113 At one point there was one ex-Mudginberri employee on the picket line. Kitay and Powe 1987 p.384

114 http://www.naa.gov.au/collection/explore/cabinet/by-year/1984-85/industrial-relations.aspx

115 The difference between the price for export and local meat was the basis for Jay Pendarvis' damages claim. Brian 1999 p.117

116 The union's funds were released from sequestration on 25 September 1985.

117 The government was also aware that a number of transport and administrative

unions – POA, WWF, SUA, TWU, APSA, NTTLC and ACTU – also supported the Meat Inspectors action and that the transport unions would not ship meat certified by non-union inspectors. The MIA would also have precipitated a national strike of their members if the government had directed them to cross the picket line.

118 *Bulletin* 16 July 1985 p.51

119 *AFR* 17 July 1986

120 Brian 1999 p.118

121 Kitay and Powe 1987 p.389

122 Brian 1999 p.119

123 Kitay and Powe 1987 p.392

124 Brian 1999 p.119

125 The Katherine abattoir did not open in 1985 because of lack of meat due to dry conditions. The union, however believed the graziers boycotted the abattoir for siding with the AMIEU. A report in the *National Farmer* said that cattle producers had voted to boycott Katherine meatworks, though the farmers denied there was a boycott. Brian, 1996.

126 Brian 1996

127 The reason Pendarvis could seek damages under s.45D is that, instead of directly hiring workers, he hired three contractors who then hired the rest of the employees. The courts regarded the three as the employer, meaning that Pendarvis became the 'third person' affected by the dispute and therefore the subject of a secondary boycott.

128 Anderson 1966–7

129 Kitay 2001 p.194

130 Kitay and Powe 1987 p.391. See Katie Wood 2013 for details of the Clarrie O'Shea case.

131 ACTU 1987, *Future Strategies for the Union Movement*

132 All quotes from Brian 1999 p.121

133 Quotes in this section from Kitay and Powe 1987 pp.398, 365, 378

134 Kitay 2001 p.195

Chapter 3

135   Russell 1992

136   Russell p.81. Bjelke-Petersen's government opposed the Accord, part of the National Party's hostility to the ALP. The government was the only participant not to sign the April 1983 Accord Summit communiqué.

137   *Business Review Weekly* 26 April 1985 p.44

138   Gerrymandering, introduced in 1948 by the ALP to hold on to power through its base amongst rural workers, turned into a weapon against them when the National Party won in 1957.

139   Before 1974, Bjelke-Petersen ruled with only 17 percent of the vote; by the 1980s, his government ruled with 30 percent of the vote. Hamilton 1978; Willett 1986; Barrigos 2018

140   O'Lincoln 1993 p.18; Willet 1986; Bloodworth 2013.

141   Kahn 1981

142   See Russell, chapter 2 for a comprehensive history of the use of State of Emergency legislation and powers, including the famous 1965 Mount Isa strike. Bjelke-Petersen quote from his Memoirs.

143   See Russell, chapter five for further analysis of the Bjelke-Petersen government.

144   Since SEQEB had been established, energy prices had risen twice as fast as CPI. It was clear SEQEB intended shifting the blame for higher energy prices onto the workers, covering up the price gouging that became typical of energy privatisation around the country.

145   Russell p.3. ETU Document *History of the Power Dispute*.

146   McCarthy 1985

147   The next four references are to Russell, pp.3, 5, and 81. By 1985, Gilbert was also a member of the HR Nicholls Society. Doodney was a shop steward at SEQEB prior to becoming an organiser.

148   Bjelke-Petersen rang Comalco's CEO Mark Rayner. 'Mark, I'm telling the boys up here to switch off your Comalco refinery.' When Rayner protested that the refinery would be permanently damaged by this move, Bjelke-Petersen replied 'I couldn't care less.' *Courier Mail* 1.2.1986.

149   Russell p.12

150   Mark Sherry 1993 p.29. The QTLC had already raised concerns about the use of contract work and on 4 September 1984 sought urgent meetings with SEQEB

management. The leaflet, however, did argue that 'If this attack goes unchallenged then workers will have no one to blame but themselves.'

151   *Courier Mail* 1 February 1986

152   As reported in the press in late February; also interview with Senator George Georges, ALP. Mark Sherry 1995 p.169–70

153   This and the next two references from Mark Sherry 1993 pp.4, 142

154   Russell p.19

155   The Act established a new Tribunal to replace the QIC in the electricity industry; banned strikes and incitement of strikes, setting out certain conditions of work that the Tribunal could not alter. Other restrictions were placed on the Tribunal to limit its power to review sanctions.

156   Mark Sherry 1993 p.7. Reported in the press as 'Angry SEQEB Men storm Trades Hall' (*AFR* 8.3.1985); 'Sellout charges fly as power workers sweat', (*Australian* 8.3.1985); 'We were sold out, say sacked power men' (*Telegraph* 8.3.1985)

157   Carnegie was a member of the Seamen's Union of Australia, SUA, a member of the then Socialist Party of Australia (SPA) and initially a supporter of the Accord. He was arrested nine times during the dispute. He has stayed an active unionist and, at the time of writing (2019), was the State Secretary of the Queensland branch of the MUA.

158   Mark Sherry 1995 pp.160–1

159   Mark Sherry 1993 p.57–63. The Broad Left Conference, organised by the CPA to boost support for the Accord. In the build up to the conference, there were seminars held in some capital cities.

160   Guille 1985 p.383

161   Russell p.61

162   Coming into law on 29 March, this was to be the Industrial Relations Tribunal for the power industry, stripping the QIC of any jurisdiction. It met with resistance, not just by workers, but also the Chief Justice, who advised the government that judges were not prepared to sit on such a tribunal.

163   Many years later, the High Court found these police actions wrongly executed, the people wrongly convicted and wrongly having criminal records.

164   Mark Sherry 1993 p.114

165   This and following quote from Russell p.87

166   The employers weren't motivated by concern for their employees; rather, they

feared the step would entrench unionism in a largely non-unionised industry and lead to a crackdown on unofficial practices designed to avoid penalty rates.

167　*The Socialist* 178, 10 August 1985

168　Russell p.99

169　*The Socialist* 178, 10 August 1985

170　Mark Sherry 1995 p.50

171　*Courier Mail* 21.8.2018. Hamilton's comments were an appalling display of contempt for workers.

172　*Socialist Action* no.3, 1 November 1985 p.13

173　Mark Sherry 1995 p.139; Harry Hauenschild, QTLC President

174　ETU Strike Committee, *Strike Bulletin* no.6, 1985

175　*Courier Mail* 27.9.1985

176　*The Australian* 8.10.1985

177　Mark Sherry 1995 p.152

178　Mark Sherry 1993 p.11

179　In 1986, the Bjelke-Petersen government was re-elected but with a substantially reduced majority. In 1987, the Premier himself was forced to resign amid allegations of government corruption. In 1989, the ALP won office for the first time in over 30 years.

180　*Canberra Times* 23.10.1985

Chapter 4

181　Ann Sherry in Connor 1987. The roundtable included Irene Bolger, Victorian secretary RANF; Joan Corbett, Women's Officer Australian Teachers Federation (ATF); Brenda Forbath, Organiser, Hospital Employees Federation (HEF), Victoria, no.1 Branch; Anna Kokkinos, Solicitor, Slater and Gordon law firm; Ann Sherry, OH&S officer, Administrative and Clerical Officers Association (ACOA), Victoria; Louise Connor, Industrial Officer, Australian Journalists Association (AJA), Victoria.

182　Forbath in Connor p.19

183　Schofield pp.40–41. Schofield points out that the percentage gap between female and male full time workers' earnings in the period 1975–1983 increased from 76 percent to 80 percent, but, for all workers, effectively did not move from 66 percent. p.28. Following quotes from Schofield p.10 and p.2

184   Burgmann in Curran et al. *ALR* 1990 p.16

185   Stevens 1984 as quoted by Schofield p.43

186   S Jackson. *Broadly Speaking* was a broadsheet put out by a group of socialist feminist unionists for the Broad Left Conference in 1986. Many thanks to Sue Jackson for providing material for this section of the chapter.

187   Ross et al. p.11 quoting Kenneth Davidson.

188   S Jackson *Broadly Speaking*

189   At the new government's National Economic Summit, there was only one woman to speak out of 99 men. Only one of the 55 points of the Summit's final Communiqué specifically addressed women's rights: 'Given the high levels of unemployment the summit agrees that the basic rights of women should be recognised and protected and that the move towards greater equality and independence for women should be encouraged. There should be equal access to job creation programs, to employment training; retraining and education measures designed to break down occupation segregation and discrimination.' A mealy-mouthed commitment to women's rights, and no timetable to win equal pay.

190   Quoted in Ross 1984 p.14

191   McNeill et al. 1986. Comparable worth was first introduced in the 1970s in the USA. An example from America is the comparison of secretaries' and truck drivers' pay rates which resulted in a significant pay rise for secretaries.

192   S Jackson. Personal communication. CAEP arose out of the SF84 Socialist Feminist conference (1984). See also D'Aprano 1977, 1995; Wood 2015

193   Schofield p.56

194   Judge and Bottomley 2012; Wood 2015

195   Symons 2004. Symons was writing on the twentieth anniversary of the passing of the *Sex Discrimination Act* and quoted from several senators during the debate in late 1983.

196   Ross 1988

197   On 1 January 1993, the Keating government introduced a new requirement for firms failing to comply with the Act, making them ineligible for government contracts and specified forms of industry assistance.

198   Gorton and Brewer 2015

199   Ann Sherry in Connor p.19. Others such as Blackman. While sympathetic to the

Accord, her criticisms of the many shortfalls so early is telling.

200 Rosewarne 1988

201 Corbett in Connor p.21

202 Teicher p.213. On the Rosella strike see McPhillips

203 Unless otherwise stated, all quotes from Ross 'Dedication doesn't pay the rent' in Bloodworth and O'Lincoln pp. 141–158. The nurses' union was at that time the Royal Australian Nursing Federation. It became the Australian Nursing Federation and now is Australian Nursing and Midwifery Federation – ANMF. In NSW, it is known as the NSW Nurses and Midwives Association, in Queensland Nurses and Midwives Union. Because much of health is covered by the states, each state branch of the ANMF is registered under the state industrial relations system. There is also a federal branch. At the time of the strike, state enrolled nurses or SENs were covered by the Hospital Employees Federation, HEF (now the Health Services Union, HSU). Psychiatric nurses are mainly covered by the broader health unions, the then HEF, now HSU.

204 Bolger in Connor p.23

205 RJ O'Dea, HEF advocate commented on the wage rise: 'The increase may look substantial, but nurses have been underpaid for so long they [wage rises] are very disappointing.' Information about the Canberra strike from *Tribune* reports at the time (1 July 1970 p.6; 15.7.1970 p.10; 5 August 1970 p.3) and the obituary for Jan McCall, a long-term nurse activist and one of the key leaders of the 1970 strike. McCall died 11.9.2012

206 Dickenson 1993 p.188

207 By 1986, the union dropped the Royal appellation and became the ANF.

208 Bessant p.18; *Age* 18.12.1986

209 Bessant p.20; *Age* 10.12.1986

210 *Herald* 11.11.1986 p.1

211 Bolger in Connor p.23

212 At this stage in the strike, critical care staff stayed at work, and all wards had a skeleton staff.

213 Personal communication

214 *Socialist Action* February 1987

215 *Age* 12.11.1986

216 *Age* 12.11.1986

217 *Age* 12.12.1986

218 Nurses had a three year hospital-based course, comprising periods working under supervision in the wards and attendance in study periods at hospital-linked Schools of Nursing, before becoming qualified. There were also further specialist certificate courses of varying lengths. Nurses now undertake a three-year university degree, with some hospital placements before qualifying.

219 *Age* 12.12.1986. What the Victorian HEF had not factored in, however, is that SENs, in a reversal of previous trends, had begun to leave the HEF and join the RANF. They were actually out on strike themselves.

220 *Herald* 15.12.1986. The *Herald* was the afternoon paper from the Murdoch stable. It was later merged with the morning *Sun* to become *The Herald-Sun*.

221 Kahn 1986 pp.3–4. During the 1980s, roughly 92 percent of nurses were women.

222 Bessant p.19 (pagination for Bessant according to online version)

223 Fox p.95

224 Bessant p.16

Chapter 5

225 All quotes by Graeme Haynes from personal interviews with author, unless otherwise noted . This chapter draws on articles from Socialist Action written by the author or Graeme Haynes. The articles can be found at http://labourhistorycanberra.org/2015/05/wage-deal-robe-river-ructions/

226 Marian Sawer describes the core values of the New Right: 'they are united in the belief that state intervention to promote egalitarian social goals has been responsible for the present economic malaise and has represented an intolerable invasion of individual rights.' Sawer 1982 p.viii

227 Haynes 1988 p.12

228 There was an export embargo on iron ore put on by the Lyons government on 18 April 1938 as WWII loomed. In 1955, the Menzies government resisted attempts to end the ban, citing limited reserves, but then lifted the embargo in November 1960 and generally loosened restrictions over the next five years. The Pilbara is one of the biggest ore bodies on the planet. In its heyday Japan was buying between 75 and 85 percent of Robe's ore; China is now the major buyer; Vassiley 2018

229 Ellem 2017 p.41; John Kelly as cited by Vassiley p.106

230 AWU organiser Charlie Butcher, as quoted in Vassiley p.120

231 Iron Ore Production and Processing Award 1969; Cliffs Robe River Iron Associates Agreement 1972; CRRIA Iron Ore Production and Processing Agreement 1979

232 Graeme Haynes, personal communication

233 The HR Nicholls Society has an annual Copeman Medal, awarded for 'service to freedom of employment' https://quadrant.org.au/magazine/2013/09/what-charles-copeman-achieved-at-robe-river/

234 One of the most outrageous claims by Copeman and others was the supposed dispute about workers at the Cape Lambert site striking over the availability of different ice cream flavours. The reality was that, in the mess room, a temporary dividing wall was put in place between workers and staff, with fewer food options available on the workers' side. One such option was ice cream with six flavours on the staff side, versus two on the workers side. The situation was resolved by unions removing the wall. This 'dispute', as it was often written up, even appeared in a US newspaper.

235 Copeman 1987

236 *AFR* 29.8.1986 p.1, 4 'Hawke wades into Peko row'

237 Ross 1986 p.11

238 *AFR* 14 .9.86 p. 8 'New Right poses dilemma for employers, but the answer may be found in Marx'

239 McRae, quoted in Ellem 2007

240 Copeman 1987

241 Thompson and Smith 1987; *AFR* 14.8.1986 'The Pilbara confrontation: Robe closure threatens trade'

242 Graeme Haynes recalls that Marks deliberately said South Africa, because he could appeal to their opposition to the apartheid regime. Although South Africa did export some coal, everyone knew that he was really talking about Brazil.

243 Thompson and Smith 1987

244 *AFR* 15.8.1986 'In Pilbara, it's "heads I win, tails you lose"', p.6

245 Dabscheck 1995 pp.31–32

246 *AFR* 14.8.1986

247 *AFR* 29.8.1986 'Hawke wades into Peko row' p.1

248 Ellem 2007

249 Ellem 2007

250 Gethin 1990

251 Hewitt, *AFR* 19.1.1987 as quoted by Ellem 2015 (a) p.124

252 *The Age* 15.1.1987

253 Hewitt, *AFR* 1.12.1989

254 Haynes 1988 p.12

255 *BRW* 23.1.1987 'Robe River – how not to take on a union'

256 At the same time, the NSW Liberal government introduced legislation to allow non-union agreements and individual contracts.

257 *AFR* 24.8.1993; *The Australian* 31.12.1996. Ownership of Robe River: Cliffs (an American company) from 1962–1986, Peko-Wallsend full ownership 1986–1988; then North Broken Hill (BHP owned) 1988–1990; Rio from 1990.

258 Ellem 2015 (b) p.331

259 Ellem 2015 (a); Ellem 2017 for a comprehensive review of the current situation; Ellem 2003

260 Industry Commission 1991 p.473

261 *AFR* 5.9.86 p.1,4 'Labor gains the initiative in New Right debate'. In 1985, the government-commissioned *Hancock Report* had outlined a number of neoliberal measures which the government adopted over the following years.

262 Tony Abbott, 'The real lessons of Robe River.' *Bulletin* 9.2.1988. Following quotes are from this article. Abbott, more recently Australia's Prime Minister, was then a journalist

263 See endnote 10 in this Chapter, for an explanation of the ice cream myth.

Chapter 6

264 McGrath, 'Letter to an Imaginary Friend'. Another version of the second line is 'I hear the hurtling and the long thunder of money.'

265 In 1982, the new Victorian Labor government pulled out of the Royal Commission.

266 Closed shop refers to the practice of having 100 percent unionisation of a workplace, enforced by the unions at that workplace. In construction, it is called 'No ticket, no start.' Often, this union preference was included in an agreement with the employer, who could not then employ non-union labour; if they tried,

that person would be told to join the union by the workers. If either the employer or non-union worker refused the union demand, the workers would go on strike. During the late 1970s to early 1980s, some ideologically motivated workers, backed by employer groups and conservative governments, made a number of attempts to break through the closed shop. They failed.

267 *The Age* 5.2.1983

268 Bob Carr, *Bulletin* 26.4.1983. Bob Carr became an MP in 1984, later Premier and Foreign Minister in the federal Gillard government. He spoke regularly in support of deregistering the BLF. This chapter is a summarised version of my book *Dare to Struggle, Dare to Win. Builders Labourers fight deregistration, 1982–1994*, abbreviated from this point as *DTSDTW*. Quotes from BLF members came from my interviews with them.

269 *The Australian* 15.4.1983.

270 *Bulletin* 26.4.1983

271 Both NSW and Victorian governments during the 1980s relied on public works spending in the face of high unemployment levels. Three other factors were a dramatic growth in the finance, property and business services, following deregulation of the finance industry. The fall of the Australian dollar (the 'banana republic' phenomenon) facilitated an inflow of foreign investment. The October 1987 stock exchange crash prompted the Government to pump money into the economy and induced investors to desert equity markets for property. Another stimulus was from the housing industry. Housing commencements nationally rose from 84,000 in 1986–87 to a peak of 128,200 in 1988–89.

272 It was headed up by former AIRC Commissioner Allan Vosti.

273 As early as September, the MBA welcomed the dispute settling procedures in the BIA, saying that there was no reason to continue deregistration. But they did not withdraw from the case. Vic Exec Mtg 7.9.83

274 *DTSDTW* p.102, p.309 fn 10

275 The BWIU was facing its own existential crisis by the 1980s. As the nature of work on building sites was changing, particularly from the use of concrete which the BLF covered, their work was disappearing and the BWIU membership was shrinking.

276 *Economist* 6.8.83.

277 *DTSDTW* pp.105–110. Wran had been an industrial advocate for the BWIU before entering politics. His deputy Jack Ferguson had been on the BWIU executive when that union had been part of an anti-BLF Eight Union Alliance.

278	*Herald* 20.12.84; *Sun* 21.12.84.
279	Stewart West, as quoted in Mitchell p.300.
280	Keating, *Age* 26.10.85.
281	*AFR* 15.10.84
282	*DTSDTW* p.146
283	*Age* 5.4.86 and *Sun* 5.4.86. The picture of Crabb was dropped after the first edition. *The Herald* had called Crabb the 'Minister for War' a month earlier in a lengthy article about him, including his Premiership ambitions. *Herald* 11.3.86.
284	Crean said this on radio – and laughed. *Age* 26.4.86.
285	Quote from Mick Sage, a member of the smaller carpenters' union, the ASC&J. It was initially set up as a right wing breakaway from the BWIU when that union was led by members of the CPA, but during the deregistration some in the ASC&J, including Mick, were more sympathetic to the BLF.
286	*SMH* 23.4.86. Ayer's Rock is now known by its ancient Aboriginal name, Uluru.
287	*Herald* 21.5.86; *NT* 4.7.86. Many BLF members had been forced to sign forms resigning from the Federation before they could join another union. The Federation got members to sign rejection or 'duress' forms saying that they were keeping their BLF membership.
288	Technical and Further Education institutions
289	The Federal Government could only deregister the union federally. The success of the 1986 deregistration in NSW and Victoria relied on the states also deregistering the BLF. If the WA branch had won its case in the IRC, the union would have had federal coverage/registration again, and could have moved in on NSW, ACT and Victoria to claim BLs' work back from the BWIU and FEDFA. This would have derailed any attempt to refuse re-registration in the IRC, leaving the Government having to deregister the union all over again. Cook promised that he wouldn't proclaim the section of the Act affecting the WA branch's moves, but he had other plans up his sleeve. Senate Hansard pp 5889-90, 18 December 1990; BLF leaflet 'VTHC Executive Condemns…' 15.11.90.
290	The construction, mining and energy unions became the CMEU. The addition of the forestry union created the CFMEU; from 2019, amalgamation with the TCFUA and MUA produced the CFMMEU.
291	*DTSDTW* p.272
292	However, Gawenda wrote that building workers are 'like relics from a long

vanished, class ridden past' *Age* 30.8.86; 'If you don't fight you lose' is probably a modification of a saying from Bertolt Brecht, the famous German left wing playwright and poet: 'Sometimes when you fight you lose, but if you don't fight, you've already lost.' 'Dare to Struggle, Dare to Win' is one of Mao Tse-Tung's sayings and would be familiar to communists in Australia.

Chapter 7

293 White 1985. There were three unions in the federal public sector. The clerks were in the ACOA and in the Tax Office the FCU(TOB), while the clerical assistants were in APSA. The POA, covered professional officers such as engineers, librarians and social workers. Under the Accord, ACOA and APSA later amalgamated, joined by the POA. They absorbed the Tax Office workers previously covered by the FCU(TOB).

294 Kuhn 1978 p.1 For a later analysis of the public sector see Kuhn 1980.

295 In 1976, the ACOA Reform Group was founded in Victoria and stood against the Grouper leadership, winning control of the branch in 1979. In 1977, Reform Group member Ann Forward won the Federal Vice-President position. Between elections, the group met regularly, issued a newsletter and had extensive rank and file influence. When it won some positions on the Victorian Branch Executive, those members resigned, but the group itself continued, playing a strong role in the 1984–85 national pay dispute. Kuhn 1986 (b)

296 Kuhn 1986 (b). PSAG's first national conference occurred at the same time as the 1981 DSS strike and heard from some of the activists involved.

297 Harrison and Main

298 This section draws on a session at Marxism 2015 with Eris Harrison, a Grey Collar activist and ACOA delegate. Grey Collar, 'The fight for jobs. Social Security 1981'

299 In Victoria, when management arrived to stand down workers, the union strategy was for all workers to go out for coffee, so they couldn't be presented with the orders; Victoria thus lasted longer.

300 Fraser could undoubtedly have claimed that rapidly increasing unemployment levels, which reached very high levels in 1982–83, justified increased staff according to the Department's staffing formula.

301 This section draws significantly on White 1985. All quotes are drawn from here unless otherwise indicated. The Accord promised to 'ensure comparability' in wages and conditions with state government workers and those in the private sector. Fraser imposed the wage freeze on public sector workers earlier than on

other workers.

302 *Socialist Action* no.3 November 1985 p.13

303 Earlier, the pay rate awarded to one set of workers would 'flow on' or spread to others because their pay rates were set relative to the first set of workers through the awards system. The rate for a turner and fitter, a member of the AMWU, was the formal benchmark used. Because these workers were found in many different workplaces, such as factories and hospitals, a rise in this rate had an almost universal impact. Although there was no formal relativity set, when one group of workers in a factory won a pay rise or some other improvement in conditions, usually an over-award benefit, then workers in nearby factories would agitate for a flow-on. In that way, the rise would spread throughout the industry and the workforce.

304 Personal recollection. I was a delegate in DSS for the period written about in this chapter.

305 Only 18,879 voted, 15,835 for, 3,044 against. This was a typical response in the APS when a campaign defeat was in the offing. The meetings usually consisted of people who had never come to any previous mass meetings, never really supported industrial action and wanted the dispute finished, along with the more militant activists

306 This section draws on Harrison & Main 1989 and Harrison 1988 (a) (b)

307 *Green Left Weekly* 23.7.1986

308 *Socialist Action* no.12 September 1986 p.12

309 Marxism conference Melbourne 2015

310 *Socialist Action* no.32 July 1988

311 *Socialist Action* no.32 July 1988

312 *Socialist Action* no.32 July 1988

313 *Socialist Action* no.15 December 1986 p.13

Chapter 8

314 Bob Hawke *Age* 21.8.1989. Quotes, unless otherwise attributed, are from Norington 1990.

315 The two airlines policy was introduced by the Chifley government in 1945–6. Initially, TAA was meant to be a monopoly government run service, but two successful High Court challenges enabled another airline, ANA. The policy was

	formally established in 1952 by the Menzies government and took practical effect when Ansett purchased the failing ANA in 1957.
316	Paterson p.12
317	Paterson p.12
318	Wapping the bitterest of disputes https://redflag.org.au/node/5587 ; News International Wapping – 25 years on. The workers story. Exhibition and book. 2011
319	Raby had a run-in with Abeles in 1988 over the NZ pilots' industrial action. Paterson p.16. During negotiations in 1989, Abeles is alleged to have pointed at Raby saying 'I'll use every power available, including legal action, to get you.'
320	Ansett collapsed in 2001. Australian Airlines (formerly TAA) merged with Qantas in 1992.
321	AFAP President was an elected, honorary role with immense executive power. Terry O'Connell was not a pilot and joined the union in 1977 initially as research officer, then Industrial Officer and then Executive Director. Lawrie Cox had been with the Rubber Workers' Union and was aligned with the Right in the ALP.
322	Hutson 1983 p.254. The AFAP finally registered in 1981, partly in response to TWU and other union attempts to sign up pilots.
323	The August 1988 stopwork had been held over a period of days, as was the usual practice, so as to not disrupt flights.
324	A proposed career path covered broadbanding of pilot's duties, redefined bid period, preferential bidding including composite blocks and productive flight time (time spent in the cockpit).
325	Qantas pilots broke away in 1981 to form the Australian and International Pilots Association (AIPA), not registering until 1986.
326	The structural efficiency principle encouraged workers to agree to multiskilling, broadening work classifications and a reduction in demarcation 'barriers.' It was designed to 'flatten' the workplace structure, giving management more flexibility to switch workers around. It led to a more thorough award restructuring process through Accord Mark IV. See Ch.2 for further explanation.
327	The average wage was $27,000, average pay of pilots was $79,000 (NB not the median), but the starting rate was $42,000 going up to $130,000. The rises were in the order of $2,000–$5,000 per year.
328	Norington p.16
329	In fact, the AFAP put in a more extensive ambit claim towards the end of June – a

ENDNOTES

50-point log of claims which would have won pilots a 100 percent pay rise.

330 Paterson p.35

331 Kelty contacted the airlines on the eve of the 6 August national wage case, warning them that if pilots were granted 'even 0.001%' above what was allowed for other airline workers, he would seek a flow-on for every other airlines worker.

332 Previously the pilots and other flight crew's cases were heard in a specialist tribunal, the Flight Crew Officers Industrial Tribunal. It was closed down earlier in 1989.

333 Norington p.30

334 Norington p.85

335 Maddern was an employers' advocate in national wage cases during the 1970s. Kelty secured Maddern's position as AIRC President, but he later drew the ire of Kelty by refusing to grant the ACTU's claims for the introduction of a new Enterprise Bargaining phase of the Accord – Accord Mark VII. See Ch. 12

336 ABC *The World Today* 21.8.1989

337 Maddern was criticised for the speed with which he cancelled the pilots' awards, then sitting on the case for five weeks, allowing the industry to plunge into crisis.

338 Paterson p.26. Later moves by the government after the dispute was over to allow the overseas pilots to extend their visas, bring their families out and apply for permanent residency suggest Australian citizenship was a major motivator for overseas pilots. Nine of the Civil Aviation Authority's (CAA) 23 professional pilot staff also signed up to the airlines, scabbing on the pilots.

339 The use of the RAAF cost the government at least $800,000. Defence Minister Kim Beazley scandalously described using the RAAF to strikebreak as equivalent to its use in the humanitarian evacuation from Darwin after Cyclone Tracy in 1974.

340 Ansett worked out that pilots who were sacked or quit could not get access to their superannuation if previous industrial action breached the misconduct provisions of the contracts. Pilots were sent letters of advice saying that superannuation would be withheld and damages deducted from their funds.

341 According to Norington, Ansett had a plant in AFAP headquarters. The identity of the person was never discovered. At some point in the dispute, the plant went back to work at Ansett, and the airline's source of inside information dried up.

342 'Recompense' was in the form of waiving government charges, so it would just appear as losses on the CAA and Federal Airports Corporation books. The estimated cost was $100 million, based on a return to work within a month.

343 The eight unions and their leaders were George Campbell AMWU, Martin Ferguson ACTU, FMWU, Tom McDonald BWIU, Di Foggo ATF, Peter Robson ACOA, John Maitland Miners Federation, Jack Cambourn FEDFA, Graham Harris ADSTE.

344 Another threat facing the AFAP at this point was an attempt by the TWU and ATOF to claim coverage of pilots. The claims went to the AIRC and were not rejected until after the end of the dispute in May 1990, left there deliberately to pressure the pilots back into the Accord.

345 The Air Traffic Controllers (CAOOAA) had been running a dispute all this time over wages but, seeing what was happening to the pilots, decided to end their industrial action on 21 September and accept a 14 percent pay rise. Norington p.96

346 Paterson p.11. There were few pilots covered by this new award, because most Australian pilots had not gone back. At this stage, perhaps 40 of the 1,600 AFAP members had signed contracts; of those, 25 were at East-West and IPEC. Any planes flying were using management or overseas recruits.

347 One of the conditions the pilots held out for was the retention of their seniority. Without that, the scab pilots who had been employed in their absence would be in a better position financially and promotion-wise. The airlines refused to the end to agree to this demand.

348 Ross Gittins, 'ACTU pursuing a "solidaristic" wage policy', *SMH* 20.9.1989

Chapter 9

349 Price 2014

350 Mackinnon 2009

351 At the time of APPM dispute, Peko-Wallsend had quit Robe River; they later merged with North Broken Hill to become NBH–Peko.

352 This section relies on work by John Tognolini, a worker at Cockatoo Island, and the Cockatoo Island Reunion group http://cockatooreunion.com/ . Price 2014, interview with Claude Sandaljian, chair of the combined shop stewards committee, on the 25th anniversary of the occupation.

353 The island, known as Wareamah, was used by Aboriginal people. An Aboriginal tent embassy was established in November 2000, then a unsuccessful attempt made to claim back the land under native title in 2001. From the 1850s, it was used by colonisers as a penal settlement and a reform school, as well as a dockyard, also making products for power stations, bridges, dams, ports and mines.

354 The occupation lasted 10 May to 14 August 1989. The final day of work on the

ENDNOTES 289

Island was 4 June 1991.

355 Makovich 2014

356 'on the grass' is a commonly used phrase to describe a strike

357 A similar fight broke out at the Newcastle dockyards in 1988. It was also lost. Giles 1988

358 This section relies on articles by Mackinnon 2009 and Carl Jackson 2015. Quotes are assigned appropriately. This and the next two quotes are from Mackinnon 2009.

359 Unions active in the region included AWU, MEWU (AMWU), ETU, TWU, FEDFU.

360 The case was JFK Nominees, run by the hardline conservative Jeff Kennett (later Victorian Premier).

361 The CFMEU was shut out when the FEDFA and United Mineworkers Union were in the process of amalgamating with the construction unions to form the CFMEU.

362 C Jackson 2015. Unless otherwise noted quotes from here are from this source.

363 Simon Kuether, CEPU as quoted in Nicholls and Kuether 1995

364 Mckinnon

365 Mason 1995

366 In 2002, Rio Tinto moved to shift 4,000 workers in WA to a collective agreement in response to the election of a new Labor government. Rio argued that collective agreements provided flexibility, were more efficient and easier to administer, but there was no guarantee that unions would be involved in the process. There was no regret for the use of deunionising individual contracts.

367 Vassilopoulos 1997

368 Baker

369 Baker p.9

370 Oldfield

371 The union covering APPM workers was the Pulp and Paper Workers Federation, but in 1992, after a short-lived amalgamation with the timberworkers' union, both were in the process of amalgamating with the CFMEU.

372 Tierney p.70, quoting Thompson, details how the Burnie mill was 'an industrial dinosaur and the classic case of a company in a death spiral. Its machinery [was] … ancient and hopelessly inefficient.' Tierney also notes that environmental pressure groups were targeting logging and paper production in Tasmania over

sustainability and pollution.

373 Tierney p.68

374 Baker interviewed Inspector Fox, who said the police felt they had been tricked by the company and that he would not have arrested the men had he known they were workers at the mill. This incident soured relations between Burnie police and management. Baker p.10

375 Brought over by Sydney-based Toraguard Security, guards were called 'ninja turtles' by workers. They were only there for three days at the beginning of June before the company withdrew them because they became a PR disaster for APPM. NBH–Peko had used the same company at Vista Paper Products in Sydney during an eight-week picket. Tierney p.69; Baker p.17

376 Quotes about women's involvement from Tierney pp.73–75

377 *Age* 6 June 1992. As quoted by Baker p.17

378 Paul Munro was one of the many union officials, in his case from the ACOA, who were promoted from their union leadership positions to the AIRC or its state counterparts.

379 Jamieson

380 Quoted in Strauss 2011 p.142

Chapter 10

381 This chapter draws on Easson's *Keating and Kelty's Super Legacy* and Mees and Brigden's *Workers capital*. I disagree with much of their analysis and use the material often to argue for an opposing point of view. See also Humphrys 2019 for a more critical view of the Accord, including superannuation. I was involved in some of these disputes during the Accord years and have written about superannuation since: https://redflag.org.au/index.php/node/6366 https://redflag.org.au/node/6491

382 Easson 2017 p.123

383 Kelly 2009 p.146

384 NSW, Queensland and Victoria introduced means tested age pensions in 1900. The new constitution of 1901, introduced with federation, gave the federal government constitutional power to provide for age and disability pensions. The Act to implement it was passed in 1908, with payments commencing in 1909.

385 In the APS, 70 percent of workers left the scheme with only their own contribution

ENDNOTES

and the accrued interest. Easson 2017 p.12

386 Mees and Brigden outline a rich history of union-initiated attempts to win superannuation.

387 In 1974, the first ABS national survey. 32% of workforce covered, 36% male, 15% female. 24% in private sector, 58% in public sector.

388 Easson 2017 pp.6, 7, 12; Mees and Brigden pp.45, 80

389 Easson 2013 p.12

390 Easson 2017 p.14Mary Easson 2017 pp.12, 14, 16, 215

391 Easson 2017 p.16

392 Easson 2017 p.8

393 Mees and Brigden p.53, Easson, p.166 respectively

394 Easson 2017 p.66

395 Mees and Brigden p.242, frontispiece. These authors also quote Garry Weaven's 2008 remarks about the wonders of superannuation, where he said, 'Industry super funds allow working people to pool their savings so they can invest as if they are the wealthiest people on earth. They can invest for the long term. They can buy, not sell, when prices are low. Thy have access to the best advice – no deal is too big for them.'

396 Mees and Brigden p.88. Earlier, they point out that the CAI's Bryan Noakes had already warned of exactly this situation.

397 Ross 2004 p.114

398 Easson 2017 p.71

399 All quotes in this section from Ross 2004

400 Mees and Brigden p.79

401 Easson 2017 p.99

402 Easson 2017 p.101

403 This and the next quote from Mees and Brigden pp.81–82

404 Easson 2017 p.119

405 http://www.hcourt.gov.au/assets/publications/speeches/current-justices/frenchcj/frenchcj26feb09.pdf

406 Mees and Brigden p.74

407 Mees and Brigden pp.59, 78

408 Easson 2017 p.195

409 This section is drawn from Chapter 9 of *Dare to Struggle, Dare to Win*. All quotes come from this text.

410 Crabb, MBAV Seminar 3.3.87, *Age* 4.3.87. Other unions could have been as militant. Ron Owens, SA BLF branch secretary, points to the Glaziers who, because they were last on the site, could put the job in limbo if they refused to put glass in the top two floors. Nobody was going to move into a building with the top two floors open to the elements.

411 Like the BLF, because the Plumbers union refused to sign the MoU, plumbers had not been paid the 2.3 percent July national wage increase. *DA* 13.8.86; John Cummins Vic Br Mtg 10.2.87. During the dispute, the BLF put out a number of leaflets backing the Plumbers, as well as taking action on the job.

412 Bubb, MBAV Seminar 3.3.87. The impact of subcontracting was demonstrated at the White Industries site in Canberra in April 1987. The employer sacked the 180 direct employees, intending to re-employ only 16. Others would be taken on via subcontracting firms. When all the sacked workers struck, White Industries took s.45D action against them. ACT BLF leaflet 2.4.87. NSW/ACT Fight Back! Newsletter of Canberra Fightback Group No.4, 9.4.87.

413 *Age* 30.6.87; Quote from FEDFA's Malcolm McDonald *Herald* 9.4.87

414 *AFR* 14.12.87

415 National wage case April 1991, p.39

416 Easson pp.112–116

417 Retire Ready Index compiled by the Commonwealth Bank and actuarial firm Rice Warner. Similar figures from Ready to Retire study carried out by News Corp and Industry Funds. https://www.commbank.com.au/content/dam/commbank/personal/docs/commbank-retire-ready-index-full-report.pdf https://www.greenleft.org.au/content/superannuation-shameful-deceit https://www.greenleft.org.au/content/superannuation-generation-betrayed

418 Adele Ferguson, 'Grand theft, a retiree's tax on a grand scale', *AFR* 29.7.2019; Adele Ferguson and Eryk Bagshaw, 'Keating blasts "monkeys" for "grand theft" super rejig, *Age* 29.7.2019

419 Easson 2017 pp.133–139 and 180–184

420 Mees and Brigden p.2, Easson 2017 p.148 resp. First quote from Peter Drucker.

421 Retire Ready Index

422 Workers earning less than $450 per month do not receive any superannuation, and women on parental leave are not paid for their time away.

423 As reported in Jessica Irvine, 'Let's end the unlucky lottery', *Age* 17.2019. Productivity Commission, *Superannuation; Assessing Efficiency and Competitiveness* no.91, 21 December 2018

424 Easson 2017 pp.151, 155

425 Easson 2017 p.145. Kelty added: 'The day he agreed our relationship changed forever. I became Keating's greatest supporter. I realised Keating was a very rare person.'

Chapter 11

426 The *Industrial Relations Act* was amended in 1992 and 1994. The enterprise bargaining sections, s.112 and s.115 were replaced by s.134 in July 1992; s.134 was replaced by s.170 MC in 1993 and then s.170 MA in April 1994. There are a series of s.170 M sections under the Act.

427 Kelly 2009 p.136. Less elegantly, Kelty said: 'The decision we took was that the unions couldn't live forever off the tit of the Arbitration Commission and we couldn't have judges deciding the wage increase in every industry. This was a judgment made by the trade unions.' Kelly p.135

428 O'Neill 1994, pp.5, 6. Buchanan was deputy director of the Australian Centre for Industrial Relations Research and Teaching (ACIRRT), which co-hosted a 1994 conference on enterprise bargaining. O'Neill's document is a report of that conference.

429 Wilson et al. 2000 p.29

430 Many businesses employing fewer than 20 workers saw little need for EFAs; they were usually non-union and generally didn't adhere to the award either, although some did have over-award pay and conditions. Managerial prerogative was a given in such workplaces. Ron Callus in O'Neill 1994 pp.1–3

431 Kelly 2009 p141. Brereton noted that 'There was lots of animosity. On one occasion I was booed by the ACTU congress in the Sydney Convention Centre.'

432 Kelly 2009 p.138

433 Kelly pp.138, 139

434 Ewer et al. p.xii

435 Gray 1990 pp.17, 19

436 Accord thirtieth anniversary

437 Since 2013, private sector enterprise agreement coverage has halved to 11 percent, triggering a 'dramatic and lasting deceleration in wages', down to less than 2 percent in 2016 and 2017. https://d3n8a8pro7vhmx.cloudfront.net/theausinstitute/pages/3100/attachments/original/1572229868/IR_Reform_Briefing_Note_FOR_RELEASE.pdf?1572229868

438 Kelly 2009 p. 138; O'Neill 1994 p.5

439 O'Neill 1994–95 p.3

440 Bramble 2008 pp.176–7. See also O'Neill 1994–95 pp.4–7

441 Bramble 2008 pp.160–168. This was also my experience and that of fellow workers in the federal public sector. Ron Callus in O'Neill 1994 p.3 points to some workplaces winning child care or access to child care and training as examples of 'quality of life' conditions being incorporated in EBAs which were not allowable under awards from 1988.

442 Fellows in Wilson et al. 2000 p.36

443 O'Neill 1994 pp.8–9

444 Bramble 2008 p.170

445 O'Neill 1994–95 p.1. Iain Ross, former ACTU assistant secretary, was on the Full Bench when the ASAHI decision was made in 1995.

446 Wright and Ryan 1994. All quotes in this section are from this article. The authors interview several public sector workers in the Department of Social Services (now Centrelink and the Department of Social Services) and the Department of Veterans' Affairs.

447 Flexitime meant that you could work extra hours in a day, not as overtime, and then use those hours at a time of your choosing. Under the new agreement the department was offering eight-week periods where you would work specific combinations of hours that then became non-negotiable.

448 I am indebted to Luke van der Meulen for his insights and information on the Latrobe Valley disputes. Information in this section comes from interviews with Luke van der Meulen and notes and draft chapters for a book on the history of the FEDFA during his time in the Latrobe Valley.

449 As a result of amalgamation, this became the CFMEU M&E sub-branch

450 In the amalgamation process, unions were assigned Principal, Significant and Other status. Principal meant that most workers had to join that union. Significant

meant that the union could remain with its existing members, but could not recruit any new members. In many cases –certainly in the Valley – the 'principal' union was the union most prepared to agree with the employers on most issues.

451 Shortly after the Loy Yang B privatisation and signing of their EBA, three ASU officials, including the state secretary, quit the union to take up managerial positions with the new owner, Edison Mission Energy.

452 As M&E leader, van der Meulen argued against the proposed industrial action, warning other union leaders of the advantages this would give the company through the *force majeure* and ability to do maintenance work on the site, effectively undercutting the industrial action.

453 In 2013, a rejuvenated CFMEU M&E sub-branch took a stand, with 75 striking workers at Yallourn joined by supporters. After a 100-day lockout, they won a new EBA which clawed back some of the earlier losses.

454 'Coles workers approve landmark new agreement', Duncan Hart, *Red Flag* 8.3.2018 https://redflag.org.au/node/6238

455 All Kelty's quotes from Hannan 2013

Chapter 12

456 Burford 1984

457 Cook 1991 p.7

458 *AFR* 13.9.1989; the quote in the chapter heading was the *AFR* Headline 7.3.1990

459 Ross et al. 1986 p.14

460 Ross et al. 1986 p.11

461 Dabscheck 1995 pp. 31–32

462 Lucas 2013

463 *AFR* 5.9.1986 pp.1,4 'Labor gains the initiative in the New right debate'

464 http://www.abc.net.au/4corners/stories/s72787.htm 19.2.1997

465 Crean, ACTU Presidential Address 25.9.1989

466 Ewer et al. 1991 p.63. Keating gave the 1990 McKell lecture as part of the McKell lecture series begun in 2011 to pay tribute to Sir William McKell, NSW Labor leader during the 1940s and later Governor General.

467 Humphrys 2016 pp.242–3

468	O'Lincoln 1985 (b); Mark Sherry 1995 pp.99–100
469	Crean, ACTU Presidential Address 25.9.1989
470	McDonald and McDonald 1998 p.289
471	Queensland in 1987, NSW 1991, Victoria 1992, Tasmania 1992 and WA in 1993
472	Cited in O'Lincoln, 'Trade Unions and Revolutionary Oppositions'
473	Gramsci as quoted by O'Lincoln 'Trade Unions and Revolutionary Oppositions'
474	Dean Mighell, personal communication. In a DSS branch delegates' meeting, I and two other Socialist Action members put the case against the Accord. Except for one other delegate, we were in the minority, like Dean. Like him, we remain unrepentant.
475	Personal communication
476	Strauss 2011 p.155
477	The Social Rights Campaign was a joint attempt by the SWP and the anti-Accord SPA to build anti-Accord forces. The Defend the BLF campaign later became a Defend the Unions campaign, meeting regularly for some years, to defend unions under attack. (See chapter 7.) For the SPA position on the Accord, see Jack McPhillips 1985.
478	Clarrie O'Shea – Wood; BLF – Burgmann and Burgmann
479	Arch Bevis in 'Labor, unions no longer in accord', Australian 6.3.2000; Ged Kearney at 30th anniversary.
480	https://www.marxists.org/archive/marx/works/1853/07/14.htm Thanks to my comrade Sebastian for alerting me to this wonderful quote. Of course, the slaves did revolt, but some of that history was unknown in Marx's time.

BIBLIOGRAPHY

Accord. Thirtieth anniversary http://www.youtube.com/playlist?list=PLRl3LQExZ1f1ABfME8VZfYrVkw0wFdhWc

ACTU, *Future Strategies for the Trade Union Movement*,1987

ACTU-TDC Australia Reconstructed: ACTU/TDC mission to Western Europe: a report by the Mission Members to the ACTU and the TDC. AGPS 1987

Albrechtson, J., 'An antidote to union sob stories', *The Australian*, 4 January 2006.

Anderson, A., 'Mudginberri: confronting, contracting and the secondary boycott provisions, *Hummer*, Summer 1996–7, https://www.labourhistory.org.au/hummer/vol-2-no-7/mudginberri/

Archer, V., 'In search of the Australian dole bludger: Constructing discourses of welfare, 1974–83', PhD thesis, ANU, June 2006. Available from: https://pdfs.semanticscholar.org/3aab/bfc24256dee648efba5c3cbcdcd4978bee8a.pdf

Armstrong, M., 'Disturbing the peace: riots and the working class', *MLR* no.3 (Winter), 2012, https://marxistleftreview.org/articles/disturbing-the-peace-riots-and-the-working-class/

Baird, J., 'Skill and fines and "rock and roll": the metal trades margins campaign of 1967–8', *Hummer*, Summer 1996–7, https://www.labourhistory.org.au/hummer/vol-2-no-7/skill-and-fines/

Baker, D., 'Community police peacekeeping amidst bitter and divisive industrial confrontation: the 1992 APPM dispute at Burnie', https://pdfs.semanticscholar.org/0ef8/8a400c65732828bc5df6b2cfb25e9904567b.pdf.

Barrigos, R., 'Why Queensland is different', *Marxist Left Review*, no.15 (Summer), 2018, pp. 61–86, https://marxistleftreview.org/articles/why-queensland-is-different/

Bessant, J., 'Good women and good nurses: conflicting identities in the Victorian nurses strikes – 1985–1986', *Labour History*, no. 63. 1992, pp.155–173, https://www.jstor.org/stable/27509144?seq=1#page_scan_tab_contents

Blackman, D., 'Women and the Accord', *ALR*, no. 89, 1984, pp.17–23.

Blackmur, D., *Strikes: Causes, conduct and consequences*, Federation Press, 1993.

Bloodworth, S., 'An activist's life in Joh's Queensland', *Red Flag*, 29 November 2013, https://redflag.org.au/article/activist%E2%80%99s-life-joh%E2%80%99s-queensland

Bloodworth, S. and T. O'Lincoln (eds), *Rebel Women in Australian working class history*, Red Rag, 2008.

Bramble, T., *Trade Unionism in Australia. A history from flood tide to ebb tide*, Cambridge University Press, 2008.

Bramble, T. and R. Kuhn, *Labor's Conflict. Big business, workers and the politics of class*, Cambridge University Press, 2011.

Brewer, P. and P. Boyle, 13 years of hard Labor: Lessons from the Accord experience, http://www.dsp.org.au/node/135#Promises

Brian, B., 'Mudginberri revisited: a case study of a secondary boycott', *Green Left Weekly*, no. 257 (4 December), 1996, https://www.greenleft.org.au/content/mudginberri-revisited-case-study-secondary-boycott

Brian, B., 'The Mudginberri Abattoir dispute of 1985', *Labour History*, no.76 (May), 1999.

Brian, B., 'The Mudginberri Abattoir dispute of 1985: Response', *Labour History*, no. 80 (May), 2001, pp.197–200.

Burford, M., 'Prices and incomes policy and socialist politics', *JAPE*, no. 14, 1984.

Burgmann, M. and V. Burgmann, *Green bans, red union: Environmental activism and the New South Wales Builders Labourers' Federation*, UNSW Press, 1998.

Burgmann, M. and V. Burgmann, *Green bans, red union: The saving of a city*, 2nd edn, NewSouth, 2017.

Coghill, K. (ed.), *The New Right's Australian fantasy*, McPhee Gribble/Penguin, 1987.

Coleman, P., 'Australian noties', *The Spectator*, 8 February 2014, https://www.spectator.co.uk/2014/02/australian-noties/

Connor, L., 'What's in it for women. A roundtable on women in unions', ALR, no. 100 (July–August), 1987, pp. 17-23.

Cook, P., *The Accord: an economic and social success story*, Occasional Paper no.1, Centre for Economic Performance, December 1991, https://core.ac.uk/download/pdf/6489398.pdf

Copeman, C., 'The Robe River Affair', in HR Nicholls Society, *Light on the Hill: industrial relations reform in Australia : the proceedings of the Queen's birthday weekend conference at Mooloolaba*, 6th–8th June, 1987, http://archive.hrnicholls.com.au/archives/vol3/vol3-8.php

Costello, P., 'Dollar Sweets: confronting union power', *IPA Review*, 1985, pp. 49–52.

Costello, P., *In search of the magic pudding: The Dollar Sweets story*, HR Nicholls, 5–7 August 1988, http://archive.hrnicholls.com.au/archives/vol5/vol5-5.php

Costello, P., 'Fred's place in political history', *SMH*, 26 July 2006.

Costello, P., with P. Coleman, *The Costello Memoirs*, Melbourne University Press, 2009.

Crean, S., *ACTU Presidential Address 1989*, https://www.actu.org.au/actu-media/speeches-and-opinion/presidential-address-simon-crean-actu-congress-1989

Crosby, M. and Michael Easson (eds), *What should unions do?* Pluto, 1992.

Curran, C. et al., 'Unions at the Crossroads', *ALR*, July 1990, pp. 10–19.

Dabscheck, B., *The struggle for Australian industrial relations*, Oxford University Press, 1995.

D'Aprano, Z., *The becoming of a woman*, North Carlton, Victoria, Z. D'Aprano, 1977.

D'Aprano, Z., *Zelda*, Spinifex Press, 1995.

Dickenson, M., *An unsentimental union: The NSW Nurses Association 1931–1992*, Hale & Iremonger, 1993.

Easson, Mary, 'Present at the creation: the origins of the Australian system of superannuation', Masters Thesis, UNSW, 2013. Available at: http://unsworks.unsw.edu.au/fapi/datastream/unsworks:12592/SOURCE02?view=true

Easson, Mary, *Keating and Kelty's Super Legacy: The birth and relentless threats to the Australian system of superannuation*, Connor Court Publishing, 2017.

Ellem, B., 'New unionism in the old economy: community and collectivism in the Pilbara's mining towns', *JIR*, vol. 45, no. 4, 2003, pp. 423–441.

Ellem, B., From Robe to Workchoices: the productivity myth. 10th National Labour History Conference. ASSLH 2007

Ellem, B. (2015a), 'Robe River revisited: geohistory and industrial relations', *Labour History*, no. 109 (November), 2015, pp. 111–130.

Ellem, B. (2015b), 'Resource peripheries and neoliberalism: the Pilbara and the remaking of industrial relations in Australia', *Australian Geographer*, vol. 46, no. 3, 2015, pp. 323–337.

Ellem, B., *The Pilbara: from the deserts profits come*, UWA Publishing, 2017.

Evatt Foundation, *Unions 2001: A blueprint for union activism*, 1995.

Ewer, P. et al., *Politics of the Accord*, Pluto, 1991.

Ewer, P., W. Higgins and A. Stevens, *The Unions and the Future of Manufacturing in Australia*, Allen & Unwin, 1987.

Ferrier, C., 'SEQEB: Can the workers beat Bjelke?' *Socialist Action*, no.1 (September), 1985, p. 9.

Ferrier, C., 'We workers must spit on their false unity!' *Socialist Action*, no. 2 (4 October), 1985, p. 12.

Ferrier, C., 'SEQEB: officials throw in the towel', *Socialist Action*, no. 3 (1 November), 1985, p. 13.

Ferrier, C., 'Coal miners dig in to fight Joh's strike ban', *Socialist Action*, no.19 (May), 1987, p. 5.

Forsyth, A., 'The enduring myth of the industrial relations club', *The Conversation*, 27 November, 2014.

Fox, C., 'Enough is enough: the 1986 Victorian Nurses Strike', *UNSW Studies in health service administration*, 1991.

Fritjters, P. and R. Gregory, 'From golden age to golden age. Australia's "great leap forward"?', *Economic Record*, vol. 82, no. 257 (June), 2006, pp. 207–224.

Gardner, M., 'Australian Trade Unionism in 1985', *JIR*, March, 1986.

Gethin, P., 'The power switch at Robe River', *AIPP*, 1990.

Giles, G., *Bitter Bread: The fight to save Newcastle State Dockyards*, Newcastle Trades Hall Council, 1988.

Gorman, P., *Weipa: Where Australian unions drew their 'line in the sand' with C.R.A.*, WISC–CFMEU, 1996.

Gorton, C. and P. Brewer, *Women of steel: Gender, jobs and justice at BHP*, Resistance Books, 2015.

Gray, S., 'Unfinished business', *ALR*, July, 1990, pp. 17,19.

Grey Collar, *The fight for jobs: Social Security 1981*, Public Servants Action Group.

Guille, H., 'Industrial relations in Queensland', *JIR*, vol. 27, no. 3 (September), 1985, pp. 383–398.

Hamilton, H., 'Democratic Struggles in Queensland', *ALR*, vol. 1, no. 65 (August), 1978, pp. 4–11.

Hancock, K.J., C.H. Fitzgibbon and G. Polites, *Australian Industrial Relations Law and Systems, Report of the Committee of Review*, vol. 2, AGPS, 1985.

Hannan, E., 'We're all to blame, including me, unions own worst enemy', *The Australian*, 31 May 2013.

Harrison, E. (1988a), 'DSS workers back in the wars', *Socialist Action*, no. 31 (June), 1988, p. 11.

Harrison, E. (1988b), 'Lessons of a historic strike', *Socialist Action*, no. 32 (July), 1988, pp. 7–9.

Harrison, E. and D. Main, *Fighting Labor's cuts – the NSW Social Security strike, May-June 1988*, https://labourhistorycanberra.org/2015/09/fighting-labors-cuts-the-nsw-social-security-strike-may-june-1988/

Haynes, G., 'We can fight back, say Robe River workers', *Socialist Action*, May, 1988, p. 12.

Houlihan, P., *A brief history of Mudginberri and its implications for Australian trade unions. Arbitration in Contempt*, HR Nicholls Society. http://archive.hrnicholls.com.au/archives/vol1/vol1-4.php

Humphrys, E., 'Australia's Accord, the labour movement and the neoliberal project', Phd Thesis, University of Sydney, 2016, https://ses.library.usyd.edu.au/handle/2123/14965

Humphrys, E., *How labour built neoliberalism: Australia's Accord, the labour movement and the neoliberal project*, Chicago, Haymarket, 2019.

Hutson, J., *Penal colony to penal powers*, rev. ed., AMFSU, 1983.

Industry Commission, *Mining and minerals processing in Australia Report*, no. 7, vol. 3, Issues in Detail, 25 February 1991.

Jackson, C., 'The Weipa strike', *Red Flag*, 2015 https://redflag.org.au/node/5036

Jackson, S., *ACCORDing to some* Broadly Speaking Broadsheet, nd (c.1985–6).

Jamieson, I., 'APPM dispute ends in stand-off', *GLW*, 17 June 1992. https://www.greenleft.org.au/content/appm-dispute-ends-stand

Jerrard, M., 'Exporting animals, exporting jobs: 30 years of campaigning against live exports', *Brisbane Labour History Group, Conference Proceedings*, 23–25 September 2017.

Judge, C. and A. Bottomley, 'Still fighting for equal pay', *MLR*, no. 4, 2012, pp. 177–188, https://marxistleftreview.org/articles/still-fighting-for-equal-pay/

Kahn, A., 'The Fraser years', *International Socialist*, no. 11 (Autumn), 1981.

Kahn, A., 'Nurses' strike: sisters are doing it for themselves – and us', *Socialist Action*, no.15 (December), 1986, pp. 3–4.

Kelly, J., *Rethinking industrial relations: mobilization, collectivism and long waves*, Routledge, 1998.

Kelly, P., *The end of certainty: The story of the 1980s*, Allen & Unwin, 1992.

Kelly, P., *The march of patriots: The struggle for modern Australia*, Melbourne University Press, 2009.

Kitay, J., 'The Mudginberri Abattoir dispute of 1985: Response', *Labour History*, no. 80 (May), 2001, pp. 191–196.

Kitay, J. and R. Powe, 'Exploitation at $1000 per week? The Mudginberri dispute', JIR, vol. 29, no. 3 (September), 1987, pp. 365–400.

Kuhn, R., 'Class struggle in the public service: class and labour process in the Australian public service', unpublished BA thesis, Monash University, 1978.

Kuhn, R., 'Thin cats and socialism: Class struggle within the state', *International Socialist*, no. 10 (August), 1980, pp. 5–19.

Kuhn, R., 'Whose Boom: Left Nationalism and the Resources Boom', *International Socialist*, no. 12 (Summer), 1981–82, pp 18–30.

Kuhn, R., 'Strategies: Left Nationalism and Revolutionary Marxism', *JAPE*, 12/13, 1982, pp. 93–109.

Kuhn, R. (1986a), *Militancy uprooted: labour movement economics 1974–86*, Socialist Action pamphlet, 1986.

Kuhn, R. (1986b), 'White collar, red ties', *Socialist Action*, no. 13 (October), 1986, pp. 7–9.

Kuhn, R., 'Industry Policy and the Working Class', *Politics*, vol. 22, no. 2 (November), 1987, pp. 97–102.

Lavelle, A., 'In the Wilderness: Federal Labor in Opposition 2003', Published Thesis at Griffith University, available at: https://research-repository.griffith.edu.au/bitstream/handle/10072/366181/02Whole.pdf?sequence=1

Lucas, C., '30 years on: Accord deal "a bitter time", says Kelty', *The Age*, 31 May 2013.

McCarthy, P., 'Power without glory: the Queensland electricity dispute', *Journal of Industrial Relations*, vol. 27, no. 3 (September), 1985, pp. 364–382.

McCreadie, S. and A. Booth, 'Towards 2000 in the TCF industries – a bold experiment', in M. Costa and M. Easson (eds), *Industry Policy – what policy?* Pluto, 1991.

McDonald, T. and A. McDonald, *Intimate Union: Sharing a revolutionary life. An autobiography*, Pluto Press, 1998.

McGrath, T., *Letter to an imaginary friend*, Copper Canyon Press, 1997.

Mackinnnon, B.H., 'CRA/Rio Tinto in the 1990s: a decade of deunionisation', *Labour History*, no. 97, 2009, pp. 75–96.

McLachlan, I., 'After Mudginberri: the turning of the tide', *IPA Review*, Feb–April, 1988, pp. 29–32.

McLachlan, I., 'We used to run this country and it wouldn't be a bad idea if we did again: In praise of a "comrade"', http://archive.hrnicholls.com.au/archives/vol28/vol28-1.php.

McNeil, K., S. Jackson and P. Morrigan, 'A new phase for equal pay. "Comparable worth" signals a new approach to a long campaign', *Australian Society*, January, 1986, pp. 22–26.

McPhillips, J., *The Accord and its consequences: Trade union experiences*, New Age Publishers, 1985.

Makovich, M., 'Cockatoo Island strike and occupation', *The Guardian*, 25 June 2014.

Marr, J., 'Peter's Principles', http://workers.labor.net.au/features/200602/b_tradeunion_costello.html

Mason, B., 'Weipa miners vow to maintain blockade', *GLW*, 31 October 1995, https://www.greenleft.org.au/content/weipa-miners-vow-maintain-blockade

Mees, B. and C. Brigden, *Workers' Capital: Industry funds and the fight for universal superannuation in Australia*, Allen & Unwin, 2017.

Mitchell, G., *On strong foundations: The BWIU and industrial relations in the Australian construction industry, 1942–1992*, Harcourt/Brace, 1996.

Nichols, D. and S. Kuether, 'Weipa strikers fight for equal pay for equal work', *GLW*, 28 November 1995, https://www.greenleft.org.au/content/weipa-strikers-fight-equal-pay-equal-work

Norington, B., *Sky Pirates: The pilots' strike that grounded Australia*, Crows Nest, ABC Enterprises, 1990.

Oldfield, C., 'For the labourer is worthy of his hire: The APPM dispute', http://archive.hrnicholls.com.au/archives/vol12/vol12-12.php

O'Lincoln, T. (1985a), *Into the mainstream. The decline of Australian Communism*, Stained Wattle Press, 1985.

O'Lincoln, Tom (1985b), 'The BLF: making of a maverick', *Socialist Action*, no. 2 (October), 1985, pp. 7–10.

O'Lincoln, T., *Years of rage: Social conflicts in the Fraser era*, Melbourne, Bookmarks, 1993.

O'Lincoln, T., 'Trade unions and revolutionary oppositions: a survey of classic Marxist writings', http://sa.org.au/marxism_page/intros/ol-tu.htm

O'Malley, N., 'The sweets of a famous victory', *SMH*, 25 July 2006, http://www.smh.com.au/news/national/the-sweets-of-a-famous-victory/2006/07/25/1153816182414.html?page=fullpage#contentSwap2

O'Neill, S., 'Enterprise Agreements: myths and realities' (Conference report), Parliamentary Research Service, Current Issues Brief no. 27, 1994, https://www.aph.gov.au/binaries/library/pubs/cib/1994-95/95cib27.pdf

O'Neill, S., 'Future directions for unions after ASAHI', Parliamentary Research Service, Current Issues Brief no. 38, 1994–95, https://www.aph.gov.au/binaries/library/pubs/cib/1994-95/95cib38.pdf.

Passant, J., 'Dollar Sweets verdict menaces right to picket', *Socialist Action*, no. 5 (February), 1986, p. 11.

Paterson, A., 'A pilot's perspective of the Australian pilots dispute of 1989', 2008, http://www.vision.net.au/~apaterson/aviation/pd89_document.htm

Peetz, D., *Unions in a contrary world; The future of the Australian trade union movement*, Cambridge University Press, 1998.

Petersen, E., 'The legal antecedents of the workplace relations act: From the Plague to Reith', http://sa.org.au/interventions/law.htm

Price, S., 'The Cockatoo Island occupation – 25 years on', *Red Flag*, 2014, http://redflag.org.au/article/cockatoo-island-occupation-%E2%80%93-25-years#sthash.T1OBX1nt.dpuf

Productivity Commission, *Superannuation: assessing efficiency and Competitiveness. Report no. 91*, 21 December 2018, https://www.industrysuper.com/assets/FileDownloadCTA/d62c256bec/Super-Scandal-Unpaid-super-guarantee-in-2016-17-formatted-versio-for-final-compliance-tick-V5.pdf

Rafferty, M., 'Union amalgamation: the enduring legacy of Australia Reconstructed?' *JAPE*, no. 39, 1997, pp. 99–105.

Rosewarne, S., 'Economic management, the Accord and gender inequality', *JAPE*, no.23 (August), 1988, pp. 61–86.

Ross, L., 'Courting equal pay...a case for "comparable worth"', *Socialist Action*, no. 2 (4 October), 1984, p. 14.

Ross, L., 'Peko: against a ruthless boss, more was needed', *Socialist Action*, no. 13 (October), 1986, p. 11.

Ross, L., 'Sisters are doing it for themselves...and us', *Hecate*, vol. 13, no. 1, 1987, pp. 83–99.

Ross, L., 'Equality? Only for profit!' *Socialist Action*, no. 28 (March), 1988, p. 12.

Ross, L., *Dare to struggle, dare to win: Builders Labourers fight deregistration 1982–1994*, Vulgar Press, 2004.

Ross, L., T. O'Lincoln and G. Willett, *Labor's Accord: why it's a fraud*, Socialist Action, 1986, http://www.reasoninrevolt.net.au/objects/pdf/d0135.pdf

Russell, B., 'A spark of hope', unpublished thesis, University of Queensland, 1992.

Sawer, M. (ed.), *Australia and the New Right*, George Allen and Unwin, 1982.

Schofield, J., *Freezing history: Women under the Accord, 1983–1988*, Industrial Relations Research Centre Monograph, UNSW, 1990.

Sheen, R.L., 'Patterns in Australian industrial conflict: 1973–1989', unpublished thesis, Australian National University, 1992, https://openresearch-repository.anu.edu.au/handle/1885/123354?mode=full

Sherry, M., *Sellout: The story of the SEQEB strike*, R&F Press, 1993.

Sherry, M., 'Agency and discourse in labour history: a case study of the SEQEB dispute', Master of Arts thesis, University of Queensland, 1995, https://www.textqueensland.com.au/item/thesis/53db52ec7f4a0a02004a8214f1f3d81d

Stevens, J., 'Women's work – undervalued, underpaid', *ALR*, Spring, 1984.

Stone, J. and L. Walker, 'Queensland miners "champing at the bit" to take on Joh', *Socialist Action*, no. 20 (June), 1987, p. 15.

Strauss, J., 'The Accord and working-class consciousness: the politics of workers under the Hawke and Keating governments, 1983–1996', PhD thesis, James Cook University, 2011, http://eprints.jcu.edu.au/29816/

Symons, E-K., 'Sex revolution leaves "some sisters poorer" and it's one tough act to follow', *The Australian*, 30 July 2004.

Teicher, J., 'Union compliance and incomes policy: the Australian social contract', *NZJIR*, no. 13, 1988, pp. 213–325.

Tierney, R., 'Class struggle and the "community of families": The 1992 dispute at Associated Pulp and Paper Mills', *JIGS*, vol. 4, no. 2, 1999, pp. 64–80.

Thompson, H., 'Australia Reconstructed. Socialism deconstructed', *JAPE*, no. 23 (August), 1988, pp. 87–96.

Thompson, H. and H. Smith, 'The conflict at Robe River', *Arena*, no. 79, 1987, pp. 76–91.

Tognolini, J., 'The Cockatoo Island strike', https://www.youtube.com/watch?v=Lmc6-dgFYsA&feature=em-upload_owner

Tracey, R., 'Section 45D of the Trade Practices Act and Primary Boycotts: A case study in the meat industry', in H R Nicholls Society Forum, *For the labourer is worthy of his hire*, http://archive.hrnicholls.com.au/archives/vol12/vol12-10.php

Trebick, D., 'The industrial significance of the live sheep export dispute', in HR Nicholls Society Forum, *No Ticket, No Start*, http://archive.hrnicholls.com.au/archives/vol6/vol6-7.php

Vassiley, A., 'Establishing trade unionism in the emerging Pilbara mining region of Western Australia: 1965–72', *Labour History*, vol. 115 (November), 2018, pp. 105–127.

Vassilopoulos, J., 'Union renewal at Weipa', *GLW*, 25 June 1997, https://www.greenleft.org.au/content/union-renewal-weipa

White, P., *From tragedy to farce: The sorry story of the 1984–1985 ACOA pay campaign*, ACOA Reform Group, November, 1985.

Willett, G., 'Is Queensland different? The roots of Joh's regime', *Socialist Action*, 14 (November), 1986, pp. 7–9.

Wilson, K., J. Bradford and M. Fitzpatrick (eds), *Australia in Accord: An evaluation of the prices and incomes Accord in the Hawke–Keating years*, South Pacific Publishing, 2000.

Wood, K., 'Fighting anti-union laws: the Clarrie O'Shea strikes', *MLR*, no. 5 (Summer), 2013, http://marxistleftreview.org/index.php/no5-summer-2013/87-fighting-anti-union-laws-the-clarrie-oshea-strikes

Wood, K., 'Australian unions and the fight for equal pay for women', *MLR*, no. 10, pp. 51–78, 2015, https://marxistleftreview.org/articles/australian-unions-and-the-fight-for-equal-pay-for-women/

Wright, S. and M. Ryan, 'Enterprise bargaining in the public sector', *Reconstruction*, no. 2 (July), 1994, pp. 15–26

ALSO BY INTERVENTIONS

Without Bosses
Radical Australian Trade Unionism in the 1970s
Sam Oldham
Interventions 2020

'The book demonstrates that labour militancy and the practice of worker control is not an antediluvian form drawn from the early 20th century, but a compelling force in more recent times with a powerful legacy in the present... activists in the present should take heart in the fact that the urge for workers' power is never far from the surface.'

– Immanuel Ness, Professor of Political Science, Brooklyn College, City University of New York

ALSO BY INTERVENTIONS

**Dare to Struggle, Dare to Win!
Builders Labourers Fight Deregistration, 1981-94**
Liz Ross
First published by Vulgar Press 2004

The first steps to destroy the militant Builders Labourers Federation occurred in 1981, but it was Labor – backed by many union leaders – which finished the job. After a Royal Commission, legal attacks and anti-union laws, in 1986 the union was shut out and its members forced into other unions. The BLF fought back. This story of the unions fight for its life, much of it in the words of BLs, also provides a left-wing analysis of the major players and issues. Fighting back then and now – this book has lessons for us all.

ALSO BY INTERVENTIONS

Years of Rage
Social Conflicts in the Fraser Era
Tom O'Lincoln
Interventions 2012

It's 1975, and Malcolm Fraser makes his ruthless grab for power. Workers resist, opening up seven years of bitter class conflict. From the upheavals of the Constitutional Crisis through the strikes in defence of Medibank and on to the 1981 "wage push", Tom O'Lincoln traces the industrial and political struggle, complemented with studies of social movements against oppression, unemployment, environmental destruction and war. Joh Bjelke-Petersen's crisis-ridden Queensland gets a chapter of its own, as do major debates on the left. The book shows how the exhaustion of the two sides after years of unrest set the scene for a Hawke Labor government that replace Fraser, yet brought nothing but disappointment to his opponents.

www.ingramcontent.com/pod-product-compliance
Lightning Source LLC
Chambersburg PA
CBHW070419010526
44118CB00014B/1823